# An Afrocentric Manifesto

# An Afrocentric Manifesto

## Toward an African Renaissance

MOLEFI KETE ASANTE

polity

First published in 2007 by Polity Press

Reprinted in 2008

Polity Press
65 Bridge Street
Cambridge CB2 1UR, UK

Polity Press
350 Main Street
Malden, MA 02148, USA

ISBN-13: 978-07456-4102-7
ISBN-13: 978-07456-4103-4 (pb)

A catalogue record for this book is available from the British Library

Typeset in 11.25 / 13 pt Dante
by Servis Filmsetting Ltd, Manchester
Printed and bound in the United States by Odyssey Press Inc., Gonic, New Hampshire

The publisher has used its best endeavours to ensure that the URLs for external websites referred to in this book are correct and active at the time of going to press. However, the publisher has no responsibility for the websites and can make no guarantee that a site will remain live or that the content is or will remain appropriate.

Every effort has been made to trace all copyright holders, but if any have been inadvertently overlooked the publishers will be pleased to include any necessary credits in any subsequent reprint or edition.

For further information on Polity, visit our website www.polity.co.uk

# Contents

1 Introduction     1

2 Ama Mazama and Paradigmatic Discourse     9

3 Afrocentricity: Notes on a Disciplinary Position     31

4 In Search of an Afrocentric Historiography     55

5 Kemetic Bases: The Africanness of Ancient Egypt     68

6 The Afrocentric Idea in Education     78

7 Sustaining a Relationship to Black Studies     93

8 Afrocentricity and History     105

9 The Black Nationalist Question     122

10 Race, Brutality, and Hegemony     132

11 Blackness as an Ethical Trope: Toward a Post-Western Manifesto     153

*References*     167

*Index*     174

# 1

## Introduction

## An overview

The African people of Georgia tell the story of a mother eagle that was flying low over a chicken yard holding her newly born baby eagle in her claws as she joined a large flock of eagles. A gust of wind forced the young eagle out of the mother's claws and it fell into the chicken yard. Although she looked for the baby eagle she could not find it. All she could see when she looked into the chicken yard were chickens. So after a long and exhaustive search, she reluctantly left the baby eagle and flew away with the large flock of eagles.

As the baby eagle grew in the chicken yard, it began to see itself as a chicken. Surrounded as it was by chickens, the little eagle received a chicken education, wore chicken clothes, ate chicken food, and attempted to imitate the walk and mannerisms of the chickens. Every day the little eagle practiced its chicken education. Its curriculum was a strictly chicken curriculum, one made expressly for chickens, to assist chickens in living in the chicken yard as good chickens. When the little eagle spoke, it spoke chicken language because it did not know eagle language. It carried its head like the chickens because it had only a faint knowledge, elementary knowledge, of what an eagle style or fashion or idea might have been. All traces of its earlier eagle training had been forgotten. In everything, the little eagle acted like a chicken until one day it started to think of itself as a chicken.

It tried to mimic the chickens. Whatever the chickens did, it did. If the chickens laughed, it laughed. If the chickens said, "It is a good day outside," the eagle said, "It is a good day outside." In everything that mattered the eagle saw itself as a chicken. It did not recognize itself as an eagle. In fact, all eagle consciousness was lost. Although it questioned why it looked different from the rest of the chickens, it just thought it was a funny-looking chicken. Soon it never thought of itself as anything but a chicken, strange-looking and all. There were physical characteristics it did not like because they were not the characteristics appreciated by the chickens. It never saw itself in the light of its eagle history; it was simply a chicken.

One sunny day an old eagle flew over the chicken yard. It had no special mission and was not looking for anything in particular. However, as it was leisurely flying over the chicken yard, something caught its attention. It looked down and saw what it thought was an eagle. It flew closer and looked with keener sight and saw what it was sure was an eagle. It then flew to a tree just next to the chicken yard and it called out to the bird that looked like an eagle. "Come up here and talk with me, young eagle," the old eagle said. The eagle in the chicken yard ignored the old eagle because it knew it was not the eagle that was being called because it was a chicken. But the old eagle persisted and at last the eagle in the chicken yard recognized that he was being called. Whereupon the eagle in the yard turned and said to the old eagle, "I'm not an eagle, I'm a chicken." The old eagle, with knowledge that stretched back through generations of eagles, said "I know an eagle when I see one. You're an eagle. Open your wings and fly up here to this tree and let us talk." The young eagle in the chicken yard said, "I cannot fly because I am a chicken." After the old eagle had asked it several times, the young eagle stretched its wings and flapped them and flew up to the tree. It looked down at the chicken yard and said, "I did not know that I could do that." The old eagle asked the young eagle to fly and they flew effortlessly toward the setting sun.

## Pinpointing the issue

I am a child of seven generations of Africans who have lived in America. My entire life, including career, struggle against oppression, search for ways to overturn hegemony, political outlook, fortunes and misfortunes, friends and detractors, has been impacted by my Africanness. It is an essential reality of an African living in America. Sometimes one has to learn what it is to be and this learning is how something seemingly essential can be translated into culture.

Afrocentricity is a paradigmatic intellectual perspective that privileges African agency within the context of African history and culture transcontinentally and trans-generationally. This means that the quality of location is essential to any analysis that involves African culture and behavior whether literary or economic, whether political or cultural. In this regard it is the crystallization of a critical perspective on facts (Asante, 1998). I do not present Afrocentricity as a settled corpus of ideas, as a worldview or as a closed system of beliefs. It remains important that we hold back any reductive misunderstanding of the nature of human interaction and the creation of reality. The vast academic corporate grab for uniformity, rooted in the tradition of the assertive American reach for hegemony in thought, leads to the inevitable confrontation between Afrocentrists and those who would like to subsume all new ideas under one form or the other of Eurocentrism (Keita, 2000). What is now plain to see is that some scholars are nervous about the possibility of a perspective on data, that is, a locative thesis, which does not adapt to the overarching ideas of a European hegemony. At this moment in intellectual history there is a critical reading and an assessment of Afrocentricity in all disciplines. Every one has something to say and normally what they have to say is critical of the fact that Afrocentricity appears "outside" the mainstream. What is meant by this notion of being "outside" is that Afrocentricity traces its theoretical heritage to African ideas and African authors. It is not a Eurocentric idea because, for it to be, it would mean that Europe would be assaulting its own patriarchy and sense of superiority in language, content, and structure. Clarence Walker, a leading Eurocentrist, who happens to be black in color, writes in his book, *We Can't Go Home Again* (Walker, 2001, p. xviii), something quite naive and nonsensical when he says: "Although some of its advocates may claim that Afrocentrism is history, the methods by which its proponents reach their conclusions are not historically rigorous." The naïveté occurs because Walker knows no Afrocentrist who claims that Afrocentricity is history. What is nonsensical about this charge is that any conclusion reached by Afrocentrists is usually based on the best arguments in the literature or orature. Clearly what would have been useful here is for Walker to cite some reference, some argument made by Afrocentrists, which suggested the lack of rigor. I accept the fact that he could not produce such an argument and therefore resorted to the most incredible example of the lack of rigor: the assertion without proof.

Walker's unfortunate intervention is built around two themes: (1) if everybody was a king, who built the pyramids? Afrocentrism and Black American History; (2) All God's Dangers Ain't a White Man, or Not All Knowledge is Power. With these two shadow pillars, Walker constructs a myth without foundation in the literature. He seeks to rewrite the intellectual history of African thought and to recast the Afrocentric movement in a negative light. For example, he claims that "Afrocentrism is a mythology that is racist, reactionary, and essentially therapeutic" (Walker, 2001, p. 3). While it is true that Afrocentricity is centered on the lived experiences of a particular group of people, namely Africans, it is not a mythology that is racist or reactionary. On the other hand it might serve as therapy to some people, and that is alright, so long as the therapeutic nature of the intellectual activity of Afrocentricity does not stand in the way of advancing science. I think where Walker and I part company is on the question of white privilege in intellectual matters. It is difficult it seems for Walker to accept the possibility that a theoretical idea, based on African traditions and concepts, could exist apart from the European experience. He would probably come to the same conclusion about Asian ideas and traditions as well. The work of the Asiacentric theorist Yoshitaka Miike has advanced an Asian critique of humanity, culture, and communication that must challenge Walker's own self dislocation (Miike, 2004, pp. 69–81). Nevertheless I am willing to give Walker the benefit of any doubt in this area and to consider some of his other points. He assumes a position closely resembling mythomania when he tries to "steal" the Afrocentrist's core in order to divest it of any relationship to what he is calling history. It is a devious and ingenious statement to say "good history should give its actors agency, show the contingency of events, and examine the deployment of power" (Walker, 2001, p. 4) when he knows or should know that one of the strongest arguments for Afrocentricity is African agency (Asante, 1998, p. 177). Is Walker really trying to argue that Afrocentricity has demonstrated what good history ought to be or is he seeking to muddy the waters? I think that it is the latter course that he professes because he is unable to discover any significant philosophical error in the Afrocentric construction. Regardless of Walker's program for good history, the Afrocentric scholars have maintained that in all experiences where African people are discussed we look for African agency. In the book, *The Afrocentric Paradigm*, Ama Mazama discusses agency in connection with the philosophy and activism of Marcus Garvey (Mazama, 2003a, pp. 10–14).

The principal weakness in Walker's critique of Afrocentricity is that he engages a discourse that was put to bed several years earlier by my book, *The Painful Demise of Eurocentrism* (Asante, 1999). This discourse was based on the reaction to Afrocentricity written by Mary Lefkowitz in a book called *Not Out of Africa* (1996). As I will show in a later chapter, it was Lefkowitz's objective to reassert the idea that Greece did not receive substantial contributions from Africa through Egypt. Furthermore, it was her purpose to challenge the blackness of the ancient people of Egypt. These are the same arguments that Walker reiterates in his book.

Lefkowitz was put to rest after several biting rebukes of her book and numerous debates (three or four with me) over her ideas. Walker has avoided this discussion until now and it will be important to show how he differs from Lefkowitz. My comment regarding Lefkowitz's book could be applied to Walker's when I said, "tragically, the idea that Europeans have some different intellectual or scientific ability is accepted doctrine and some scholars will go to any lengths to try to uphold it" (Asante, 1999, p. 53). But they always commit four fundametal flaws:

1 They attack insignificant or trivial issues to obscure the main points in a discourse.
2 They will make assertions and offer their own interpretations as evidence.
3 They will undermine writers they previously supported in order to maintain the fiction of a Greek miracle.
4 They will announce that both sides of an issue are correct, then move to uphold only the side that supports European triumphalism.

A serious reading of Walker demonstrates that he is a victim of these flaws. What is more frightening is that Walker's argument calls for a special category for those Africans who are victims of self-hatred. He writes that "Afrocentrism is not a record of the black past, but a therapeutic mythology based on the belief that there is an essential blackness in black people" (Walker, 2001, p. 23). This is a strange statement because there are no Afrocentrists who claim that Afrocentricity is a record of the black past. There are those who claim that it is a quality of thought (Karenga), a paradigm (Mazama), a perspective (Asante), or a metatheory (Modupe), but no theorist has claimed that it is a record of the black past (Mazama, 2003a). There is no one who claims that it is a therapeutic mythology based on the belief that there is an essential blackness in black people. This is unreal. In the first place, many events, activities, behaviors, programs, and philosophies might be therapeutic. I can find no fault in therapy, if one needs it. But this is not the Afrocentric Manifesto. I do not call for therapy, although I have often seen the need for it, and I am confused by a historian's use of the phrase "essential blackness in black people" because I think he has different axes to grind than literary theorists. It appears to me that we do not speak of the essential brownness in brown people or the essential whiteness in white people. Alas, self-hatred is a particular orientation of African people, or any people, who have been so destabilized by being "off-center" and "out of location" within their own culture that they have lost all sense of direction. I think that the ordinary African person on the streets of London, Philadelphia, or Paris will have a fairly good idea what it means to be an African in the Western world. They may not articulate it the same way that an Afrocentrist would with theoretical concepts but they would definitely speak to the uniqueness of the black person in a white-dominated environment. The fact that Walker cannot see this may be a reflection of the environment he has created for himself; it is certainly not the case with the majority of African people.

There are some ludicrous arguments made by Walker that indicate he has rarely read any Afrocentrist or, if he has, he has not read reflectively. For example, he claims without proof that Afrocentricity is Eurocentrism in black face (Walker, 2001, p. 4). This is certainly an insult because Afrocentricity is not the reverse of Eurocentrism; neither is it a counter to Eurocentrism. Even if Eurocentrism never existed, there would be a need for African people to operate from their own sense of agency. With other options one might want to assume an Asian identity and Asian agency or, in the distant future, a Martian or alien agency. This would also be an escape from African agency. One does not have to pose Afrocentricity as a counter to Eurocentrism since the dislocation of Africans is a fact that should be corrected at any rate. While it is true that the cultural and intellectual dislocation of Africans has a lot to do with the fact that Europe colonized and enslaved Africans, it must be understood that for the African to assert his or her own agency is not a racist act, but a profoundly anti-racist act because it liberates the African from the dislocation that may have been created by Europeans and undermines any sense of European hegemony.

To render Afrocentricity more meaningful it might be useful to discuss what the options are if Africans particularly, and those who are studying Africa specifically, seek to resolve the intellectual issues surrounding the acquisition of knowledge. In the late 1970s, I wrote on Afrocentricity as a way of conceptualizing what we had called in the 1960s' Black Power Movement "the black perspective." The convergence of two influences worked to produce the idea that the "black perspective" needed a fuller, rounder theoretical construction. The first influence was the critical insight of the philosopher Harold Cruse who suggested that it was critical for the African community in the United States to articulate a political, social, cultural, and economic idea consistent with its own history (Cruse, 2005 [1967]). The second influence was that of Kwame Nkrumah who had argued in his book *Consciencism* (1964) that Africa itself had to come to terms with its own personality and create a scientific response to national and international issues based on the interest of Africa. I will examine how Cruse and Nkrumah contributed to the maturing of Afrocentricity in later chapters.

Of course, it should be observed that I was not the only person thinking along this line in the late 1970s. In many respects the Kawaida Movement founded by Maulana Karenga had articulated a vision based on the twin ideas of tradition and reason grounded in the African experience during the

1960s. Karenga's political essays and philosophical works, particularly around the importance of culture in true liberation of the mind, became useful guides in the evolution of my own theory of Afrocentricity.

I have written elsewhere, namely in *The Afrocentric Idea* (1998), of the struggle over definitions. Thus, it came as no great surprise to me that the Oxford dictionary defined "Afrocentric" as believing "that black culture was pre-eminent" (*New American Oxford Dictionary*, 2005). Needless to say, this is precisely the kind of distortion that led to the creation of the Afrocentric School of Thought in the first place. Many definitions of African people and their ideas appear to be either outright distortions or deliberate negations. For example, nowhere in the corpus of works called "Afrocentric" is the statement ever made that "black culture is pre-eminent," and the Oxford consultant who claimed such as the case misread the evidence and usage of the word. However, this is not unique and is quite representative of the way African ideas are discussed and defined by European and American writers. On the other hand, Eurocentric is defined by the *Encarta World English Dictionary* (1999) as "focusing on Europe or its people, institutions, and cultures, sometimes in an arrogant way."

As we shall see in following chapters, the sociolinguistics of racism and cultural imperialism have to be challenged and neutralized in order to produce an arena of respect where Africans assume more than a marginal role in their own discourses. Conversely, Europeans will see that respect cannot be created from aggressive linguistic adventures that seek to define and determine the boundaries of non-European experiences and ideas. Humility, often lacking in intellectual work, is the necessary trait of the person who would reach toward a reasonable arena of respect.

I think that it will become clearer as we proceed that a multiplicity of dislocations, disorientations, and distortions are at the foundation of the generative and productive system that demonstrates the strain of an imperialistic and triumphalist vision of the world. Afrocentricity, if anything, is a shout out for rationality in the midst of confusion, order in the presence of chaos, and respect for cultures in a world that tramples on both the rights and the definitions of the rights of humans.

Out of an experience of great inquietude over the past 500 years, Africans have now put into place, with great resistance as we shall see, the elements necessary for a truly African renaissance founded on African principles and the centrality of African interests. What is at stake is clear. Either the African people will escape the intellectual plantation that has paraded as universal or will be stifled in every attempt to express their own sense of culture.

## Other centric expressions

The original work of Yoshitaka Miike on Asiocentric communication is instructive. Miike, alongside Jing Yin, has articulated a view of Asian culture that seeks to liberate the discourse around Asian communication ideas and rhetorical concepts away from being forced into the straitjacket of Western ideas. This is a remarkable undertaking that will have far-reaching effect on the course of social science and humanities discussions about culture.

My aim is to examine the relevance of Afrocentricity in a time when many intellectuals and activists are clients of two overlapping prisons of vision. While the dominant attitude that imprisons most of us may be called a Eurocentric worldview that gives rise to the spread of a particularism as if it were universal, we are also constrained by the infrastructures, by which I mean the maintenance systems, of dominance and privilege. They represent ideas such as globalization, postmodernism, modernism, structuralism, feminism, cultural materialism, and cosmopolitanism. Although this list does not exhaust the numerous manifestations, it should be a demonstration of the kinds of ideas that have served to enrich particularism as a universal value. I mean one does not have to be a genius to understand that the experience of Europe intellectually may not be the experience of Asians or Africans. Notice I said "may not" because I recognize the insidious nature of cultural ideas in a world where the control, as Samuel Huntington says in *The Clash of Civilizations* (1996), of almost all critical areas of power is in the hands of Europeans, whether in America or on the continent of Europe itself.

My intention has been to pinpoint the issue that we will return to in the following chapters. From here on out, it will be important to discuss the conceptual idea of Afrocentricity, place it in its own historical and philosophical context within African thought, and demonstrate how it operates in relationship to pedagogical, sociolinguistic, historical, multicultural, and gendered discourse. This means that I will have to discuss education, identity, class, and economics, and the meaning of blackness as a new construction for a human manifesto. But I am unable to do any of this without attention to the arguments for and against Afrocentricity. I shall try to deal with all arguments with equanimity, but I shall be especially careful to quote those who have taken an anti-Afrocentric view. In the end, what *The Afrocentric Manifesto* intends is to provide the reader with a clear, coherent, and persuasive argument for a reconceptualization of the way Africans view themselves and the way others have viewed Africans.

# 2

# Ama Mazama and Paradigmatic Discourse

In her book, *The Afrocentric Paradigm*, Ama Mazama explains that Afrocentricity is not merely a worldview nor even a theory as such, but rather it is a paradigm that results in the reconceptualization of the social and historical reality of African people (Mazama, 2003a). Actually, what she suggests is that the Afrocentric paradigm is a revolutionary shift in thinking proposed as a constructural adjustment to black disorientation, decenteredness, and lack of agency.

Ama Mazama is an African who was born a French citizen in Guadeloupe, educated at the Academy of the Antilles in Guadeloupe, Bordeaux and La Sorbonne, where she obtained a PhD with highest distinction in linguistics. She became a professor in African American Studies at Temple University after making professorial stops at the University of Texas in Austin, Howard, Georgetown, and the Pennsylvania State University. Growing up as she did in the intellectual environment of French philosophical and linguistic studies but with the political and social radicalization of the Guadeloupean and Martinican campaigners for autonomy, Mazama reacted to colonial indoctrination that suggested the superiority of European culture over African culture. No one could convince her that the language of the black people of Guadeloupe was simply bad French nor could they influence her to believe that the Congo-based language of the people was inferior to any other language. In *Langue et Identité*, she establishes in a sustained argument the point that the Guadeloupeans were not merely imitators of French nor were they trying to speak French; they were speaking a language that had its roots deep in the continent. They were not creoles and there was no real creole identity. Maryse Conde, also a Guadeloupean, had argued a view that elevated and privileged creole status. In rejecting this formulation, Mazama was laying the foundation for her future work in Afrocentric theory. Already by the time she was getting her first Master's degree at Bordeaux, she had begun to see the damage that was done to the psyche of black people in Guadeloupe by the insidious work of the cultural elitists. By the time she arrived in the United States to teach linguistics at the University of Texas, Ama Mazama had developed a clear plan for overturning the reigning paradigm in so-called Creole Studies. It was with deftness that Mazama established a formidable array of intellectual weaponry with books, monographs, and articles that attacked the very construction of creolization. In challenging creolization she was challenging the idea of white racial supremacy.

This work was soon followed up by lecture tours each year in Guadeloupe, interviews on the radio and television, and speeches to community groups. The masses of people were thirsty for the information, particularly the African connection that Mazama was now prepared to give them from her own travels and studies in Africa. But it was her philosophical and theoretical orientation, more than anything else, which grounded her in the tradition of Cheikh Anta Diop, Amilcar Cabral, Kwame Nkrumah, Marcus Garvey, Anna Julia Cooper, and others who have always believed that African people were not white people in color. Mazama knew that the horrendous situation of black people in Africa and in the Americas was not just a political and economic crisis, but a crisis of culture, theory, and philosophy. Of course, the French authorities would soon ban her from appearing on television in the land of her birth, but her videotapes and audiotapes would be played and used by the people to raise the consciousness of their children. While Mazama found the small island of Guadeloupe more and more difficult to navigate in terms of access, she found ample opportunity in France itself and also in Africa for her intellectual ideas. Her works soon became popular in France, Canada, Guyane, Benin, and other Francophone countries. Yet it is in the United States, as a leading theorist of the Afrocentric School, that she has made her greatest impact on students and colleagues. Because she understands the intersections as well as the centers and margins in the discourse around hegemony and domination, she has become one of the most prominent theorists.

Mazama's argument for Afrocentricity is therefore grounded in practical and intellectual experiences. Since she has both philosophical and linguistic training, her approach to the same general problem of African dislocation will be slightly different from my own. I am much more stilted, if not structural, in my approach to the phenomenological problem of agency.

Let us see if we can outline Mazama's principal argument. Although colonization of Africans has ended, Africans are still mentally subjugated. The reason for this sad mental state is that we have been fighting against the evil of colonization as an economic and political problem rather than a total conceptual distortion leading to confusion. Mazama further contends that colonization "must be analyzed within the broader context of the European cultural ethos that generated the economic exploitation and political suppression" in the first place (Mazama, 2003a, p. 4).

The tension between the colonizer and the colonized is explicitly reiterated in Mazama's work in much the same way as Albert Memmi and Frantz Fanon had done earlier. A hyper-valorized dominating culture and a "systematically denigrated" oppressed or colonized community is the standard formulation for the mental confusion of the dominated. This ontological reduction of colonized people was a necessary part of the process of bankrupting the intellectual and cultural space of the colonized.

Mazama contends that there is another aspect of the process of colonization that is more significant than ontological reduction that has gone relatively unrecognized because the leading critiques of colonization have been by those who operated within the framework of European thinking. For example, Fanon was a Marxist and accepted the idea of evolutionary change which led him to believe, along with Europeans, that Africans needed "development." Because neither Fanon nor his countryman, Aime Césaire, constructed European development as problematic they never questioned the use of language such as "normal," "natural," and "universal," all terms that Europeans had constructed to relate to themselves as normative. Mazama understands this phenomenon and insists that the "Afrocentric idea rests on the assertion of the primacy of the African experience for African people" (Mazama, 2003a, p. 5).

In a riveting critique of authors who have misappropriated the term "Afrocentricity," Mazama highlights the obvious mischaracterizations in the literature. For example, Patricia Hill Collins, as early as 1991, misunderstood the idea of Afrocentricity as having "core African values." This leads immediately to a misunderstanding that creates bad conclusions. There is a difference, as Mazama explains, between Africanity, which is what Hill Collins must have been writing about, and Afrocentricity. Africanity refers to the traditions, customs, and values of African people. But Afrocentricity is a much more self-conscious approach to the agency of African people within the context of their own history.

The special contribution that Mazama makes to the advancement of Afrocentricity has to do with the application and extension of the Kuhnian notion of paradigm. She argues that "Afrocentricity, within the academic context, will best be understood as a paradigm" (Mazama, 2003a, p. 7). She takes the idea of the cognitive and structural elements of a paradigm and applies them to Afrocentricity. Under the cognitive aspect of a paradigm are three constituents: metaphysical, sociological, and exemplary. Of course the Kuhnian idea was not complete in Mazama's construction because it did not have a functional aspect. However, it is impossible Afrocentrically to conceive of a paradigm that would not have a functional aspect and it is clear that "a paradigm must activate our consciousness to be of any use to us" (Mazama, 2003a, p. 8). To be engaged in the process of liberation one must not assume that activities are for the sake of activity; they must be for the sake of achieving liberation.

Mazama claims that Marcus Garvey, a deeply spiritual man who was committed to the ancestors, was seeking to develop a civil religion. In fact, taking her lead from other scholars who have made this case, she argues that Garvey's emphasis on agency was "largely predicated upon his conception of God as one who had made all people equal and masters of their destiny; a God who would be content only if his children lived up to their divine origin and exercised fully their will in determining their life conditions" (Mazama, 2003a, p. 11). It was Garvey, she contends, who first saw that the black man must be hero and subject in his own history.

Mazama is critical of Frantz Fanon. She argues that Fanon understood that the fundamental characteristic of colonization was violence. It was a process of dehumanization that was pursued with rationality to confer inferiority to the colonized. For Fanon, the white man was the purveyor of violence and all the violence on the globe could be traced to some white man. It would take the end of whiteness to destroy the idea of violence against other people because the construction of whiteness and blackness was a creation of whites to exploit blacks. To assert humanity, the colonized must kill his oppressor. What Mazama discovers is that while Fanon is correct on some aspects of his analysis, he is woefully lacking in his re-humanization project because he has a limited role for African culture. She writes "It is clear from reading Fanon that he believed that the role of culture was to be minimal" (Mazama, 2003a, p. 14). One could claim, however, that Fanon did not seek to eliminate culture, only to place it in a position where it was seen as a resource for dealing with the materiality of racism. Yet it was Fanon's belief that the recovered culture could only be a caricature because culture is to be lived not exhibited. He argued that he would not be a man of the past and would not exalt his past, or any past. Mazama brilliantly points out that Fanon was struggling with his own dislocation. Inevitably, because he did not exalt his own past, he participated in the past of Europe. One cannot divest himself of the past, and if a person seeks to divest himself of his own past or if that past has become distorted in his mind, then he will participate in the past of another. This was one of Fanon's problems. To be sure, it must be asserted, as Lewis Gordon has understood, that Fanon problematized development and normality and did not accept either without criticism. Fanon had argued in *The Wretched of the Earth* (*Les Damnés de la terre*, 1961) that development was imposed on the African communities rather than emerging from the organic nature of those communities.

This was not the case with either the Negritude or the Kawaida movements, as Mazama found. Both movements engaged the intellectual and cultural ideas that had been formulated by those who had written and acted before. They were not stuck in the past; they were able, however, to use the past as a resource.

What Ama Mazama envisions is an Afrocentricity that is free to pursue the total liberation of African people from the degradation of Europe. Léopold Senghor, Aime Césaire, and Leon Damas were struck by the overwhelming nature of French culture. They had been raised in colonized nations and had imbibed French culture. By the time they were university students they were exhausted with French culture, so they erected their defense by projecting what was their own from their ancestors. They were liberated from the strictures of European culture when they embraced themselves and saw themselves as beautiful, something wonderful to behold. But they were unable to carry this project through to completion and often found themselves back in the bosom of whiteness. They wanted, as Mazama notes, to retrieve a precolonial consciousness, a true Negritude (Mazama, 2003a, p. 17). She would discover that Kawaida brought other gifts to the table. Maulana Karenga sought to reconstruct African culture and Kwanzaa, an international holiday, represents a concrete activity brought into being by the persistent teaching of Maulana Karenga that Africans needed to revisit the cultural question since Europe had deliberately destroyed and distorted much of that culture.

Mazama's critique of Kawaida is that it was not sufficiently robust to deal with the Pan African issues confronting the interactive networks of Africans. In fact, she writes that Karenga's focus was on the New African, Afro-Americans (Mazama, 2003a, p. 20). There is no doubt, however, that Kawaida and Negritude were influences on Afrocentricity.

No other author exemplifies the paradigmatic shift more than Cheikh Anta Diop (Diop, 1974). Mazama places him in the context of the Hegelian notion that Africa was outside history because the African people did not have, according to Hegel, a historical consciousness. What she saw in Diop was "a conscious elaboration of a paradigm whose main principle is the reclaiming of ancient Egypt, Kemet, for Africa," p. 20). It was this main principle that agitated the West and created an avalanche of criticism for Afrocentricity (Mazama, 2003a). It was as if a great horse had broken free of its captors and was now on a mission to remain free and to expose the captors.

In the writings of Clenora Hudson-Weems and Nah Dove, Mazama finds new instruments and ideas that undergird her thesis on relationships which could best be understood as complementarity between women and men. Therefore, she reports favorably on Hudson-Weems's claim that for women to be against men is to endanger the African community. "African women do not apprehend African men as our enemies," she writes (Mazama, 2003a, p. 27). Hudson-Weems was the first theorist to call for Africana Womanism in place of feminism which is so badly tainted in the African American world with the idea that women are against men. Although Mazama believes that discrimination against women is pervasive in the Western society, she also knows that the controls of the West are in the hands of white men. To be against black men is a short-term solution to a much larger narrative of relationship.

Nah Dove, a brilliant analyst and Africana Womanist, argues that all discourse on relationships between men and women must be examined through the prism of the doctrine of white racial supremacy. If one fails to see that this is the dominant thrust of Western culture, then there will be no understanding of the cultural underpinnings of relationships between black men and black women. Dove's work converges with the insights that Mazama makes in her own analyses of relationships, culture, and identity.

In fact, Mazama makes two general scientific advances in the development of theory: (1) she launches the paradigmatic shift in the discourse on Afrocentricity and shows how it is a revolutionary concept for the African world, and (2) she infuses the older ideas of Afrocentricity with a functional, actionable, practical component that energizes the concept. These two achievements are central to an understanding of the Afrocentric idea.

The mission of Mazama's essay on the Afrocentric Paradigm is straightforward and clear. She weaves a tapestry of exuberant intellectual ideas that span the most abstract theories in the Afrocentric paradigm to the concrete educational proposals of Asa Hilliard. But the ultimate objective of the essay is to suggest that the liberation of the mind of the African person must precede any other type of liberation. One is convinced by Mazama's construction of the argument for a paradigm shift because to carry on as usual would be to enthrone white supremacy indefinitely. The only way to break the chains and to claim victory is to strike the blow for freedom that comes when African intellectuals say that they are no longer willing to ride the slow train to mental death any more; we are truly, then, on our own. By taking this course of action, Mazama is proposing not an evolution but a revolution in our thinking.

Afrocentricity is revolutionary because it casts ideas, concepts, events, personalities, and political and economic processes in the context of black people as subjects and not as objects, basing all knowledge on the authentic interrogation of location. One might contend that it elevates the cultural and historical location of the African and uses that as a source for surveying knowledge. Because of Afrocentricity it is possible to ask, "Where is the sistah coming from?" or "Where is the brotha at?" or "Are you down with overcoming oppression?"

## An intellectual *djed*

One can claim that the revolutionary idea of Afrocentricity creates what the ancient Egyptians referred to as a *djed*, and the ancient Greeks as a *stasis*, meaning in both cases a strong place to stand. It is a paradigm in the Mazamian sense because it enthrones the centrality of African agency, thus creating an acceptance of African values and ideals as expressed in the highest forms of culture while terminating always in a creative function bent toward mental liberation. As such it activates our consciousness as a functional aspect of any revolutionary approach to phenomena. The cognitive and structural aspects of a paradigm are incomplete without the functional aspect (Mazama, 2003a, p. 31). There is something more than knowing from the Afrocentric perspective; there is also *doing*. Only in this functional aspect does one wrest the idea from "shallow discursive spaces" to place it in a proper revolutionary context to change the actual lives of the oppressed.

One of the chief arenas for *doing* in contemporary society is the educational system. It is the locus of all definitions that maintain the society and the institutions, commercial, religious, or social, that are used to sustain the society. But, of course, the Afrocentrist understands that all definitions are autobiographical. It should come as no surprise that this is a *djed*ian position given the fact that education in a Western sense is the largest and most effective institution for creating group thought.

But it is not only education that announces a pattern of group thinking in the Western world; it is a factor in every aspect of the societies of the West. For example, there is a reason for Europeans to claim that permanent architecture is one of the principal keys to societies having culture because they have built buildings that have lasted for generations. How would this definition fit in the lives of the Yaqui Indians of Mexico? Would we have to conclude that they did not have culture or civilization because they did not build a St Peter's basilica or Notre Dame? Furthermore, what goes for functional architecture in one society may be different from that in another. One can see the Golden Temple in Bangkok and claim that its elaborateness is unlike anything in Western culture, but one cannot say that it is better or not; this is really a question of difference, not of good or bad. Civilization, like other terms, is a victim of Western particularist expansiveness.

For now it is critical for us to see that Afrocentricity assumes that all relationships are based on the interplay of centers and margins and the distances from either the center or the margins. When Africans, continental or diasporan, view themselves as centered and central in their own history then they see themselves as agents, actors, and participants rather than as marginals on the periphery of the political or economic experience of Europe. To be an African is to be a part of a community, in contemporary terms, that was historically enslaved, exploited, and colonized because of skin color, and a community that lost some of the control of the intellectual, social, philosophical, and religious ideas it had inherited. To establish a new intellectual *djed* is an act of revolution, as Mazama understands, because by its very existence it critiques and unsettles five hundred years of mental enslavement prosecuted through language (Mazama, 2003a, p. 210).

Using this paradigm, human beings have discovered that all phenomena are expressed in the fundamental categories of space and time. Furthermore, it is then understood that relationships develop and knowledge increases to the extent that we are able to appreciate the issues of space and time. Now this leads us to the very edge of discovery: what is the meaning of Afrocentricity itself?

I have defined Afrocentricty as a consciousness, a quality of thought, and an analytical process based on Africans viewing themselves as subjects, that is, agents in the world, but with the intervention of Mazama it now becomes clear that there has to be a functional component to the concept. *Afrocentricity is therefore a consciousness, quality of thought, mode of analysis, and an actionable perspective where Africans seek, from agency, to assert subject place within the context of African history.* All other explanations or elaborations of the Afrocentric idea begin with this foundation; there is no Afrocentricity without an emphasis on African agency in the context of African history.

One is allowed to make a number of commentaries about the Afrocentric paradigm based on the scope of the preceding definition. For example, it is possible to say Afrocentricity is the quality of viewing phenomena from the perspective of the African person as an agent of history, not as an object of European creation. But it is also the quality of seeking in every situation involving Africans the appropriate centrality of the African person (Asante, 1998).

One must not assume that Afrocentricity is the opposite of Eurocentricity (Asante, 1998). In fact, Afrocentricity is not an ethnocentric valorization to the degradation of other perspectives as Eurocentricity tends to be. Eurocentricity imposes its consciousness as universal, making a particular historical reality the sum total, in the European's view, of the human experience (Asante, 1998). I see this as a warrior mentality intent on conquest and triumphalism where it is acceptable to dominate others. This is contrary to the Afrocentric way of participating in human life. Karenga argues that Afrocentricity is about values and interests and puts it this way: "Afrocentricity is a quality of thought, practice and perspective that perceives Africans as subjects and agents of phenomena acting in their own cultural image and human interest" (2002). Of course, one should realize that it is not simply affecting African styles and manners, but something deeper, more conscious. In fact, it is necessary to separate Africanity from Afrocentricity. The idea of conscientization is at the center of Afrocentricity because this is what makes it different from Africanity. One can practice African customs and mores and not be Afrocentric because Afrocentricity is conscientization related to the agency of African people. One cannot be Afrocentric without being a conscious human being

By way of distinction, Afrocentricity should not be confused with the variant Afrocentrism. The term "Afrocentrism" was first used by the opponents of Afrocentricity who in their zeal saw it as an obverse of Eurocentrism. The adjective "Afrocentric" in the academic literature always referred to "Afrocentricity." However, the use of "Afrocentrism" reflected a negation of the idea of Afrocentricity as a positive and progressive paradigm. The aim was to assign religious signification to the idea of African centeredness. However, it has come to refer to a broad cultural movement of the late twentieth century that has a set of philosophical, political, and artistic ideas which provides the basis for the musical, sartorial, and aesthetic dimensions of the African personality. On the other hand, Afrocentricity, as I have previously defined it, is a theory of agency, that is, the idea that African people must be viewed and view themselves as agents rather than spectators to historical revolution and change. To this end Afrocentricity seeks to examine every aspect of the subject place of Africans in historical, literary, architectural, ethical, philosophical, economic, and political life. Afrocentricity precedes Afrocentrism, that is, it is older as a term in the intellectual discourse.

Afrocentricity is not a religion, worldview, or a closed belief system but rather a standpoint, and it is not founded on any revealed mysteries. The titles of my earlier books on the subject suggest nomenclature: *Afrocentricity*

(2003a), *The Afrocentric Idea* (1998), *Malcolm X as Cultural Hero and Other Afrocentric Essays* (1995), and *Kemet, Afrocentricity and Knowledge* (1990). Indeed, two books by the important Afrocentric scholar, Ama Mazama, have the titles *The Afrocentric Paradigm* (2003a) and *L'imperatif Afrocentrique* (2003b). It is unclear why those who insist on debating the issue prefer to use the term Afrocentrism. One can usually assume that the user of the term Afrocentrism is staking out a negative position on Afrocentricity. In English, there is a difference between Afrocentricity and Afrocentrism, and it is a difference the English scholar Stephen Howe understood when he wrote the book *Afrocentrism* (1998), a diatribe against the most progressive elements of African thought. Mary Lefkowitz, in the United States, had written in the same vein. While her book concentrated on the ideas she thought misinterpreted European thought, she never resorted to the *ad hominem* attacks of Stephen Howe. Yet both understood that by seeking to demonize Afrocentricity into Afrocentrism they would be able to more easily deal with its arguments. I do not know if this difference in language holds in Spanish, French, Portuguese, Yoruba, or Kiswahili. However, the point is that Afrocentricity is not a closed system; it is not a belief system that one has to adhere to in order to reach the kingdom of heaven or any other kingdom. As an open system it allows for discussion and debate over the meanings of the key presumptions and assumptions. This is as it should be in any intellectual discourse.

Patricia Hill Collins has written an intriguing, if rambling, book, *Black Power to Hip Hop* (2006), where she jumps on the bandwagon of those who fail to establish what they mean by Afrocentricity and then set up a false concept that they name Afrocentrism. They then stride toward the false concept with the idea of demolishing it or creating a black version of Eurocentricity. This is not only poor scholarship; it is a form of self-hatred because it is usually engaged in by vulgar careerists whose plan is to distance themselves from African agency. This is an unexpected turn in the writing of Hill Collins since her visit to the sociology Department of Boston College in 2002 is written up by Jeffrey Littenberg in the following manner:

> On the evening of February 18th, Patricia Hill Collins gave a public lecture on the future of feminist thought. At the start of this lecture, Collins reiterated a central theme of her work – the utility of thinking about complex social issues from a particular standpoint – for Collins, this is the standpoint of women of African descent. By orienting research toward a particular standpoint, it is possible to develop empirically grounded knowledge claims that are socially situated, rather than relying

on the assumption of an Archimedean worldview for pretension to scientific authority. (Littenberg, 2003)

If Littenberg can be believed, Hill Collins took a centered position from the standpoint of women of African descent. Literally this means that she understands and obviously appreciates the possibility of building grounded knowledge claims that are socially situated. What is the meaning of her lapse in understanding how the Afrocentrist, female or male, black or white, can view "complex social issues" from the standpoint of African agency in her book, *Black Power to Hip Hop: Racism, Nationalism, and Feminism*?

In the second part of this book, "Ethnicity, Culture, and Black Nationalist Politics," Hill Collins concentrates on two main themes. The first is "Black Nationalism and African American Ethnicity: Afrocentrism as Civil Religion," and "When Fighting Words are Not Enough: The Gendered Content of Afrocentrism." There are some obvious problems with this section of the book, including the lack of clear definitions of Black nationalism, African American ethnicity, Afrocentrism (by which I take *her* to mean Afrocentricity), and civil religion. Let us now turn to Hill Collins's arguments.

I will lay out the essential arguments made by Hill Collins in her recent work and then demonstrate how they support an artificial intellectual agenda that is founded on the most negative reactionary politics in contemporary American history. In the first place, Hill Collins pays the necessary homage to Black Nationalism for, as Michael Dawson has shown in his study, it remains the most adhered to political ideology of the African American community despite numerous attempts to wipe it out of the African imagination. She writes:

> Black nationalism's appeal may lie in its usefulness to individual African Americans searching for meaning within their everyday lives; in its utility in mobilizing African Americans as a collectivity for quite diverse activities that are not overtly political; and in its versatility to have diverse meanings for segments of African American civil society distinguished by social class, color, gender, immigrant status, and religion. (Hill Collins, 2006, p. 76)

Although Hill Collins's claim that her view of Black nationalism "constitutes a major departure from standard approaches," her assessment comes out at the same place as that of those who speak of revolutionary nationalism, cultural nationalism, black feminist nationalism, and religious nationalism, the four distinct "standard" forms that Hill Collins abhors.

Nothing said in her statement about the appeal of Black Nationalism to African Americans is not contained in some aspect of the arguments of the adherents to one or all of the four standard divisions. Thus, one of the first things we learn in this new analysis by Hill Collins is that she has established a straw argument to blow over. There is no real, no essential, difference between her creation of an approach to Black Nationalism and what African intellectuals have written for more than a hundred years.

But let us see Hill Collins's argument in detail. She contends that race and religion played an important role in the creation of the identity of the American nation. Furthermore, it is argued that external racism was directed against the indigenous peoples and internal racism was directed against African people, creating a nation that privileged whiteness (Hill Collins, 2006, p. 76). National identity, her argument goes, was embedded with racial identity and vice versa. America, thus racialized, had Native Americans, blacks, and whites, the latter being the privileged group. Hill Collins contends that the religion of the country was projected in the idea of the separation of the church and state and the freedom of religion. Thus, there was crafted an American civil religion that celebrated and worshipped the idea of American identity. In reality, Hill Collins argues that civil religion is the worship of a form of civil government and the political principles that are associated with it (Hill Collins, 2006, p. 78).

As Hill Collins sees it, the reality facing immigrants from Europe was to decide how to become "white" and the reality facing immigrants from the Caribbean was to decide how not to become "black." Soon, however, the black immigrants to the United States became participants, along with the Africans residing in the United States, in the Universal Negro Improvement Association and African Communities League, the largest mass movement of Africans in history.

Observing whiteness in the American culture as an operation toward un-racing whiteness, Hill Collins points out that, although white was constructed in such a way as to receive European ethnicities, the idea of whiteness became un-raced because whites had the power to erase their own notion of race. They became, in effect, the only Americans because they enjoyed the status of being the racial majority who could define themselves as "individuals," not as a part of a group. They could even choose optional identities, become Native American, or part-Irish, or part-Italian. The only thing they could not do was become part-African. On the other hand, there was nothing but race for African Americans, no ethnicity.

Hill Collins seems bewildered by the "new" racism that appears to operate in the context of desegregation, an illusion of equality, and a logic of colorblindness. She then jumps completely off the train that while chugging along might have got us to a proper place and onto a boat going in the wrong direction. Hill Collins takes a quote from one of the greatest minds the African American community has produced, C. Eric Lincoln, and uses it to bolster her argument about Black Nationalism. The problem is that the quote is one of the few things that Lincoln was wrong about. The idea Hill Collins quotes approvingly from Lincoln seems to suggest that African Americans cannot distinguish between black religion and Black Nationalism. In fact, Lincoln is quoted as saying that these two ideas are the same in the minds of the black masses (Hill Collins, 2006, p. 82). Now Hill Collins is prepared to make her case for Black Nationalism as a part of some religious movement or some political movement with a religious character.

From this argument Hill Collins attempts a mighty leap; she contends that "The Nation of Islam under the leadership of Louis Farrakhan and Molefi Kete Asante's Afrocentricity constitute two prominent manifestations of contemporary Black nationalism since the mid-1970s" (Hill Collins, 2006, p. 82). She falls into the water and is in danger of drowning with the follow-up statement that "Both black nationalist projects simultaneously draw on the historical religiosity of African Americans yet do so with an eye toward developing ethnic identification among African Americans" (Hill Collins, 2006, p. 82). These are bad facts and bad reasoning.

In the first place, Afrocentricity and Black Nationalism are two different concepts. One concept refers to a philosophical paradigm and the other refers to a political ideology. This much has to be clear in order to proceed with any reasonable possibility of discovering truth. *Afrocentricity* is an intellectual idea that suggests that African people must be viewed and must view themselves as agents in the historical process. *Black Nationalism* is a political ideology that asserts that African people must be self-defining, self-determining, and self-actualizing within the context of a collectivity born out of struggle. You cannot collapse one idea onto another and hope to have any clarity. My political ideology is my own business. What does it matter that I am a Black Nationalist, Marxist, Democrat, Republican, Socialist, or Anarchist? My religious faith is my own business. What does it matter that I am an Atheist, Agnostic, Christian, Jew, Yoruba, Muslim, or Shintoist?

The point of this is that you cannot blur the idea of Afrocentricity with the idea of Black Nationalism. These are two very powerful ideas with separate functions and spheres of operation. Afrocentricity as a way of interpreting reality begins with the idea that it is teachable and accessible to anyone who cares to learn it. Just as you would not turn away an individual who wants to learn Marxist theory or methodology or capitalist theory or methodology, the Afrocentrist will teach anyone how to become a scholar who begins the study of African people and African phenomena from the standpoint of Africans as subjects rather than objects of history. It is easier for a white person to become an Afrocentrist than a Black Nationalist; one depends on study and science; the other is grounded in the essential reality of being black in America.

Hill Collins is wrong again in her understanding of Afrocentricity when she implies that it draws upon the "historical religiosity of African Americans" (Hill Collins, 2006, p. 82). Supposedly, the Afrocentric idea searches for a way to develop ethnic identification. This is not the case and never has been the case with Afrocentricity. The Afrocentrists did not care one iota about African American religion or "historical religiosity" when the idea was launched and Afrocentricity has not depended upon this notion in its present form. Black people do not need an Afrocentrist to tell them that they are African. There is nothing in Afrocentricity that speaks to the idea of a political ideology although many Afrocentrists are Black Nationalists by political orientation; of course, they do not have to be, and many are not. A Black Nationalist is definitely not necessarily an Afrocentrist. To be an Afrocentrist, one has to make a self-conscious effort to interpret, explain and analyze the world from the perspective of African agency.

Hill Collins has articulated a view of Afrocentricity that is clearly off-center and disoriented. She claims, again linking Afrocentricity with the Nation of Islam in an overreach, that both "offer . . . highly idealistic proposals – one explicitly religious, the other quasi-religious – for group empowerment" (Hill Collins, 2006, p. 83). All proposals that seek to overturn the paradigm that has victimized thinking about African phenomena trans-generationally and transnationally can be called idealistic. But idealistic is not a negative term; it is a profoundly positive term although I am sure that is not what Hill Collins meant in her use of the term. In fact, she claims that Afrocentricity was quasi-religious, but this is untrue.

In a remarkable rhetorical display, Hill Collins rephrases the entire Afrocentric paradigm with the question, "How does Black Nationalism assume the character of religion to address the oppression and suffering caused by the new racism?" But this is a false question about a false issue. In the first place, Hill Collins speaks of "Afrocentrism" instead of "Afrocentricity." What is telling about this shift is that Afrocentricity has never claimed the status of a religion, quasi- or formal; therefore, to use the word "Afrocentrism" in the sense of a belief system is to miss the entire point of the discourse on Afrocentricity that is going on in the African world. There is an eagerness here to define the idea as a religion. Only those who are anti-Afrocentricity define the idea as Afrocentrism.

Patricia Hill Collins sets up another shell game when she writes "Within American higher education, Asante and other African American academics refashioned the main ideas of black cultural nationalism to guide fledgling Black Studies programs. Despite Afrocentrism's expressed function as a social theory within American higher education, its actual use more closely resembled that of a civil religion" (Hill Collins, 2006, p. 93). There was no "refashioned" anything. Black Studies itself was an outgrowth of the Black Nationalist political tradition; there was no need to refashion any ideas in this regard. Black Studies as an idea pre-dated the development of Afrocentricity so it was not around to "guide" Black Studies.

What is correct in Hill Collins's statement is that Afrocentricity is a social theory in the sense that it explains the dislocation, disorientation, and mental enslavement of African people as being a function of white racial hegemony. The idea of the enslaved serving the master even as the master whipped him or her was clearly the picture the Afrocentrist tried to reveal in analysis. The betrayal of the slave master was impossible with a mentality that considered the African inferior, second-class, and incapable of theorizing without religion. The only possibility left for individuals like that was to praise the master for teaching them how to attack themselves intellectually. Self-mutilation is the highest form of dislocation.

Now we are at the core of Patricia Hill Collins's new approach. She claims that Afrocentricity took the framework of American civil religion and stripped it of its American symbols and substituted a black value system (Hill Collins, 2006, p. 84). As one of the earliest proponents of Afrocentricity, I can say that if we did what Hill Collins said we did, we did not know that we were doing it. There was no conscious attempt on the part of the earliest Afrocentrists, Nah Dove, C. Tsehloane Keto, Ama Mazama, Kariamu Welsh, Terry Kershaw or any others of the Temple Circle nor scholars such as Maulana Karenga, Wade Nobles, Asa Hilliard, Clenora Hudson-Weems, Linda James Myers, or others that I know, to create a civil religion. Perhaps this is just the newest concept in Hill Collins's considerable bag of clever attachments upon which to hang black intellectual ideas.

To create a civil religion you must have civil power. White people have been able to create a civil religion because they control the purse strings of the municipal, state, and federal government. They also have the largest private foundations. With this type of institutional control and power a people can create a civil religion. They can organize remembrances and have memorials to contain their wishes and desires, they can create rituals and ceremonies to highlight their achievements, they can establish parks, statues, and memorials in the name of their ancestors and get others to pay reverence to them. All of these things can be done by whites, but they cannot be done by black people in a racist society where blacks do not hold the purse strings.

Now this is the point. Black Nationalists argue that black people should be self-defining and self-actualizing so those things that we can do for ourselves to honor our ancestors we should do without waiting for money from white institutions. Of course, this is a Black Nationalist argument, not one made by Afrocentrists who may accept that the Black Nationalists' position is correct. However, to state as Hill Collins did that Afrocentrists seek to create a civil religion is way off base. It is, as the Nigerians say, full stop, an intellectual paradigm.

What I find curious is the attempt to make Afrocentricity conform to some form of Christian religion. I find this problematic for several reasons. In the first place, it appears as a projection of Hill Collins's own religious orientation. Secondly, it has no basis in fact in the theoretical work that I do or others do in the field. Thirdly, being neither Christian, nor Muslim, nor Jew, I find the insertion of a religious idiom in the discourse about Afrocentricity to be a subversion of the explicatory energy of this paradigm.

Finally, it is not the identifying or not identifying with blackness that is at the core of Afrocentricity. This is almost a deliberate misunderstanding of the arguments that have been made in connection with the intellectual paradigm. It is not blackness per se that is at issue here, but place, *djed*. I can only believe that Hill Collins misinterpreted this concept because she conflated it with Negritude. There is a difference between Negritude and Afrocentricity. The first is associated with the idea that black people have art, culture, music, dance, and song as beautiful as any in the world. It is a philosophy of the aesthetics of African art and literature. Blackness is not negative in the minds of the Negritude writers; it is a valuable part of the world. Afrocentricity begins with the idea that African people should be at the center of their own history in every conceivable situation where Africans are involved. Both of these ideas are important, but the distinction must be made or else Hill Collins's mistake will be magnified. So it is not a "re-centering on blackness" that is at the heart of Afrocentricity, but the re-centering of the African person in the center of his or her own historical context, reality, and time. We are not on the margins of any other people's history; we are profoundly in our own time and space and if we view ourselves outside of this reality, we are disoriented and decentered.

# Acting from a centered position

What is any better for Africans than operating and acting from a centered position, one of agency and accountability? Who is to say that the historical experiences of the African world are less valid for Africans than others? What resonates more than the centrality of Africans to their own history, not someone else's? It is not unreasonable to hear an African say, "If we can, in the process of materializing our consciousness, claim space as agents of progressive change, then we can change our condition and assist in changing the world."

But how is this possible given the persistent categorical and philosophical confusion that exists in African communities throughout the world? Perhaps it is necessary for African people to explore their own reality as the primary locus of change. Just today I opened my email and saw a beautiful note from a Zimbabwean studying for a doctorate in London. He claims to have read my works and to have felt quite insufficiently educated by the European system of training because it taught him little or nothing about his own culture and did not integrate his knowledge, that is, what he already had as knowledge into the general system of knowledge promoted by Europe. I was struck by his letter because I realize the great mental and cultural pain that he must have experienced during his academic career. It is the problematic of Africans being educated away from their centers.

# Implications for method

I have asserted that there are five general characteristics of Afrocentric research that engages the serious scholar. In the first place, one assumes, based on historical analysis, that no phenomenon can be apprehended adequately without first being located. Thus, location is a principal activity of the Afrocentric analyst. A phenom, that is, any situation, event, text, or personality, must be studied and analyzed in relationship to psychological time and space. It must always be located. This is the only way to investigate the complex interrelationships of science and art, design and execution, creation and maintenance, generation and tradition, and other areas bypassed by theory. Furthermore, Afrocentricity considers phenomena to be diverse, dynamic, and in motion and therefore it is necessary for a person to accurately note and record the location of phenomena even in flux. This means that the researcher must take an auto-locative stance in order to know where she or he is standing in the process.

If we are beginning to have elements of an approach that gives us some-thing we call the Afrocentric method, then we reveal it as a form of cultural criticism that examines etymological uses of words and terms in order to know the source of an author's location. This allows us to intersect ideas with actions and actions with ideas on the basis of what is pejorative and ineffective and what is creative and transformative at the political and economic levels.

I remember being invited to write an entry for the *Encyclopedia of African Religion* on the subject of "reincarnation." In researching the issue in African philosophy and after reading the works of Opoku, Gyekye, Onyewuenyi, and Idowu, I was struck by the difficulty of the task brought about because of the term "reincarnation" as understood in the West as the return of a person's spirit into another being. This was not found in the African notion of deathlessness which I believe more adequately describes how Africans view the idea of ancestors reappearing.

The difficulty is the Western bifurcation of the spirit and body, a Platonic invention that produced the notion that the body dies but that the spirit goes somewhere else. During the rise of Christianity, a major tag for Western culture, it was thought that good spirits go to heaven and bad spirits go to hell. This separation of spirit from body became a part of the language of Europe and in consequence the language of those cultures that were conquered by Europe. Reincarnation came to mean the re-entering of a body of the spirit that had left the dead person. This is inex-plicable from an Afrocentric point of view because African cultures, including the Akan with their own relationship to community, believe that an ancestor is not a ghost, or spirit, but a person who lives, speaks, makes decisions, and can present in many different individuals at the same time and never leave the world of invisibility. It is therefore impossible to speak of a one-to-one reincarnation when the ancestor appears, perhaps, in several descendants. In a system where the *okra, sunsum*, and *mogya* are interpreted as representing three different "pieces" of the human, one can see great confusion. This is the Akan construction of the person as soul, personality, and blood. However, this cannot be understood in a Platonic sense; it must be seen as inseparable forces of the human. There are no split humans in African culture. One can discuss this further but reading on it should consider the writings of Innocent Onyewuenyi and others. My main contention here is that the Western notion of language is often a trap for explaining African concepts.

To start from a place where we assume that the way Europe has struc-tured its own thoughts is exactly as it should be for the rest of the world is the most acute form of imperialism. Afrocentricity is one formula for overcoming this problem.

The Afrocentric method seeks to uncover the masks behind the rhetoric of power, privilege, and position in order to establish how principal myths create *place*. The method enthrones critical reflection that reveals the perception of monolithic power as nothing but the projection of a cadre of adventurers. For example, it would be wrong to assume that the whole of Europe is engaged in the imperial project that has become the globalizing vision of a new group of conquerors. One cannot lay at the feet of all the whites in America the damnable deeds done against Africans, Mexicans, and Asians in their name. What we are speaking about when we speak of the mask is a facade that has been created for control.

Finally, I think that the Afrocentric method *locates* the imaginative structure of a system of economics, bureau of politics, policy of government, expression of cultural form in the *attitude, direction, and language of the phenom*, be it text, institution, personality, interaction, or event. To locate a phenom as peripheral or central to the African experience allows the researcher to begin from an orientation that will have meaning for the ultimate analysis of a situation or condition. One of the perennial complaints of Africans who have lived in Francophone areas of Africa or in France itself is that the educational system teaches students that their ancestors were the Gauls. This is certainly decentering for African children and an example of a system that was put in place for French descendant and origin children. It is disorienting for African children and ultimately makes them "insane" by disconnecting them from reality. A black child who goes around thinking that the Gauls were her ancestors has already begun on the wrong path to sanity. In fact, it is the road to a terrorizing psychology that will be unrelenting in its hold on the person throughout her life.

What is absolutely necessary for the person who seeks to use the assumptions and principles of Afrocentricity for critical analysis is an emphasis on the analytic aspects of the idea. For example, it becomes important for the Afrocentrist to understand how to use the Afrocentric method in textual analysis. It goes without saying that the Afrocentrist cannot function properly as a scientist or humanist if he or she does not adequately locate the phenom in time and space. This means that chronology is as important in some situations as location. Both aspects of analysis are central to any proper understanding of society, history, or personality.

An Afrocentrist must always know what time it is otherwise his analysis may be off the mark. If you are referring to a particular cultural phenomenon that has occurred in Africa or anywhere in the African world it is crucial to know when the phenomenon occurred. Without this information you are playing in the fog and will not be able to see correctly the meaning or interpretation of the phenomenon. Inasmuch as phenoms are active, dynamic, and diverse in our society, the Afrocentric method requires the scientists to focus on accurate notations and recording of space and time. In fact, the best way to apprehend location of a text is to determine where the researcher is located in time and space first. Once you know the location and time of the researcher or author, it is fairly easy to establish the parameters for the phenom itself.

Another aspect of the analytical enterprise of Afrocentricity is etymology of words and terms. The value of etymology, that is, the origin of terms and words is in the proper identification and location of concepts. The Afrocentrist seeks to demonstrate clarity by exposing dislocations, disorientations, and decenteredness. One of the simplest ways of accessing textual clarity is through etymology. In a larger, more universal sense, etymology is a part, only a small part, of the process of myth-making in society. Myths tie all relationships together, whether personal or conceptual. It is the Afrocentrist's task to determine to what extent the myths of society are represented as being central to or marginal to society. This means that any textual analysis must involve the concrete realities of lived experiences, thus making historical experiences a key element in analytical Afrocentricity.

Closely allied to this etymological process is the operation of reclamation of names, places, and concepts that create dislocation in the African world. When Europe colonized Africa, it also colonized the language used to speak about Africa. Thus, at the very beginning of Greek domination of African interpretation one finds that the name of Kemet is changed to Egypt. An African original becomes in the writing of the Greeks a Greek epithet for "houses of Ptah." Subsequently, the appropriation of African cultural forms, places, and concepts such as *shenu, bennu, tekken, hormarkhet, Waset, Mennefer, neb ankh* (Europe claims these as *cartouche, phoenix, obelisk, sphinx, Thebes* or *Luxor, Memphis*, and *sarcophagus*) and thousands of other terms disrupted the common understanding of African realities. This was not simply a process that infected thinking about ancient Egypt; it was an ordinary process of European control. Cities in Africa lost their African names only to be re-introduced with European names: Rhacostas becomes Alexandria, Harare becomes Salisbury, and so forth. Where African names seemed difficult for Europeans to pronounce, they gave completely new ones such as Leopoldville, Stanleyville, and Elisabethville. Natural formations lost their names as Europe colonized mental territories by calling *Mosi wa tunya*, "the smoke that thunders," by the name of *Victoria Falls*. How to combat dislocation in the thinking and writing of Africans and Europeans becomes the task of the researcher who must explore all information from the standpoint of Afrocentricity if he is to discover the proper *djed*. One can only do this by discovering certain mental and psychological markers.

In examining attitude, direction, and language the Afrocentrist is seeking to uncover the imagination of the author. What one seeks to do is to create an opportunity for the writer to show where he or she stands in relationship to the subject. Is the writer centered or is the writer marginalized within his own story? It is in answering this question that the researcher establishes the author's first response to their own works because the answer to the questions about centeredness and marginalization assists the researcher in making an analysis. Do I really know you? Can I know you if you do not know yourself? Where do you stand in this text or outside this text? Where are the people of this text?

## A reconciliation

Afrocentricity cannot be reconciled to any hegemonic or idealistic philosophy. It is opposed to radical individualism as expressed in the postmodern school. But it is also opposed to spookism, confusion, and superstition. As example of the differences between the methods of Afrocentricity and postmodernism, consider the following question, "Why have Africans been shut out of global development?"

The postmodernist would begin by saying that there is no such thing as "Africans" because there are many different types of Africans and all Africans are not equal. Furthermore, Africa is an invention of the last five hundred years and as such cannot exist as an entity apart from its creation. The postmodernist would go on to say that if there were Africans and if the conditions were as described by the questioner, then the answer would be that Africans had not fully developed their own capacities in relationship to the global economy and therefore they are outside the normal development patterns of the world economy. On the other hand, the Afrocentrist does not question the fact that there is a collective sense of Africanity revealed in the common experiences of the African world whenever Africa was invented. Thus, by the trappings of texts, history, language, wars, and imperial designs, one can still say Africa exists. Of course, there are tendencies against this position in Europe; I mean there are those who see too much speaking about speech and too much writing about writing, intertextuality. I do not go quite so far because I think there is a great degree of knowledge to be gained by this type of inquiry. However, I do not know of any caprices of language that can eliminate the realities of Africa itself. The Afrocentrist would look to the question of location, control of the hegemonic global economy, marginalization, and power positions as keys to understand the deliberate, assertive, and imperial underdevelopment of African people.

But what is an Afrocentric response to the economic situation of the African world? Economic development is the issue of producing and using food, shelter, clothing, and utilities to sustain a human way of life. How humans have produced food and how humans will produce food constitute a question of time and space. What is possible given the space and time humans have to produce and distribute food? What about the weather, the geo-political realities? When Africans are able to produce their own food for the continent, there will be a different orientation toward Africa. In fact, food production and distribution are at the center of any problem concerning Afrocentric location of the economy. There will be, as the Marxists claim, a new reality when the modes of production change. But there is a new reality when the producer assumes a central rather than a marginal role in society.

# 3

## Afrocentricity: Notes on a Disciplinary Position

As we have seen in the preceding chapter, the Afrocentric idea is essentially about location (Asante, 1998; Mazama, 2003a). Since Africans have been moved off terms culturally, psychologically, economically, and historically, it is important that any assessment of the African condition in whatever situation or condition or estate be made from an Afrocentric location. Perhaps this is the central idea of discipline when it comes to pedagogy as well as other aspects of life. The problem of effective response to the condition of oppression, literally mental oppression, which is the first-order oppression, has needed a pre-emptive strike. Afrocentricity provides the necessary instruments to transform the condition of the colonized, the victimized, the wretched, and the nihilistic (Fanon, 1961; Okafor, 1994; Asante, 2006).

Lewis Gordon claims in the book *Disciplinary Decadence: Living Thought in Trying Times* (2006, p. 3) that "the term discipline originally meant to educate. Its connotation over the millennia has shifted considerably, now referring in English to processes of control, at times linked with punishment in one instance and sycophantic allegiance and followers, as in disciples, in another." However, there is an element of certainty, centeredness, in the concept that introduces *djed* or stasis, the place where one stands. I do not see either the idea of location or the concept of centeredness as a characteristic of control or punishment; rather both are reasonable positions for an individual committed to discovering the power of the center.

There could be no true understanding of the role of pedagogy without some appreciation of where students and teachers are located culturally and psychologically. The latter is more important when it comes to the question of centrality and marginality. Both locations assist in determining what types of pedagogical interventions are useful.

Stating a definition does not exhaust the power of a concept; it may in fact create further difficulties unless it is explained in such a way as to elucidate the idea. Afrocentricity is about location precisely because African people have been operating from the fringes of the Eurocentric experience. Much of what we have studied in African history and culture, or literature and linguistics, or politics and economics, has been orchestrated from the standpoint of Europe's interests. Whether it is a matter of economics, history, politics, geographical concepts, or art, Africans have been seen as peripheral to the "real" activity. This off-centeredness has impacted Africans as well as whites in the United States. Thus, to speak of Afrocentricity as a radical redefinition means that we seek the re-orientation of Africans to a centered position (Asante, 1998) in their own history.

## Conscientization

Afrocentricity emerged as a process of political consciousness for a people who existed on the edge of education, art, science, economics, communication, and technology as defined by Eurocentrists. If the process were successful, then the re-centering of the people would create a new reality and open another chapter in the liberation of the minds of Africans. Two philosophers of culture had already predicted this phase of the Afrocentric movement: Kwame Nkrumah and Harold Cruse, a continental and a diasporan African. My aim with the publication of *Afrocentricity* was to strike a blow at the lack of consciousness, not simply the lack of consciousness of our oppression but the lack of consciousness of what victories were possible on the basis of Nkrumah and Cruse's formulations. One could begin to analyze human relationships, multicultural interactions, texts, phenomena and events, and African liberation from the standpoint of orientation toward facts.

No one can question the fact that Kwame Nkrumah was the most important political philosopher to lead an African nation. His philosophy of *Consciencism* had been born out of his experience in the United States of America. He had come into contact with an advanced hegemonic society that was bent on asserting its intellectual and cultural dominance. Indeed, when he arrived in London he discovered that, just as in the United States, there were individuals in the United Kingdom whose ambition seemed to be extending the thinking that Europe was superior to Africa. Nkrumah writes in his introduction to *Consciencism*:

> It was at the Universities of Lincoln and Pennsylvania that this conscience was first awakened. I was introduced to the great philosophical systems of the past to which the Western universities have given their blessing, arranging and classifying them with the delicate care lavished on museum pieces. When once these systems were so handled, it was natural that they should be regarded as monuments of human in intellection. And monu-

ments, because they mark achievements at their particular point in history, soon become conservative in the impression which they make on posterity. (Nkrumah, 1964, p. 4)

Like so many young African students, Nkrumah recounts how he was introduced to Plato, Aristotle, Descartes, Kant, Hegel, Schopenhauer, Nietzsche, Marx and other European intellectuals. He knew as a student from a colony, the Gold Coast, that these philosophers were being promoted against all forms of African knowledge and experience. What the white teachers were doing was stamping in his chest for ever the superiority of their own intellectual immortals. He would never be without the effects of this teaching; he would be a victim of the propaganda of the conquerors. But how does one regain a sense of balance?

Nkrumah knew that he was being made to question his own intellectual origin and he had nothing in his memory that could combat the incessant attack. He writes that:

> The colonial student can be so seduced by these attempts to give a philosophical account of the universe, that he surrenders his whole personality to them. When he does this, he loses sight of the fundamental social fact that he is a colonial subject. In this way, he omits to draw from his education, and from the concern displayed by the great philosophers for human problems, anything which he might relate to the very real problem of colonial domination, which, as it happens, conditions the immediate life of every colonized African. (Nkrumah, 1964)

Whatever ability the African student has and whatever attempt he makes to meander through the intellectual systems which are provided, he can never fathom all the intricate ways the Europeans have devised to keep him marginalized. Clearly one has to remember that even "philosophical systems are facts of history" (Nkrumah, 1964). Nkrumah calls the type of education received by colonial students defective education. In effect, this is similar to Carter G. Woodson's expression of "the mis-education of the Negro." Nothing could be worse for the young colonial student than to be miseducated about the world. Most of these students were hand-picked by colonial officials and carried certificates of value with them to the European schools. These certificates were used to say that these students would make good colonial subjects. They were fit to become knowledgeable of the European way of life. Indeed, Nkrumah writes that "By reason of their lack of contact with their own roots, they became prone to accept some theory of universalism, provided it was expressed in vague, mellifluous terms" (Nkrumah, 1964, p. 4).

These students, selected by the colonial administrators to receive "white" education, would soon carry their weapons of European knowledge back home with attitudes at variance with their elders and ancestors. They would be lost to the concrete struggles of their people. They would challenge all forms of knowledge that might liberate them and their people. They would use abstractions instead of concrete realities to speak about the conditions of the people. Thus, Nkrumah wanted to see a new African evolve who would practice the philosophy of consciencism and make Africa the center of their ambitions. But to do this, the African has to revise Marxism, which Nkrumah believed to be the most combative ideology for challenging colonialism, and demonstrate that African communalism could move through its traditions to African socialism. None of this could happen without having political and cultural space and, just as Nkrumah was moving in the direction of discovering this space with Marx, another philosopher in the African world was going in the opposite direction after long years with Marxism.

The objective has always been to create space for conscious human beings who are, by virtue of their centeredness, committed to sanity. This is the key to re-orientation and re-centering so that the person acts as an agent rather than as a victim or dependant. Clearly the most practical theorist in this regard was Harold Cruse, who was the philosopher abandoning Marxism for a kind of revolutionary nationalism in the 1960s. When he died in 2005 at the ripe old age of 89 he had written two important books, *The Crisis of the Negro Intellectual* and *Rebellion or Revolution*, and scores of articles laying out his view about the intellectual and cultural direction of African people. I believe his contribution rests in several places and at several levels of inquiry. Cruse is concerned with culture, politics, education, and economics. By virtue of his concern with the African American community exercising its own volition in terms of culture and economics, Cruse was a nationalist. The plea he made in *Rebellion or Revolution* (Cruse, 1969, pp. 48–67) for a radical cultural theory indicates that he was a forerunner of the Afrocentric idea. He sees these issues from the standpoint of African American history and investigates the various dimensions of the issues from the standpoint of political maturity and cultural consciousness. When one reads his works, the principal ones, *The Crisis of the Negro Intellectual* and *Rebellion or Revolution*, his concept of the crisis in the African American community is clear. For Cruse, the fundamental question facing the community is a cultural one, not simply one of singing and dancing, but one concerned with the sum total of our behaviors, artistic, social, and communal. He asks, "Whose culture do we uphold, the Afro-American or the Anglo-American?" (Cruse, 1969, p. 48). Only the recent Afrocentrists have answered the question in the manner Harold Cruse would appreciate because the Afrocentrists believe that the cultural crisis provides the greatest opportunity for the loss of liberty. If we are able to resolve the cultural question, we will be able to confront all other issues such as economic unity, political redemption, that is, the choice for ourselves, and social maturity and protocols. In this sense culture becomes genetic to the intellectual and political achievements of people who accept and give agency. In Cruse's construction of the problems in the African American community everything was clear. Africans had denied, lost, or given away agency in order to become different from our historical selves. Like the black women who sit for hours at the hair stylist getting their hair straightened in the painful perm process, Cruse says that we have become victims of the worst form of cultural propaganda (Cruse, 1967, pp. 420–43). Some blacks did not support African American culture because in their minds it was separatist; they wanted to demonstrate that they were Americans, meaning that they supported Anglo-American culture. This confusion Cruse recognized before others and sought to explore ways to neutralize this destructive attitude.

The message of Harold Cruse is especially poignant because this is pre-eminently the age of "no race" and "interrace" and "fluid cultures." We are profoundly affected by this postmodern appeal to forget culture, not even to build new cultures, just forget African culture. This is predominantly a phenomenon of the black elite; it is not an attitude found among the Chinese Americans, Japanese Americans, Korean Americans, Italian Americans, or French Americans. This seems to be a peculiarly African American problem enhanced by the lack of a strong sense of cultural identity promulgated by Africans who have lost their sense of cultural ground.I am convinced that the enslavement was more effective as a maker of slaves, mental slaves, than is imagined. As other cultures recognize the value of their own and in some cases, like the French, continue to legislate ways to preserve their culture, many African American intellectuals still suffer, as Harold Cruse understood, from cultural dualisms, split personalities, and lean toward the worship of an iconic whiteness. I can think of no example of people of other cultures urging the abandoning of their culture or refusing to practice their culture. This is obviously a behavior of those who feel inferior or have been made to speak as if their culture is inferior because of their own cultural condition.

Because Cruse is a strict African Americanist, he does not view the relationship of Africa or the Caribbean to the African American as important; this is a crucial flaw in his conception and one that the Afrocentrists have corrected in their own theories. Therefore, the powerful cultural analysis of Cruse is outstanding in its reach but it is incomplete. This is his biggest hurdle and one that makes it impossible for him to understand the response of the African American Negro intellectuals of the 1950s and 1960s. Cruse had deliberately separated Africa from African Americans and in so doing believed that he was following Du Bois' notion that the African American was truly an American product (see Du Bois, 1982 [1903]). But Du Bois was wrong and Cruse's support of him was to compound the problem of culture and further conceal the source of the lack of cultural will. It is to be regretted that Harold Cruse did not see this mistake because in so many other insights he is brilliant. Yet he thought that the ocean was an insurmountable barrier between the African and African American. Since we Africans in the Americas had been de-tribalized, he thought we could not search for Africa and indeed he believed we would never find it because of the complications of the Americanization of the Negro. But the Negro was to be a transitory person, an artificial creation, an inauthentic African, one without groundedness and thus only a passing phase in the evolution of cultural change. The cycle would be completed only with the return to centeredness in the African's own cultural grounding, which is not some esoteric back-to-Africanity idea, but the genuine operation of our psychocultural center from our own reality, experience, and perspective.

But this is the crux of the cultural problem. The African people who landed, against their wills, in the Caribbean and North and South America, were Africans – Mandinka, Ibo, Yoruba, Asante, Fante, Ibibio, Congo, Angola, Wolof, Ijo, and so forth – not African Americans. We were never made European, though some came fairly close to being so made. As John Henrik Clarke, the late dean of African American Studies would say, "We were Africans who retained much of Africa even through the slavery institution and we also were deeply affected by Europe in America, but we remained Africans." Wolof wisdom says, "Wood may remain in water for ten years but it will never become a crocodile." In respect to the cultural question, Cruse's project would have been stronger had he seen that the real issue was the lack of Afrocentricity in the African. Although we could not escape our inherent Africanity in the way we talked, walked, danced, or made music, we did not often consciously choose to be Afrocentric. Therein is the cultural difficulty he failed to see.

Cruse's lament is that African Americans have not achieved what we should have achieved culturally given what he sees as our artistic genius. However, he argues the necessity for a new type of culturalist with specific characteristics. I have drawn from his analysis three factors that the culturalist should possess: (1) a commitment to cultural agency; (2) the lack of economic or moral fear; and (3) the willingness to pursue the objective of freedom. What Cruse understood in this regard was that only artists or just plain humans who were capable of supporting these ideas could be depended upon for cultural liberation.

The African American community, male and female, continues to be marginalized in the context of culture and economics, just as the African continent continues to be marginalized globally. What is the role of the artists in such a situation? Does it mean that artists should place their own personal ambitions ahead of the masses of African people? The debate about individual freedom and community responsibility has often deteriorated into a lament about the inability of artists to understand that culture is the centerpiece of communal rehabilitation. To indulge oneself in non-committed art is certainly within the freedom of the individual artist but Cruse argues that it is socially non-redemptive. Great art emerges from the soul of the creator and the best creator is the person who knows who he or she is at the moment of creation. This is self-conscious art, the highest form of creating the new and making the innovative. The enslaved Africans could produce the Spirituals because they recognized the existential reality of their situation. They were not confused about their identity and knew precisely who they were and who the white slave masters were.

Obviously, the future of the heterogeneous United States is not one giant amalgamation of cultures as some suggest, but rather a multiplicity of cultures without hierarchy resting on certain political and social pillars that support racial and cultural equality and respect. This multiplicity of cultural centers revolving around respect and equality is the only viable future for the United States. In some ways, this could be a model for the world where we know the nearly 2000 ethnic groups will not disappear but could live in a peace where there is mutual respect.

But for this to work effectively it means that humans must have a mature attitude toward culture. Harold Cruse's concern about this in relationship to African Americans was real. He saw a state of cultural malaise where the popular culture did not enrich the community and where artists had degenerated into peddlers of the most vacuous nonsense to gain fame and money. Surely Cruse was brutal in his estimation of the contemporary artists whose art was merely narcissistic. For him, having grown to maturity in the communist tradition, the best art had to be performative in the service of the community. Thus, even when he had abandoned communism, he appropriated the most severe forms for the artistic discipline.

I believe that Harold Cruse understood long before the present Afrocentrists the dislocation that occurred because of the forced migration of the African people. The enslavement of African people created, inter alia, a permanent class of revolutionaries against the racist order. Cruse understood this and while he was more acutely impacted by the integrationists than he admitted, he was still profoundly convinced that the African American community needed a cultural revolution. But he knew also that the only way that such a radical change could occur was with a new philosophy of culture.

Harold Cruse did not believe that the Marxists or radical democrats could bring about the type of cultural revolution he envisioned. They are captured by the ideology of failure and the inability to redefine the relationship of the African American to American society. Understanding the history of Marxism, Cruse examined it as inapplicable to the condition of African American culture. According to Cruse, Marx relied upon the basic principle of the law of unity and the conflict of opposites to underscore his idea of the dialectical principle of theory and practice. The idea is that capital production creates two classes, the capitalists and the workers. Since the capitalists will try to increase their profit by exploiting labor, labor will revolt with strikes, work stoppages, and other protests. When this occurs in advanced capitalist societies it means that there will be revolution.

The problem is that there has never been a workers' revolution in an advanced capitalist society. All of the previous communist revolutions have been in less advanced capitalist societies. Thus, Cruse understood something that many contemporary leftists fail to understand, and that is that white labor is pro-capital, anti-immigration, and anti-African. Yet the Marxists and their political descendants believe in some radical reconfiguring of the American political landscape where white and black labor will unite against white capital. Cruse knew, as the Afrocentrists contend, that the situation was much more complex, perhaps nuanced in new ways, than the strict white labor and white capital uniting. The rewards were now far more global.

It is my contention that the Marxists were in turmoil in the United States long before the writings of Cruse, although there are a lot of Marxists who would accuse Cruse of red-baiting. The international crisis of Marxism during the past two decades or so is just an indication that it could not have succeeded in the case of African Americans. The de facto radical movement in the United States has always been the African American movement for justice and equality. The Marxists as communists never ascended to the level of posing a political threat to the American government or the established order, despite the harassment and persecution they received at the hands of American authorities. Many prominent Marxists have been black and it has been estimated that 40 percent of the communists of Harlem were African Americans. Despite the incarceration rate, the bullying, the raids on their homes, they were never able to galvanize the black masses. In fact, we have no history of a communist movement in the United States where communists put their bodies and lives on the line for black liberation as African Americans themselves did. What does this mean? Was class not a strong contradiction in the American society or was race the fundamental contradiction for which people were willing to die for resolution? Were there no white workers willing to give up their lives for the class issue? In the United States race remains the one characteristic which has confounded the Marxists. It is this situation that confounds the radical democrats today as they scurry to find a place to be. Because the Marxists as communists or Trotskyites were unable to lead any type of revolution, they became "twin branches on the withering tree of Marxism," according to Cruse.

The Afrocentrists are the legitimate children of Harold Cruse's appreciation of the role of culture, though they differ with his understanding of the complexity of the oppression, the internationalization of the hegemony, and the role of Africa in the rise to consciousness in Africans in the Americas. Nevertheless, we seek to assert Cruse's notion of a radical cultural theory in every context of African life. But what is the principal element of this radical theory? It is the fact of agency, that is, the activity of a subjectivity based on one's orientation to culture.

What Cruse does not see, I believe, is that it is impossible for this radical theory and practice to emerge from the conditions of mental slavery. The slave must overcome this condition in order to advance to a higher degree of cultural expression. Thus, Frantz Fanon of Martinique, a political psychologist and a supporter of the Algerian Revolution, understood this more clearly than any of the Negritude writers though ostensibly they were concerned with culture. On two occasions, once in 1968 at the University of California, Los Angeles and again in 1985 in Miami at the Negritude Conference organized by Carlos Moore, I heard Léopold Sédar Senghor expound on culture and each time I felt that he did not effectively address the question of cultural encapsulation, that is, the fact that one could never rise above the condition of mental slavery without a radical re-orientation.

Harold Cruse does not even venture down this road but he raises the question of a radical social and cultural theory. Aime Césaire, Leon Damas, Alioune Diop, and Senghor attempt to address it with Negritude but this is ultimately an artistic movement, perhaps, even only an artistic statement that we have a culture, that our culture is rich, and that we declare our cultural maturity. As an assertion and indeed a demonstration in the works of the poets and essayists this is a positive advance but it could not deal with the confrontation of Cruse's cultural malaise.

The theory that Cruse prophesied would have to have five aspects: (1) psychological orientations; (2) emotional commitments; (3) political implications; (4) collective textual revision; and (5) socio-economic redefinitions. Aiming to redefine the cultural landscape used by African Americans the new theory would be oriented toward African motifs, designs, concepts, languages, and styles. In this psychological orientation it would take on dimensions of personality and spirituality that would direct any thrust into personal or collective transformation. As an emotional commitment it would mean that the African American would be saturated in historical knowledge so as to understand the nuances and intricacies of the culture and not merely participate without some emotional attachment to the knowledge. Only with this kind of emotional orientation could self-interested political actions be possible. Otherwise the African American person could conceivably become anti-African American in political situations. The collective textual revision that would take place in this case would change the ethos and image of African Americans as beggars after the culture of others and would promote and project us as agents, actors, artists, in our own right who operate in keeping with our cultural and ethical standards. Implications for socio-economic achievement should be self-evident in such case. Those who are transformed into agents would also seek to make agents out of others through economic activity centered in the interest of liberation. What Cruse calls into being is a radical theory, not merely an assertion of culture, and in this instance those who have obliged him the most are the Afrocentrists.

## The agency concept

An agent, in our terms, must mean a human being who is capable of acting independently in his or her own best interest. Agency itself is the ability to provide the psychological and cultural resources necessary for the advancement of human freedom. In situations of un-freedom, oppression, racial repression, the active idea within the concept of agent assumes the primary position. What does this mean practically in the context of Afrocentricity? When one interrogates issues of place, situation, milieu, and occasion that involve African people as participants, it is important to look for the concept of agency as opposed to dis-agency. We say that one has found dis-agency in every situation where the African is dismissed as a player or actor within his or her own world. I am fundamentally committed to the view that African people must be seen as agents in economic, cultural, political, and social terms. What we can argue about in any intellectual discourse is the degree to which Africans are weak or strong agents, but there should not be any question that agency exists. When agency does not exist we have the condition of marginality, and the worst form of marginality is to be marginal within your own story. Take the story of David Livingstone in Africa where the entire history of a region of the continent turns on what happened to a white man in the midst of hundreds of thousands of Africans. Is there no agency to any of the African personalities? Should the writing of the history of Central Africa be the writing of Livingstone's history? Are there no other ways to approach a topic such as this?

Africans have been negated in the system of white racial domination. This is not mere marginalization, but the obliteration of the presence, meaning, activities, or images of the African. This is negated reality, a destruction of the spiritual and material personality of the African person. Therefore, the African must, to be conscious, be aware of everything and seek to escape from the anomie of fringeness. This is a linguistic problem at one level but at another level it is a problem of dealing with the reality of constructed economic and cultural situations.

Afrocentricity is not religion and that is why the constituents of African values are debatable, even though they are central to Afrocentric inquiry. There are no closed systems; that is, there are no ideas that are absolutely seen as off limits for discussion and debate. Thus, when Afrocentricity is employed in analysis or criticism, it opens the way for examination of all issues related to the African world.

## Minimum characteristics

In the previous chapter I argued that the minimum characteristics for an Afrocentric project should include: (1) an interest in psychological location; (2) a commitment to finding the African subject place; (3) the defense of African cultural elements; (4) a commitment to lexical refinement; and (5) a commitment to correct the dislocations in the history of Africa. However, Danjuma Sinue Modupe has presented additional ideas identified from my earlier work which he believes help create a more robust list of characteristics of Afrocentricity. He lists the communal cognitive will, African development, a consciousness matrix, psychic liberation, cultural reclamation, Africanity, African personalism, Afrocentric praxis, Afrocentric framework, framework integrity, cause, effect, alleviation, theoretical constructs, critical theoretical distinctions, structural gluon, victorious consciousness, and perspective (Modupe 2003: 55–72).

# An interest in psychological location

This is fundamentally a perspectivist idea. The Afrocentrist argues that one's analysis is more often than not related to where a person's mind is located. For example, you can normally tell if an African is located in a culturally centered position vis-à-vis the African world by how that person relates to African information. If he or she speaks of Africans as the "other" then you have an idea that the person views the African as other than herself or himself. This is one way the dislocation works. Of course, if a person is not African but seeks to make an Afrocentric analysis, what you look for is the ability of the person to view African phenomena from the standpoint of Africans themselves. One who seeks to construct an Afrocentric curriculum for schools, an Afrocentric social work practice, or an Afrocentric literary text must give attention to the idea of psychological or cultural location.

The use of the term location in the Afrocentric sense refers to the psychological, cultural, historical or personal place occupied by a person at a given time in history. Thus, to be in a location is to be fixed, temporarily or permanently, in a certain historical space. When the Afrocentrist says that it is necessary to discover one's location, it is always in reference to whether or not the person is in a centered or marginal place with regards to his or her culture. An oppressed person is dis-located when she operates from a standpoint, that is, location that is centered in the experiences of the oppressor. As Memmi understood, once the colonized is out of the picture, he "is no longer a subject of history anymore" (Memmi, 1991, p. 92). The aim, of course, of the Afrocentrist is to keep the African in his own story.

# A commitment to finding the African subject place

The Afrocentrist is concerned with discovering in every place and in all circumstances the subject position of the African person. This is particularly true in cases where the issues of significance, that is, the themes, topics, and concerns are of African ideas and activities. Too often the discussion of African phenomena has moved on the basis of what Europeans think, do, and say in relation to the phenomenon rather than what the Africans themselves are saying and doing. Thus, the aim of Afrocentric agency is to demonstrate a powerful commitment to finding the African subject place in almost every event, text, and idea. This is not easy because the complications of identity of place are often discovered in the interstices between who we are and who we want to be. While we may determine what a person is at one given moment, we may not know all that he or she can become tomorrow. Yet we must have a commitment to discovering where the African person, idea, or concept enters a text, event, or phenomenon, as subject.

## The defense of African cultural elements

The Afrocentrist is concerned with all protection and defense of African cultural values and elements as part of the human project (Schiele, 1994, p. 284; Schiele, 1996, p. 150; Schiele, 1997, p. 800). One cannot assume an orientation to African agency without giving respect and place to the creative dimension of the African personality. This does not mean that all things African are good or useful; it means that what Africans have done and what Africans do represent human creativity. Such a pronouncement speaks to the embarrassing fact that many past scholars and writers dismissed African creations, whether music, dance, art, or science, as something different from the rest of humanity. This was decidedly racist and any interpretation or analysis of African cultural elements or contributions that employed negations of African cultural elements was suspect.

However, the Afrocentrist uses all linguistic, psychological, sociological, and philosophical elements to defend African cultural elements. Given the arguments against African values, habits, customs, religion, behaviors, or thought, the Afrocentrist discovers as much as possible the authentic African understanding of the elements without imposing Eurocentric or non-African interpretations. This allows the scholar to have a clear appreciation of the African cultural element.

## A commitment to lexical refinement

Typically the Afrocentrist wants to know that the language used in a text is based upon the idea of Africans as subjects. This means that the person who creates the text must have some understanding of the nature of the African reality. For example, when the American or English person calls the African house a "hut," he or she is misrepresenting reality. The Afrocentrist approaches the question of the living space of Africans from the standpoint of African reality. The idea of a house in the English language leads one to assume a building with kitchen, bedrooms, bathrooms, and recreational spaces, but in the African concept one has a different representation. Thus, the house must be conceived of as a compound of structures where there is one structure for sleeping, one for storage, and another for guests. The cooking and recreational areas are typically outside the sleeping space. Therefore it is important that any person considering African cultural ideas pay close attention to the type of language that is used. In the case of the domicile of Africans one must first of all ask what do Africans call the place where they sleep? This is the only way to prevent the use of negative terminology such as "hut" when referring to African living places. One could also extend the analysis by examining the differences in understanding the concept of house, home, and so forth in various African cultural communities. Thus, the genuine Afrocentrist seeks to rid the language of negations of Africans being agents within the sphere of Africa's own history. This should not have been perceived as a problem in scholarship and literature except the condition of Western education was such that all references to Africa or African people, with the exception of a limited number of progressive thinkers, sought to see Africa as helpless, second class, inferior, non-human, not a part of human history, and indeed, in some instances, savage. This was Europe's contribution to the lexicon of African history.

## A commitment to a new narrative of Africa

One assumes now that the Afrocentrist is clear that one of the primary obligations of the scholar is to make an assessment of the condition of research and then to intervene in the appropriate manner. With regards to African literature, history, behavior, and economics, the Eurocentric writers have always positioned Africa in the inferior place with regards to every subject field. This has been a deliberate falsification of the record. It is one of the greatest conspiracies in the history of the world because what was agreed upon, tacitly, by writer after writer was that Africa should be marginalized in the literature and downgraded when it seemed that the literature spoke with high regard to Africa. We see this at the very root of the problem in the study of Kemet, classical Egyptian history.

After Napoleon, the emperor, and Dominique Vivant Denon, the leader of Napoleon's cadre of writers, had made their conquest of Egypt, an entirely different orientation to African knowledge was undertaken. We were at once introduced to a new field of human inquiry, Egyptology. With Champollion's deciphering of the language of the ancient Egyptians, Europe was off to a dismantling of Egypt's history as African and of African history as being related to the Nile Valley. The only river on the African continent that was made a part of the European experience was the Nile. It was as if Europe had taken the river drop by drop out of the continent and dumped it onto the European landscape. All African contributions from the

Nile Valley became European contributions and Europe began the task of confusing the world about the nature of ancient Egypt. This was the biggest falsification and the one that appears at any discussion of the great civilizations of antiquity.

## Egypt v. Greece

Perhaps one of the abiding myths to sustain the European hegemony has been the Greek origin of civilization. This has now been shown to have been an exaggeration promoted by scholars intent on proving the superiority of Europe. Martin Bernal's book, *Black Athena*, shattered the idea that Greece preceded Africa, particularly Egypt, in human civilization (Bernal, 1987). What Bernal did in relationship to the origin of Greek civilization, Cheikh Anta Diop had done with regards to civilization in general (Diop, 1974).

In other words, Diop demonstrated that the African origin of civilization was a fact, not fiction. He further showed that the ancient Egyptians were black-skinned people, using evidence from written texts, scientific experiments, and cultural analysis (Diop, 1981). What is more is the fact that the evidence has been pouring in since the death of Diop in 1986 that he was correct in his theories (Poe, 1998).

Indeed, we know now with even more certainty that the origin of the human race is on the continent of Africa. Even more, biology has shown that the mitochondrial DNA of all humans can be traced to one African woman who lived about 200,000 years ago in East Africa.

Thus, two arguments that would not have been made fifty years ago have now been made and have changed the way we look at the ancient world. The first argument is that the ancient Greeks owed a great deal to ancient Africans. Indeed, Plato, Homer, Diodorus, Democritus, Anaximander, Isocrates, Thales, Pythagoras, Anaxagoras, and many other Greeks studied and lived in Africa (Asante and Mazama, 2002). The other part of that argument is that the ancient Egyptians were black-skinned Africans. The proof had been given by Herodotus, Aristotle, Diodorus, and Strabo. They did not set out to make a case for the blackness of the ancient Egyptians to support modern arguments; yet their words are there to contradict the opinions of modern critics of Afrocentricity.

The second argument is that all humans are derived from an African source. This is the monogenetic theory of human origin that has grown in recent years because of numerous research finds. The polygenetic theory claiming that humans emerged in several locations simultaneously has been shown to be false. It is not possible for us to establish the fact that

Cheikh Anta Diop's views were almost prophetic. He understood the interconnections of Africans as well as the relationship of the rest of the world to Africa itself.

Thus, rewriting this history becomes a challenge to the Afrocentric scholars who have mastered Africa's classical ancient language. It is also a fact that the writing of the history of other African communities cannot be undertaken without some serious intellectual intervention of African scholars who with an Afrocentric eye will rescue the teaching of Africa from the clutches of the anthropologists whose only intent it seems to me is to develop their ethic of comparison. The idea of comparison is not necessarily the source of the Eurocentric error though there is no doubt in my mind that it is a contributing factor.

There can be no mistake about African origins. Classical Africa must be the starting point for all discourse on the course of African history or else scholars have no grounds for a coherent understanding of the events on the continent. Kemet is directly related and linked to civilizations of Kush, Cayor, Peul, Yoruba, Akan, Congo, Zulu, and Bamun through languages, rituals, and art. This much we know. There is still much more that we do not know because our focus of study has only recently turned to the study of Africa for its own sake. In the past we studied Africa as it related to Europe, not as African cultures related to each other, and certainly not as Africa related to Asia. This was the colonial model of research. It was perfected by the French and English explorers, missionaries, and adventurers of the nineteenth century at the height of the imperial moment. If the English studied West Africa and looked at the Akan, they examined the people of Ghana as if they had no relationship to the Baule people of Côte d'Ivoire. The French did the same; they studied the Baule but not the Asante-Akan. This has produced a kind of direct beam research that does not permit the researcher to understand the interrelationships with adjacent or contiguous cultures. Afrocentricity has already begun to change this type of research and the work of numerous scholars must be seen as contributing to a Tarharkan revival in African research.

## Assumptions

Clearly what I have discussed in the preceding paragraphs are the minimum requirements for approaching any subject Afrocentrically. There are some assumptions that I have had to make in regards to intellectual methods; however, they are also important as we interrogate the facts of African life experiences in economic, social, political, and cultural terms.

The first point that should be emphasized is the complexity introduced into discourse by the term "African." This is not an essentialist term, that is, it is not something that is simply based upon "blood" or "genes." It is much more than that as a construct in knowledge. An African at the basic level is a person who has participated in the five-hundred-year resistance to European domination of the African continent. Sometimes a person may have participated without knowing that he or she has participated but that is where conscientization enters the picture. Only those who are consciously African, given to appreciating the need to resist annihilation culturally, politically, and economically, can claim to be adequately in the arena of Afrocentricity. This is not to say that they are not Africans, just not Afrocentric. Thus, to be African, Afrocentrically located, is to claim a kinship with struggle and to pursue an ethic of justice against all forms of human oppression. At another level we speak of Africans as those individuals who argue that their ancestors came to the Americas, the Antilles, and other parts of the world from the continent of Africa during the last half of the millennium. There is an internal African connection as well as an external African connection. Those who live on the continent at the present era are the internal connection and those who live on other continents are the external connection. Whites on the continent of Africa who have never participated in the resistance to white oppression, domination, or hegemony are indeed non-Africans. Their outlooks, attitudes, rituals, holidays, and missions are often at odds with those of the people who do call themselves Africans. Domicility alone does not make one an African. In the end, we have always argued that consciousness, not biology, determines our approach to data. This is the place from which all analysis proceeds.

Now the Afrocentrist argues that there can be no anti-place. One is either involved from one place or another; one cannot be in a place that does not exist since all places are positions. I cannot conceive of an anti-perspective because whatever I perceive of I am using a place, a position, a location, even if it is called an anti-perspective perspective in European terms.

In a powerful ethic of subject-to-subject communication and interaction, the Afrocentrist establishes the African agency as comparable to that of any other human in the world. If you want to talk science, we will talk science. If you want to talk astronomy, we will talk astronomy. Whatever the condition and the situation with human beings in any part of the world, African people must acknowledge themselves as players of the world stage, not as junior citizens in the halls of theoretical or practical knowledge. The five hundred years of European domination may have crippled our march toward human progress but those years could not erase the contributions of thousands of years of history before the European stepped foot on the African continent.

We already know that there has been a tremendous attack on African scholarship over the past few years. We know also that the recent assaults have been a part of the pattern over the centuries. This aggressiveness toward Africans, who have never enslaved, colonized, or dominated another group of people simply because of biology, is meant to belittle Africans and to prevent us from expressing ethics, values, and mores in a positive way to the world. Ultimately, the objective is to recreate the plantation model where Africans neither know who they are nor where they are; in effect, we will have become people loosed from our moorings and sent on new ships of fools.

The anti-spiritual and pro-material views of the West have driven the world to the brink of destruction more than once. It is certain that Western technology will not save the world; in fact, it may be that technology, along with its new adherents in the East, will hasten the destruction of the world. The corruption of the earth, from the poisoning of the air and water to the killing of innocent people as collateral victims of warfare, attests to the sense of terror that sits at the door of the Western world. Humans have been on the earth less than 300,000 years, hominids have been here less than 8 million and it is not guaranteed that we will be here another 300,000 years. As the trees and protozoa outlasted the dinosaurs they may truly outlast humans, given the blind movement toward Ragnarok. The Afrocentrist cannot abandon ethics to those whose pattern of greed and destruction threaten human annihilation; this is the lesson of the most advanced thinking about centricity.

All African experiences are worthy of study. When the Afrocentrist speaks of "all African experiences," this is not a statement that is to be taken as representing the patriarchal point of view. Women are not relegated to some second-tier realm as they have been in Western thought. The reason for this stems from the idea that men and women derive from the same cosmological source in Africa. The linguistic fact that African languages do not distinguish between the pronouns "he" and "she" as is done in Western languages suggests an entirely different conception of the place of women and men in community. If one looks at the African rulers of antiquity, it is difficult to find any society where women have not held high positions. For example, the queens who ruled in Kemet, Punt, and Nubia (and there were more than forty who ruled in Nubia) represent the earliest known examples of women ruling nations. Indeed, when the rulers of Kemet and Punt held diplomatic relations during the eighteenth dynasty, it was the first recorded interchange between women rulers. Women and men are equally important in any Afrocentric construction of knowledge.

One also assumes that a homologous relationship exists between the study of African phenomena and the study of humanity. We are a part of humanity and therefore wherever people declare themselves to be African we are involved with the creation of human knowledge. Thus, Afrocentricity recognizes and respects the transitory nature of the self, and acknowledges it without being anti-self; it is rather oriented toward the personal. In fact, one may even declare that Afrocentricity is fundamentally dedicated to the collective self and is therefore proactively engaged in the creation and the re-creation of the personal on a grand scale. What African people do in Brazil, Colombia, Costa Rica, Nicaragua, Panama, Venezuela, the United States, Nigeria, Ghana, Cameroon, Congo, and France is a part of the general and collective rise to consciousness so long as what is done is toward the process of liberation.

In the Afrocentrist's idea of agency, all knowledge must be emancipatory. How do we break open the psychological and intellectual prison that holds humans in mental bondage? How do you bring about justice in situations where there is only injustice? How do you create conditions of freedom when the ruling powers deny people the resources for life? These are the critical questions of a progressive and revolutionary paradigm for liberation.

Afrocentricity is not data, but the orientation to data. It is how we approach phenomena. Sometimes critics argue that Afrocentrists are not presenting data on such and such a topic. Or they indicate that they do not have information on a particular subject. We respond, as Afrocentrists, that it is not so much the data that is at question but how people interpret the data, how they perceive what they confront, and how they analyze the African issues and values that are contained in the data. If you do not approach the data correctly, then you are prone to poor conclusions. Furthermore, it is clear from reading the various assaults on Afrocentrists that some people assume that since there is no evidence, for instance, that Africans in the Congo region interacted with Africans in the Nile region that means it did not happen. Absence of evidence, however, does not mean evidence of absence.

History is not Afrocentricity; history is a discipline within its own sphere. It possesses certain attributes, assumptions, methods, and objectives that may or may not be consistent with those of Afrocentricity. The debates over historiography that have arisen in history over the last few years have been due to the increasing challenges of Afrocentric historiography (Keita, 2000). The implications of this transformation are tremendous and cannot be gainsaid. Consequently, the new orientations to data are engendering a robust intellectual discipline that has long left history behind. This is not to say that there should not be expressions of historical interest or attention to some of the key contributions of historical methods, but that Afrocentricity has imposed new criteria on research documents, interpretation of texts, and orientation to data (Conyers, 2003). One reason Ama Mazama has called for "l'imperatif Afrocentrique" is that we have been too busy rediscovering a Europe that appears exhausted to move beyond the traditional frameworks of the West. Our objective as scholars is to provide the world with the most valid and valuable analysis of African phenomena we can, leaving aside the moribund legacies of colonial and postcolonial studies. What this means is that we must abandon many of the elements of historical research, particularly its overemphasis on written texts, and introduce new ways of ferreting out meaning in the lives of African people in the *favelas* of Rio de Janeiro and the rich suburbs of Lagos. Indeed, in *Kemet, Afrocentricity, and Knowledge* (1990), I proposed a series of Afrocentric responses to history that have yet to be fully examined. In the first instance, I suggested an entirely new periodization of history. Secondly, I dismissed the Hegelian assumption that Africa was no part of human history. Thirdly, I have proposed the re-direction of our emphasis on the orature of the continent, particularly as it is expressed in the wisdom seeds often called proverbs. Only the second challenge has been adequately taken up in subsequent discussions. I am sure that new scholars will re-evaluate much of the early work done in Afrocentric theory. Already Mazama's *The Afrocentric Paradigm* (2003a) and James Conyers's *Afrocentricity and Its Critics* (2003) have attempted in different directions to deepen our knowledge and appreciation of Afrocentricity.

## Subject fields

Several subject fields of Africology were derived from an examination of the diverse research and writings in African and African American Studies. As those fields emerged in the early 1990s, they were social, communication, historical, cultural, political, economic, and psychological. A number of scholars have written on Africology as a way to demonstrate the power of the concept in actual analysis of texts and phenomena (Okafor, 2002). Karenga articulated an idea of cultural reconstruction that made it possible to overturn the most dangerous aspects of social and political victimization. Karenga was significant as a philosopher of culture and his demonstration of the fields of Black Studies powered a revolution in the scientific discourse about African Studies. One of the predecessors to Karenga was the eminent Cheikh Anta Diop who had also made a division of our studies, suggesting that instead of social studies we should have created family studies. My work must be seen as a synthesis of the central ideas of conceptualization as found in Karenga's and Diop's works.

Cheikh Anta Diop's importance resides in his pivotal position as the African intellectual who confronted the most powerful myth the Europeans had created about African history. In 1948 he had written an explosive article for *Présence Africaine*, "When Shall We Be Able to Talk of an African Renaissance?" Of course, it is fair to say that no African nation was independent at the time except Liberia and Ethiopia, and both these were struggling to maintain their independence from foreign intrusion. But already Diop had seen the implication of a new birth for the continent, a new beginning after the Europeans, a renaissance of ideas, ideals, concepts, images, symbols, inventions, and relationships. All that had been broken down since the separation of the Nile Valley cultures from the rest of Africa and all that had occurred at the hands of the oppressors had to be restored, repaired, and resurrected. Who would be the Africans who would do this job? Who are they now? The African Union under its current manifestation has assumed the burden by launching the first historic conference of African Intellectuals in Dakar in October, 2004. Why would it take so many years for the African people to respond to this challenge? Later Diop had embarked on the long journey to re-educate the masses with his work, *Nations nègres et culture: De l'Antiquité nègre égyptienne aux problèmes culturels de l'Afrique noire d'aujourd'hui*, published by *Présence Africaine* in 1954. Perhaps from this time forward he knew that he had placed himself in the long train of African intellectuals who sought neither glory nor wealth but the conscious and historic acknowledgement of the achievements of black people.

My concern has been to seek a place from which to examine African phenomena so that we would not end up on the trash heaps of older disciplines unable to secure footing in the thick mud and gluey debris of failed analyses that sought to render Africa and Africans objects of Europe. Thus, Africology, which I called the Afrocentric study of African phenomena, was a discipline with several subject fields. When one sought to approach any of these fields the best methods, based on what I had seen in the best practices of the emerging scholars as well as the best Afrocentric work of older scholars, were grouped as functional, categorical, and etymological (Asante, 1990).

Each of these categories has specific methods. For example, the functional category would apply needs analysis, policy analysis, and action orientation.

The categorical would require a concentration of schemes, gender, class, themes, files, and other collective ideas. Finally, the etymological category would depend a lot on language, terminology, and concept origin. These were the principal methodological approaches to research.

What was necessary in terms of the Afrocentric idea was the ability of scholars to create methods that grew out of the responses to a centered theory. Without assumptions and presuppositions methods become nothing more than rules without meaning. The Afrocentrist must not be quick to adopt Eurocentric methods that fail to appreciate African phenomena. To do so would mean that the researcher would be trapped in the constructed mental prison of failed methods. I believe that Afrocentrists could use African cultural referents in order to attain a more effective analysis of realities. I am not saying that you cannot use psychological theories, sociological theories, historical analysis, or literary theory to achieve a full understanding of phenomena. What I am saying is that the Afrocentrists must seek the African agency in all methodological constructions. We live in a world where the architectonic of human investigation is constructed by concepts that have grounding in the community. I see this as a principal avenue for creating patterns of analysis based on the centered idea. Discovering centeredness is itself the primary task of the Afrocentric researcher. One must create the methods that will lead to transformations in the text, phenomena, and human lives.

## New challenges

One of our most challenging tasks is to debunk the notion that particularist positions are universal. Europe has paraded its own culture as the norm so long that Africans and Asians no longer understand that the European experience, whether the European Middle Ages, Shakespeare, Homer, or European concepts of beauty, are only particular aspects of the human experience, not universal, though they may have implications for other cultures. What Afrocentrists must always criticize is the particular offensive that thrusts Europe forward as the standard by which the rest of the world is judged. No particular culture can claim that ground. Afrocentricity seeks to critique all overreaching claims of particularists. The point has to be made that it is not necessary to resemble European culture in order to be civilized or human!

The hegemony of Europe, whether in dress, fashion, art, culture, or economics, is really a historical moment, but it is not a universalist moment. This is not to say that with the drive for globalization, Europe and the

United States of America are not seeking to enshrine a sort of hegemonic position in the world.

One other challenge facing us is the discourse around the value of multiculturalism in a heterogeneous, industrial nation. The debate around multiculturalism is richly textured because the issues are paramount in the modern world. If we say that multicultural simply refers to "many cultures," we have a fairly good starting place for a discussion about society. If "many cultures" should be the referent, then why is it that in a heterogeneous society we have the promotion of the hegemony of a monoculture? The greatest danger to a heterogeneous nation is the lack of openness to the multicultures that exist. The Afrocentrist contends that European culture must be viewed as being alongside, not above, the other cultures in the society. The glue that holds the society together cannot be the forced acceptance of the hegemony; it must be the reasoned acceptance of the similar values, icons, symbols, and institutions that have been developed in the best interests of all the people. Multiculturalism, therefore, is not white culture above or before any others; it is the creation of a space for all cultures. Mutuality is the hallmark of such a new political and intellectual venture because no one is left behind or out of the arena. To go into the arena of life, like the good footballer, is to discover the strengths and weaknesses of all the cultures that comprise the corporate body.

Despite the many challenges confronting contemporary society, Afrocentricity establishes itself as a vigorous intellectual idea in line with the best Africological thinking. In fact, Karenga (2002, p. 346) puts the situation properly when he claims that "the initial and ongoing challenge for Africana studies is to continue to define itself in ways that reaffirm its original and fundamental mission and yet reflect its capacity and commitment to continuously extend the range of its concerns to deal with new problematics and new understandings within the discipline and with an ever-changing world." Whatever theoretical thrust predominates in the future, I am certain that Afrocentricity will shape the long-term interests of the field. In accepting the challenge of the field to "extend the range of its concerns," the Afrocentrist also searches for new avenues for examining African cultural, economic, and political phenomena in places other than North America. Scholars from Brazil, Venezuela, Peru, Colombia, Nova Scotia, Panama, Guatemala, Guyana, Surinam, Costa Rica, the Antilles, and other countries with large African populations will eventually add new facts that will expand and extend our concerns.

Mazama (2003a, p. 18) contends that "it will come as no surprise that Afrocentricity does not embrace the idea of African cultural incompleteness."

Clearly Mazama's position is grounded in the belief that Africans must reconnect to the cultural matrix that helps us free ourselves from European hegemony. There is no victory in accepting the idea that Africans, after five hundred years of dislocation, must remain marginalized. Mazama has advanced the idea that Africology is a discipline devoted to the renaissance of the African world. Thus, this is not a geographic-specific quest; it is a worldwide challenge for people committed to advancing human relationships. While the fundamental transformation of African people from off-centered consciousness to fully-centered consciousness sits at the core of Afrocentric action, we know that a re-affirmation of intellectual pursuits in the interest of humanity sustains the research agenda.

# 4

# In Search of an Afrocentric Historiography

Africa remains a complex area for scholarly study because the ambiguity of the subject continues to be a source for imagination, interpretation, and debate based on what we have learned from Europe. This distorts every-thing and renders us unable to digest African thought and culture. We know, for example, that humans originated in Africa, that it is the most diverse continent in terms of human DNA, that Africa's flora and fauna are among the most extensive on the earth, that it has the world's largest number of languages, that it contains the shortest and the tallest people, and so forth but yet the voice of Africa remains distorted by ambiguity. We do not often hear this voice in history, philosophy, and politics because the world creates views of Africa that muffle the voice. Africa's paradox is that it is perhaps the richest continent with the poorest people.

In my judgment this is directly related to the fact that for many centuries Africa was forced to speak in the voice of others. My inclination is to launch a discourse on Afrocentricity as a way of approaching African renaissance, to suggest an outline for African historiography, to define Afrocentricity as an advance in discourse about Africa, to discuss the Diopian thesis in regard to this new discourse, to see what some contributions might be, and to suggest an optimistic note about the renaissance in African Studies as a pre-cursor to the complete African resurgence. The Dakar meeting of African Intellectuals called by President Wade of Senegal for December 2003 was one of the most historic congresses on the African continent. The initiative that was advanced to bring intellectuals from Africa, the Caribbean, and the Americas together to contemplate an African renaissance was an aggressive intervention in a stagnant discourse. However, all ideas about renaissance must have substantive theoretical and ideological components.

The issue during the last half of the twentieth century seemed to be: "Now that African nations are independent and African peoples through-out the world are gaining freedom from oppression, humiliation, degradation, discrimination, and inequality, what are the missing pages in the book of African redemption?"

It was clear to me before Dakar that the problem of Africa was not Africa's problem but the problem of Europe's insistence on retaining hegemony over the intellectual and cultural dominion of Africa. Thus, the issue was not merely the political independence of African nations, the integration of Africans into the body politic of the United States, the creation of new opportunities for Africans in Venezuela, Colombia, Peru, Uruguay, and Brazil, the integration of Africans into European nations, or the end of apartheid in South Africa. These were worthy objectives, based upon struggle and goodwill, and achieved, in some cases, against great political forces.

Yet there remained the problematic of agency, meaning in my view that what Europe had succeeded in doing to Africa and Africans over the past five hundred years was to remove the normal course of agency, self-assertion, and cultural definition based on Africa's own historical development, turning the continent's people and their descendants in other parts of the world into a beggar people. I do not mean this literally but intellectually, which in some senses has literal implications. If I cannot, as a person of African descent, make my own decisions within the context of my own historical experiences then I am forever dependent upon others who, as it goes, may have been my physical and political oppressors. So to be free from political oppression, free from discrimination, free from the demeaning and humiliating experience of apartheid's social and economic degradation, is only a first step to total liberation which, in my judgment, comes with being liberated in the mind. Here is the entry of Afrocentricity as a human response to intellectual oppression.

When the Portuguese came down the west coast of Africa in the fifteenth century, they found a land much like that which the Arabs coming across the desert had discovered. It was self-reliant, self-governing, agriculturally active, and had developed its own systems of commerce and constitutional governance. Ghana itself had arisen in the third century BC and by the third century AD had established urban environments at Audoghast and Kumbi Saleh. When Sundiata Keita defeated the armies of Sumanguru at the battle of Kirina around 1240, African people were still essentially self-governing although by this time the influences of Islam had begun to make their marks on the Western Kingdoms as they had in the Eastern region. By the time the Portuguese humiliated King Kwame Ansah and erected Elmina Castle in 1482, six years before Colon arrived in West Africa, and ten years before he landed in Hispaniola, the decline of African independence had become irreversible.

The subsequent tragedies of the European slave trade, the Arab slave trade, the dismemberment of the continent by the European powers at the Berlin Conference of 1884–5, and a century of imperial colonial rule on the continent with massive and brutal segregation, discrimination, and apartheid in the Caribbean and the Americas conspired to move Africans completely off of terms: political, economic, social, religious, linguistic, and cultural. There were no African terms respected and honored by the imperial forces of Europe for nearly 500 years. Thus, the colonization of Africa was not only a physical act but an intellectual one.

The education of African children in the United States, Jamaica, Martinique, Brazil, the colonies of Guinea-Bissau, Kenya, Southwest Africa, Angola, Equatorial Guinea or Nigeria was similar. The one objective was to create in the African person an individual who was European in thought, education, behavior, attitude, opinions, and taste, artistic and otherwise, while remaining black and African only in color. The success of this doctrine is written in the actions and reactions of many Africans from leadership down to the common man and woman who seeks to be European and white as the ideal in life. It is pathetic to see people who pray to a white god straighten their hair because they are ashamed of their own naturally beautiful hair, and who throw parliamentary members outside the chamber because they do not wear European clothes as they did in Kenya. These are the problems of a culturally, politically, and ideologically confused people.

I have argued in my earlier works on Afrocentricity that such a person was dislocated by virtue of being moved off of terms. All reference points for such a person were European. The consequences of such a dislocation were enormous. It meant that those Africans who had been taught in the French schools in Côte d'Ivoire or Guadeloupe that "the Gauls were their ancestors" or the Africans in the United States or Nigeria who had been told that English literature represented the highest form of art in human history or that Africans had no history were being moved farther away from their own agency and being infused, that is, indoctrinated with someone else's story. Now here is the problem with this construction of reality. It is founded upon two insidious and odious ideas, neither of which could be sustained by fair research: (1) Africans are inferior to Europeans, and (2) the only makers of history are European males. We have made progress in putting those ideas to rest. However, there remains much work to be done and many scholars have undertaken such work. This is a remarkable achievement against both European and African intransigence in the project to dislocate Africans.

We are able to indict imperial historiography for a large part of this problem, but I am not one to beat a dead horse. I know that scholars have come a long way from the old days when they argued that Colon "discovered" America or that Mungo Park "discovered" the Niger River. What is not clear, however, to me is that there has been a collective paradigm shift in the Academy. This will take even more time but it will be done. Of course, I am aware of the work of scholars such as J. M. Blaut whose book *Eight Eurocentric Historians* (2000) made such an impact a few years ago when he contended that by his reckoning there were four kinds of Eurocentric theory used to explain how Europe grew richer and more powerful than the rest of the world. These were religion, race, environment, and culture. Of course, according to Blaut, I think prematurely, racism has been rejected and religious explanations are unpopular, and therefore Eurocentrism stands only on culture and environment at the present time. Blaut says "Europe, we are told, rose and conquered the world because its environment and its culture are superior: they caused Europe to develop faster and further than every other society" (Blaut, 2000, p. 1). In his judgment this is "false history and bad geography because Europe's environment is not better than the environments of other places – not more fruitful, more comfortable, more suitable for communication and trade, and the rest" (Blaut, 2000, pp. 1–2). His thesis is that the rise of Europe is directly related to the year 1492 when Colon's explorations gave Europe a powerful incentive for expansion and conquest.

It is not my intention to take Blaut's position but rather to advance the idea that there are some scholars who are questioning the very bases that served to undermine Africa's own agency and to insert Europe's political and military dominance in the historiography and history of African people. While it is normal for those who take anti-Afrocentric positions to argue against the Diopian or Bernalian theses, few of the same critics have been as severe on the extreme Eurocentric positions that have maintained hostility toward the assertion of Africa within its own history. Both Cheikh Anta Diop and Martin Bernal achieved a good amount of visibility for their bold positions. While both sought to re-examine the manner in which European scholarship did African history, neither would declare himself an Afrocentrist. In Diop's case the idea had not occurred to him; in Bernal's case the hostility to the idea was not necessarily a battle with which he had to engage. Yet Afrocentrists have found important aspects of their works to be Afrocentric, that is, they have interrogated African sources for African voices.

Afrocentricity's critics have taken a harsh tone against the idea. The arguments remind me of the grand imperatives of the ancient imperial powers to maintain dependency among the vassals, keep subjects pliant and protected, and to sow discord among the aliens. Like their counterparts in the political and military sectors, the academic imperialists, particularly of the nineteenth century, hold to the idea that no theory could exist if it did not produce dependency upon the extreme European model. This is the crux of the arguments against Afrocentricity and the source of much debate and discourse. My desire is to demonstrate the rational and logical bases of Afrocentricity as a new approach to African reality.

Following Mazama and Karenga, I see Afrocentricity as a paradigmatic quality of thought with implications for analysis and practice where Africans are subjects and agents of phenomena acting in the context of their own historical reality, cultural image, and human interest. Now to claim this definition is not to assail Europe or Asia; it is a statement of African consciousness within the context of history based genuinely on interrogatives of social experiences. The answer to dislocation may very well be relocation within the center of one's own history.

Europe and Africa are both inventions; that much we know from the historical record. However, we also know from the political record as well as the psychological behavior of African people that the inventions are real. They exist in the heads of the people who operate on the basis of those inventions as real; therefore, we must appreciate the endurance of the conventions that have become Africa and Europe. If we take this into consideration when we discuss Afrocentricity, we will arrive at the need for the manifesto.

It is important to understand the difference as the Afrocentrist sees it. Eurocentricity has become over the centuries an imposition of a particular human experience as if that particularity is universal, thus the imposition has taken the form of ethnocentrism and often racism, presenting Europeans with privileged assertions such as the Berlin Conference of 1884–5 where they established doctrines that enshrined their particular privilege in relationship to Africa itself.

Afrocentricity has no part in such a construction and has never claimed a special privilege for Africans on the basis of race, religion, culture, or environment. At one time, Europe spoke of itself as Christendom and when it did, Christendom was seen as being superior to other religious communities. After the battle of Poitiers in 732 when Charles Martel called the members of Christendom together to prevent the Saracens from marching to Tours, Europe discovered itself but, I believe, at that time had not discovered the imperial idea. This would come soon after Colon stepped ashore in Barcelona to announce his findings and thereby set La Rambla in motion.

Now we come to the true issue. Those who are in power, whether political or intellectual, will do nothing to assist those out of power to throw off their bondage. Any attempt to modify or change the condition of oppression, enslavement, mental or physical, will be met with hostility. The enslaved must exhibit nothing less than total compliance to the will of the enslaver. To raise another possibility, one of freedom of the mind, is to assume that the historically enslaved is capable of making theory, of proposing ideas, of creating new constructs for reflection. I see this problem in the nature of the criticism of Afrocentricity.

It is not possible for me to examine all of the presumptions of Afrocentricity in this chapter but I would like to point out some key ideas. One approaches history or any other field, as an Afrocentrist, with the view that there is no anti-location or anti-perspective. All issues are richly endowed with location so we argue that the person who claims that European concert music is classical music but Akan court music is exotic "ethnic" music is representing a place, a situation, a location. Just as the person who says classical dance is European ballet, not the dances of the Zulu court or Yoruba traditions, and so forth. Each definer or classifier is making a statement of place. I have been accused of being a perspectivist, but I do not find anything wrong with such designation and, in fact, I rather like the sound of it. Furthermore, I do not know an anti-perspectivist; even my critic is a perspectivist – it just depends on which perspective he or she is writing from at the time.

Because Afrocentricity is not a closed system, what constitutes African values and ideas is debatable but they necessarily exist and they are central to Afrocentric inquiry. This also means, contrary to some critics, that the issue of Africanity must also be interrogated. What is "African" is as valid to ask as the question, what is "European?" Of course, there are no correct answers to these questions but there are general observations that have a lot to do with historical realities, geographies, and consciousness. I accept, for example, the fact that white South Africans or white Australians are more European than their black fellow citizens in those countries. This is not a biological issue but a cultural practice, an identification with certain traditions and values that are related to the European experience. In the Americas, in Costa Rica, Honduras, Mexico, Venezuela, Brazil, Cuba, Haiti, Jamaica and other places, there are people of African descent whose histories are parallel to each other and whose cultural practices are related to each other in ways that suggest commonalities. Again this is not biological, but historical, cultural, and experiential fact.

In pursuing Afrocentric historiography, we must not confuse Africanity with Afrocentricity. Afrocentricity, which is a theoretical perspective, is fundamentally based on a type of consciousness whereas Africanity is simply

African people living as African people. I mean the fact that one is born in Africa does not mean that he is Afrocentric; since Afrocentricity is a theoretical idea, it must be gained by knowledge and consciousness, not by wearing African clothes or speaking an African language. Of course, it is likely that the Afrocentric person will speak a language and wear the clothes, but these factors are not predictors of Afrocentricity. I shall revisit this issue in a later chapter.

Afrocentrists make a homological argument that the study of African people from an Afrocentric point of view contributes to the general understanding of humanity. Thus, it is human study that is at the core of our attempt to create a new approach to Africa. We discover Africa's contributions to human civilization by interrogating Africa itself, not by adjusting Africa to Europe's image of it.

Perhaps the most widely discussed issue around the Afrocentric historiography project is the role of classical African civilizations. Here it is correct to note that most Afrocentrists have taken their cue from the late Senegalese scientist and historian Cheikh Anta Diop, called by African intellectuals, along with W. E. B. Du Bois, one of the greatest African thinkers of the twentieth century. The publication of his books, *The African Origin of Civilization: Myth or Reality* and *Civilization or Barbarism* in 1974 and 1981 respectively, were major English language achievements. Scholars who could not read him in French rushed to purchase those of his books that were translated. Soon Diop was the most talked about black scholar in the United States of America. Led by John Henrik Clarke, a chorus of scholars began to sing the name and work of Diop throughout the English-speaking world. Everyone knew something about Diop but few had any deep understanding of the tremendous work that he had done. Most of his books and articles remained untranslated from the French. Nevertheless, enough had been done with five of his books in English for Africans in America to characterize him as a major voice in world scholarship. In 1974, Diop joined with the young scholar, Theophile Obenga of the Congo-Brazzaville, to argue the blackness of the ancient Egyptians at the UNESCO Conference on the "Peopling of Egypt" in Cairo. They were overwhelmingly successful in their arguments creating chaos within the ranks of the stereotypical discourse on the nature of Africa and Egypt as a black civilization. In 1986 when he went home to his "village" for his final rest, he had achieved the stature of a modern Imhotep. He had been cited widely, quoted often, and honored in the major academic institutions of the world. His work had received attention belatedly in his own home; nevertheless, his work as the Director of the Radiocarbon Laboratory of the Fundamental Institute of Black Africa soon made him a household name. I should add that he was also a political activist but, of course, in his research he was strictly a scientist.

What Cheikh Anta Diop did was to construct an approach to African history that unsettled the vast circles of traditional European thought, circles that had included and sad to say, still include, a good number of African scholars. Diop boldly articulated a view, based on extensive research and scholarship in various scientific and linguistic fields that threatened the house of cards that had been erected by hundreds of European scholars in the service of imperial and racial dreams. What was it that Diop said that caused so much reaction? Diop maintained that the ancient Pharaonic Egyptians were black-skinned people with wooly-hair. Why was this a shock to European scholarship? It was the fact that the orthodoxy in Europe had been that the black people had produced no civilization and now Diop was claiming that black people created the most majestic civilization of antiquity. This stunned the established Western order and caused a sensation throughout the European arts and sciences in the universities. What could this possibly mean? If black people are really at the very beginning of human civilization as the mothers and fathers of the monumental civilization of ancient Egypt, then what are the implications for arts, culture, and rational inquiry?

In 1799 when Napoleon's Grand Army entered Egypt, it took nearly one hundred scholars, people of science and art, along. Under the direction of Dominique Vivant Denon this group later produced the largest book ever written, *The Description of Egypt*. It immediately caused a sensation in Europe. The drawings, illustrations, and commentaries were viewed and read in the leading circles of the European elite. Soon the question was, "Is Egypt a black civilization?" A few writers argued that Egypt was not in Africa, a view that lingers till this day in some of the small hamlets of the American Midwest. Others argued that Egypt was a black civilization but the ancient Egyptians were not blacks. In fact, one argument was that "wooly hair and black skin" did not suffice to say that the Egyptians were black. Of course, here Europe was debating with itself about how to handle the most monumental civilization of antiquity. It was clearly African, but the "black" question was what troubled those who argued for the enslavement of "black" people. If ancient Egypt is black then geometry, mathematics, politics, sculpture, art, astronomy, medicine, and the names of the gods owe their existence to black people!

Cheikh Anta Diop had started his work on this subject as a doctoral thesis at the Sorbonne to prove that Africa's history had been falsified, beginning with the idea that Egypt was not African, indeed, not black. Actually, he was following a long line of writers who had stated that the Egyptians were black. These included Herodotus, Diodorus Siculus, Aristotle, and Count Volney. Furthermore, Diop wanted African scholars to show the connection between ancient Egypt and other African civilizations as a way to gain a new sense of the continental dynamism. In recent times African and other scholars have shown that the interconnectedness of Egypt with other parts of Africa is historical and geographical.

For example, it is now argued by British archaeologists who discovered 30 sites rich in art chiseled into rocks up to 6,000 years ago in the desert east of the Nile River that pre-dynastic Egypt may have had its beginnings in the savannah regions on either side of the Nile Valley. Toby Wilkinson, a Cambridge scholar who led the Eastern Desert Survey, exclaimed that the rock drawings of cattle, boats, ostriches, giraffes, and hippos suggest that the people who lived in the area in 4000 BC, centuries before the pharaohs or the pyramids, may have been the real source of the Nile Valley inspiration. This type of work is predicted in Diop's analysis and it is my belief that the work of Theophile Obenga and others serves to demonstrate that Diop had opened up an entirely new vista on the study of ancient Egypt. The people who produced the rock paintings of 4000 BC are similar to the people who produced the older rock art paintings of Africa that go back nearly 50,000 years before the present. One can tell this from the parallel styles of the paintings. Egypt began to turn to desert in about 3500 BC about the time of the conquest of the valley by the southern king, Menes. Before that time, the landscape would have been similar to the present east African savannah with seasonal rivers and waterholes used by animals for drinking. I will not spend additional pages on this issue except to say that classical Africa becomes a necessary referent point and resource for Afrocentric concept formation and research and that an adequate understanding of African history, culture, and language cannot take place without reference or responses to classical African cultures.

Thus, Egypt and Nubia are important not simply because of their monumentality but because they pre-date many of the subsequent civilizations of Africa and one can better understand and appreciate the idea of libation among the Ga by understanding the idea of libation among the ancient Egyptians. Totems are not foreign to classical Africa and our appreciation of totemic developments in other parts of the continent might be enhanced by harking back to the earlier beginnings. Most of all the moral and philosophical concepts such as *Maat, maa kheru, iri* and *ankh* are central to explaining much of the African ethical system. Who are Africans anyway? Those who declare themselves as Africans and participate in the same historical consciousness and culture as the majority of the people of Africa must be considered Africans.

By now it is accepted that Afrocentricity is the approach to data, not the data. I do not argue only about the facts of history but also about the approach to the event, situation, or personality. If I cannot find something in a written text I do not dismiss the idea outright because "absence of evidence" is not necessarily "evidence of absence." Indeed, there may be a text that is spoken or a text that is written in music. One cannot fabricate or falsify data but one can and should explain as much as possible from the existing elements.

While I recognize that as Afrocentrists we now have both currency and responsibility, I also understand the assaults on the idea. Our currency has allowed us to articulate a new approach to the issues and facts of Africa and African people. It is no longer the study of Africa for the interest of others that motivates us but the study of Africa for itself. In this sense, it is a less selfish pursuit, one based in the clearest desire to see Africa as it is, through the eyes of its own people. Basil Davidson, the long-time popular British historian of Africa, once told me that the problem with Europeans is that they cannot get out of their heads this "disbelief" when it comes to African achievements and contributions.

The new historiography is not a false or artificial contrivance. It is a legitimate approach to the place of Africa in the world. It is, therefore, a rational activity dedicated to the understanding of history. What it allows is the explanation of the flow of African history without external mediation. One can no longer speak confidently of Portuguese African history or British African history. One is obligated to write African history with African agency assuming the lead role in the story. And so we may speak of African resistance to the British, to the Portuguese, and to the French. To speak this way is not to deny the agency of the colonialists but rather to assert Africa within the context of its own historical flow. On the other hand, Europe's interventions are minor issues in the long context of Africa. For the European powers, these one hundred or four hundred year involvements can be viewed as ripples in the stream of Europe's own long history. To assert Europe in the midst of Africa is to write over the everyday experiences of the African people. One strikes out the lived histories of the African people by this brazen imposition.

Take the experiences of the various intrepid military, missionary, and merchant Europeans in Africa: Brazza, Mungo Park, Stanley, Livingstone, and so forth. They were not out of Africa's history and experiences, but out of Europe's, as well they should have been. The inspiration, impetus, and ambition which these individuals exhibited were characteristics of the societies that produced them and, though they carried out a large part of their activities on the African canvas, the shape of their work was clearly European. For me or you as a scholar to concentrate on what they did as if it were making African history is to promote a narrow, provincial, Eurocentric way of viewing African history.

This is to say that the history of Africa is not based on the actions of David Livingstone in Central Africa but on the actions of the hundreds of thousands of people through whose lands he trespassed. So the Afrocentrist must ask, "Who are these people?" What are their histories? What resistance did they display? How do they see a white man lost in the forest? What do they make of a large train of porters carrying supplies for a white man? Are we able to discover the intimate elements of African history by a close reading of the observations of a European? What special tools are required to evaluate what we read in the journals and diaries of the travelers? Perhaps in the diaries and journals of these merchants and missionaries we are able to discern how the people themselves responded. For example, we know that the name of the grand waterfalls on the Zambezi River was not Victoria Falls before Livingstone but Musi Wa Tunya, that is, the Smoke that Thunders. Yet in the consciousness of Europe and in some Africans it has become, by virtue of Livingstone's arrogance, Victoria Falls. How is this to be understood in African history? What are we to make of this development? I believe a lot depends upon your perspective, the place you take your stand, if you will, *djed*.

The Afrocentrist goes beyond the facade to tease out the agency of Africa. This is not easy but no historiography project is easy. It is a scientific enterprise that requires keen interrogatories just as one would use in examining a witness. In our case the witness may appear to be present but remain silent and we will have to discover our answers in the philosophy, dance, clothing, and material artifacts of the culture.

The battle for truth is tedious. We have often used Greece and Rome as guiding principles in Western civilization. What would the world have been like had we used Kemet and Nubia as the key classical civilizations? What if Africa itself had been free, unencumbered for the five hundred years that it saw European oppression in its space? What if Africans had been able to use Kemet and Nubia as guiding intellectual and cultural ideas? Would the world be a better place? Would globalization, mondialization, be a galloping antelope of Westernization? Would a new ethic of human relations exist based upon the principles of *maat*? One could speculate for days and never come to any conclusive answer about these issues but one thing is certain: the missing pages in the book of African redemption are closely related to a new way of looking at African historical data. I have called this Afrocentric historiography, not to be a counterpoint to Eurocentric historiography, but as a statement of Africa's assertion of its agency in Africa's own history.

I am therefore calling for a constructural adjustment where Africanist scholars assume a responsibility, regardless of national origin of the scholar, to reassert and re-establish Africa and Africans in the center of their own narratives. To me this is the noblest task of the contemporary scholar, one that will have a far-reaching impact on the way we research and study Africa in the years to come. I can see many implications for such an orientation, that is, re-orientation. In the first place, the classical civilizations of Africa will be reconnected to the rest of the continent. Secondly, the emphasis will be more on the moral and ethical content of African societies rather than anthropological studies and methods. This is the focus of the work of Maulana Karenga, especially in his book *Maat: The Moral Ideal in Ancient Egypt* (2006). Thirdly, there will be a greater appreciation of the relationship between the African diaspora and the continent, with more studies on cultural retentions and linguistic influences. I believe that this constructural adjustment will lead us to the renaissance that is necessary in African Studies and will assist in Africa's own charge toward political, cultural, economic, and social renaissance.

Finally, if this renaissance in research is to be done, let us be the ones to do it by exploring, for example, the role of Africans in philosophy, gender relations, and family sciences. I am convinced that we cannot understand Africa's contributions to its own development and the world without examining the basis for society. A list of philosophers such as Imhotep, Ptahhotep, Amenemhat, Merikare, Duauf, Amenhotep, Son of Hapu, Chaminuka, Okomfo Anokye, and others whose thoughts have rarely been exposed should be presented as examples of African achievement. Nubia, from 200 BC to 100 AD, gave the world the longest history of women rulers. More than forty queens ruled in that land, not as wives of kings, but in their own right during a time in which it was difficult for a Roman woman to be called by her own name. What are the implications of Nubia's history for the contemporary discourse on gender relations in Africa and the world? What did Africans do to minimize the creation of orphans and why were there no people without family in traditional Africa? What is the meaning of civilization if it is not what humans try to keep back chaos with?

One of the great fields of African inquiry has to be how to maintain justice, order, harmony, balance, and peace. Maulana Karenga has shown that this could not be done without truth, righteousness, justice, and reciprocity. I hope today that the Congreso Internacionale d'Estudis Africans will join the Afrocentric renaissance and bring into existence a revitalized field of African Studies that will be used to re-center African people.

# 5

## Kemetic Bases: The Africanness of Ancient Egypt

Africans must pursue in the most determined manner the practice of renaissance, that is, rebirth of the culture, philosophy, traditions, and values of the continent, not in some antiquated form but in the spirit of creative responses to the contemporary times. However, renaissance means that you have to know what it was to have been born in the first place. What is it that has to be reborn? What are the reasons for this rebirth? Africa has suffered greatly in the past half of a millennium. There has been, as a result, a loss of traditions, values, direction, and mission. But one cannot go on talking about loss as if there is never an opportunity to move forward. The past is important but it cannot be the sum total of our discourse. How do you regain a sense of place, a location of centeredness given the condition of our existence?

What are the motivations that drive those who seek not merely to interrogate the Africanity of ancient Kemet, as if it should be questioned, but to eradicate Kemet from the narrative of Africa altogether? An attack on the Africanity of Kemet is seen in the most obscene advances of commercial greed on the symbols, icons, and values of the African people. Few people have ever had their ethnicity and identity stolen from them in the clarity of daylight. Take the example of the Luxor Hotel in Las Vegas or the Sofitel Hotel located in the city of Luxor in Egypt and one will see the boldest assault on the history of Africa by commercial interests since Europe appropriated the names and images of Native Americans for profit. In the American southwest, a popular hotel stands in the desert sands with whitened images of Africans. One could check into the hotel at Las Vegas with no idea that the ancient people of Egypt were black. By the same token, the owners of the Sofitel Hotel in Luxor, Egypt commissioned local Arab artists to create royal images of Africans in the form of white people to adorn a restaurant less than a mile from the blackest representations of the ancient Egyptians in the temples at Karnak or in the tombs in the Valley of the Kings. While I believe that the principal motivation today for seeking to change the image of ancient Africans is greed, I strongly believe that the old motivation of disbelief based on an attempt to conceal the genius of Africa is still present.

I am indebted to British historian Basil Davidson who gave me this idea at a conference in Detroit, Michigan in the early 1990s. Davidson believed then that the attack on African productive and expressive arts and modes of inquiry had to do with the inability of Europeans to admit that Africans had far exceeded Europe at the very beginnings of civilization.

So long as Africa itself succumbs to the interpretations and appropriations of either European or Arab aggressions against its history, it will remain the victim, alongside its people, of external designs to control its past image and future possibilities. No intellectual crime is as great as the appropriation of another people's cultural heritage or the robbery of a people's achievements in order to claim something that does not belong to you.

Transmission of motifs, symbols, signs, and ideas is the clearest way to bring the ancestors and their visions to contemporary society. This should be a natural process but it has become for African people an unnatural one due to the cleavages in our history. One generation normally helps to perpetuate the ideals found in the previous one. This connection is organic in the sense that we know who we are by knowing to whom we are connected.

Classical Africa must be viewed as a resource for an African renaissance. What I mean is that a new revolutionary moment in which African people interrogate and locate within their own history the values, concepts, and ideals that are essential for a reinvigorated society can be advanced by seriously engaging the Nile Valley civilizations. Indeed, the implications of such an era of renaissance are numerous and multidimensional, despite the incredible obstacles against this revolution. In Egypt, for example, the black people who are the original ancient Egyptians have been marginalized by the Arab rulers, not unlike the Native Americans in the United States or Canada, or the Blackfellows in Australia were marginalized by the Europeans, yet the black Egyptians have a definite understanding that the ancient Pharaonic civilization was theirs and that their people are the direct descendants of the land. But this is not a generally well understood idea in the northern part of Egypt or in the rest of the world, mainly because there has never been a major campaign by Egypt to project the original African people as the owners of the land. Issues involving Arabs and Jews, Israel and Palestine, and the politics of land and loss, are discussed without reference to the Africans, black people, who occupied the land long before the Arabs. These individuals, not so invisible at Aswan in the south of Egypt, know the meaning of the Egyptian state's campaign to isolate them as "Nubians" by taking the modern citizenship term "Egyptian" to refer to "Arab" and to leave the question of original inhabitants unspoken. We have seen this formula in all countries where there have been invading armies seeking to claim a territory that they have occupied.

Kemet is the source for our renaissance because the position it holds is unquestioned as the energy behind the expansion of African ideas that have held us together in a unique historical situation (Karenga, 2006).

For this reason I seek to explain Kemet's unique place in the history of Africa as a source of inspiration and genius. The reason that it still creates interest in us is because it established its own will on a long period of time and shaped the succeeding civilizations with its profound discoveries.

The Egyptians believed that the search for *Maat* was the ultimate justification for human life. We do not need some greater insight, some deeper thought, some mystical *endarkenment* to understand the creation of this will to *Maat*. The Egyptians left for us a legacy of achievement that speaks to *Maat* in all of its characteristics. Whether we speak of language, architecture, art, politics, religion, or mathematics, we are speaking of the majesty of the search for *Maat* in society. Without Egyptian cultural concepts, ritual forms, and ethical ideals we would not be speaking of the possibility of an African renaissance. This much Cheikh Anta Diop understood in *Civilization or Barbarism*.

The Egyptians gave the world a concept of value, *Maat*, which was a consciously pursued objective of human agency. One may speak of Greek, Jewish, Chinese, or Indian civilizations but none of these cultures seem to have a *Maat*-like concept. While we know that the Greek Homer was the first eloquent voice of the Greeks, Moses of the Jews advanced the Ten Commandments, the Chinese Confucius laid down wisdom teachings, and the Hindu thinkers sought Dharma, none of these groups could pattern themselves after the Egyptian *Maat*ian ethics. Indeed, Egypt belongs to Africa.

*Maat* becomes a vast array of ideas in Egyptian culture. It is a mental attitude, a way of thinking about everything. African culture today cannot renew itself without being revitalized from its ancient classical past. There must be an African reality to the renaissance. Because of the petrified system of culture that we have inherited from our oppressors, a historical drive leads us to return to the philosophical resources of our national identities for our cultural and psychological salvation. I think that we can return to Kemet by going first to our own national cultures and building upon those cultures in a link to Kemet which is much more than a reflection of our study. It must become a leading edge, a symbol of our Afrocentric consciousness.

African intellectuals must not be afraid to challenge the very heart of the Western imposition on the rest of the world. The West has found in the idea of individuality its greatest source of energy. That is why most European writers posit Greece as being opposed to Egypt on the basis of the individual. The idea in their minds is that modern European society is based on the Greek idea of the individual. In fact, Werner Jaeger, writing in *Paideia*, said it best of all for Europe, that "there could be no sharper contrast than that between the modern man's keen sense of his own individuality, and the self-abnegation of the pre-Hellenic Orient, made manifest in the somber majesty of Egypt's pyramids and the royal tombs and monuments of the East" (Jaeger, 1986, p. xix). There are several things wrong with this statement from an Afrocentric and factual point of view. You see how easily Jaeger conflates the European white man with modern man and how Greece becomes his marker for all of human history when he uses the term "pre-Hellenic" to mark the epochs. Furthermore, he eliminates Africa and its classical past by trying to make Egypt the Orient, connecting it to the East, when in fact it is South and African. What he considers to be self-abnegation is often nothing more than humility, a virtue the Greeks could have learned from their Egyptian teachers.

The contradictions in the persistent exaltation of the individual are many. False equations give false results. That is true whether the people are Africans or Europeans. Our problem stems from the fact that we have often taken their beliefs as our historical truths about society. We have done this because we have been moved off of our own terms and have not sufficiently interrogated European concepts, values, or ideas.

We have to confront the ideas that say African societies suppressed the masses, that there was an unthinking adoration of the king, that the king had limited responsibilities to the people, and that the individual African was nothing. These are straw people arguments situated at the head of most laudatory discussions of ancient Greece.

The claim goes with the idea that Homer and Christianity are wedded in the holy matrimony of Western culture. Christianity was the engine that spread the doctrine of the individual rights of each soul as a value in and of itself. Furthermore, it was felt that each individual was a law to himself or herself. Thus, the Greek doctrine of individuality clashes with the African idea of collectivity. I will explore this later.

For the time being let me say that while the Greeks formulated this idea of individuality, it would be the Christian religion that would try to resolve the issue of the place of the individual within society. One could go to heaven alone, by oneself, and let everybody else go to hell. That was the new realization brought by Greeks and handed to the West as a radical departure in human history.

No wonder some European postmodern critics feel embarrassed by the essentialism expressed by the promulgators of a white supremacy paradigm. Indeed, the postmodernists have questioned these ideas. Jaeger writes that certain qualities of the Greeks "were natural, inborn" (1986, p. xx). If this is not an essentialist reading, I have never seen one. So sure Jaeger is of the Kemetic influence on ancient Greece that he repeats a hundred times in so many different ways these mantras of the Greeks that they have "more philosophical comprehension than any other nation at any other period in history," "the living ideal which had grown up in the very soil of Greece," "regarded the Greeks as the perfect manifestation of true human nature," "the Greek mind owes its superior strength," "the Greek mind's most miraculous creation," and numerous other platitudes to distance the reader from the persistent thought that, hey, Kemet is the source of most of what he is talking about. This is mythmaking in its highest form which is the shaping or asserting of a falsehood as if it is a truth to the point that the target audience agrees with the falsehood. It carries the same logic as the mantra about the weapons of mass destruction, but of course, you know that the real problem is the weapons of mass deception.

In explaining how ancient Kemet serves as a foundation for the plinth of a renaissance, I do not make a claim for an immutable, biological miracle, as the Germans did for the ancient Greeks. Yet I understand the peculiar relationship that ancient Kemet had to its environment and will show how the Kemetic people used them to advance their own civilization and to bequeath to us this science of renaissance that is now possible.

Even in ancient times Kemet influenced other African countries and, indeed, had a role in civilizing many non-African peoples. It is common to hear or read European authors speaking of Kemet's isolation in the Nile Valley, but such a position cannot be sustained by reasoning or fact. Not only did Kemet have an ongoing relationship with other societies whose leading citizens came to Kemet for study but we know that Thales, Pythagoras, Isocrates, Democritus, Anaximander, Anaxigoras, Eudoxus, and Solon were students of the Africans.

Furthermore, we know that the Per-aa (Pharaoh in Hebrew) exercised dominion and influence over adjacent lands, to the extent that during his accession and jubilees he frequently received ambassadors with delegations loaded down with gifts as they pleaded with him to give their peoples the gift of life, as he had given it to his own people in Africa. Early dynastic monuments suggest that from the Gerzean period, probably as Cyril Aldred has contended in his book, *Egypt to the End of the Old Kingdom* (1988, p. 48), the Asiatics had come to Africa to bring their gifts to the Pharaoh. So we know that the influence was not just north across the Mediterranean but also northeast into Southwest Asia.

Now comes the part where I try to think aloud with you about the process for this plinth of renaissance. I have got to do one more thing, however. I have got to locate the central conclusions that have caused us to stumble in the first place. I offer them as a set of assumptions about why we have not been able to think outside of the European box before now. Our boldness would have been considered stupidity or, worse yet, an insult to all of our teachers, black and white, who had honored Europe so greatly.

1  The Africans created gods and the Greeks created men (Jaeger's notion).
2  The Africans sought the collective good and the Greeks sought individual good.
3  The greatest work of art for the Africans was a harmonious society; the Greeks sought to make man the individual (Jaeger).
4  The African intellectual principle is *Maat;* the Greek individualism is *humanitas,* (Latin form), humane behavior.

We must regard our classical antiquity as an inexhaustible source of power, art, motifs, ideas, signs, ethical values, and dignity. Once we are convinced of this there will be a neo-Kemetic revolution in the African world. I submit that it will begin with a new ethical posture.

One way to examine this posture is to raise the question, what happens to moral practice if one accepts the ancient Kemetic moral ideal? I ask this following a reading of Karenga's *Maat: The Moral Ideal in Ancient Egypt* (2006). Karenga argues that his aim is "to focus on the moral ideal rather than the assumed moral practice of ancient Egypt" (Karenga, 2006, p. 3). I would like to suggest that the moral ideal, like all concepts of the ideal, might lead us to describe what a *Maatic* life would look like. Indeed, what are the implications for a *Maatic* society, a *Maatic* response to the environment, to relationships, to international politics, to racial oppression, to class struggle between the rich and the poor, to inter-ethnic conflict, to gender oppression, to the pollution of the sea and the air?

Karenga recognizes the potentiality in the concept of the ideal; he chooses not to focus on practice, but he understands the implications nevertheless. He writes, for example, that "there is clearly an interest in the ideal as a point of departure and motivation for philosophical discourse in the same sense the ideal motivates discourse in other religions and ethical traditions" (2006, p. 3). He goes on to make the point that *iwa*, in the Yoruba, serves such a role.

There are two possibilities for discussing the concept ideal. One could see it as a pattern, that is, a norm or standard to be modeled and followed. Or one could see it as a theme providing a point of orientation. This is a bifurcation suggested by Cua (1978, p. 137) and adopted by Karenga (2006, p. 3) that is quite useful. My discussion centers on the notion of *Maat* as a point of departure, a theme. I believe that this is central to the idea that it is not a dead concept, but a living, vital ideal. In that form it is possible that it could generate ideas and concepts for an African renaissance.

Clearly all forms of renaissance, whether African, Asian or European, must tap into the past and sometimes rediscover among the once discarded and seemingly exhausted ideals points of orientation that will become points of departure and points of destination.

One can speak of the regeneration and the revitalization of Kemet throughout its history. We know that it went through several periods in which the intellectuals and spiritual leaders had to put their heads together to remember what was written in the old books. These were periods of reformation, reclamation, and renewal. Almost always after some great war or occupation it was necessary for the people to re-think their history and mission.

Piankhy, a Nubian king, united Kemet under the rule of the Nubians, becoming the predecessor to the twenty-fifth dynasty. He defeated Tefnakht, prince of Sais, and compelled his surrender, but some regions of Lower Kemet were still not subdued. It would take another king to completely conquer the entire land and become the first king of the twenty-fifth dynasty. He would be called Per-ao Shabaka. This king secured permanent rulership over Kemet and Nubia. It was Taharka, however, who sought more than anyone else to restore the glory of Kemet. He had seen a country that was still reeling from the effects of the period of instability, war exhaustion, and petty land crises among its citizens, and intellectual waywardness. Amen had been cast down from his high place in the hearts of the people, many in the priesthood were corrupt, the statues of the great kings lay in waste, some having remained defiled by neglect for years. Taharka sought the advice of the wise men and women of Waset, re-established the systems that had been abandoned, set in motion a return to the old books, and followed an orientation that led him to introduce a renaissance. Karenga has remarked "the Nubians saw themselves as restorers of the ancient tradition of Kemet. Thus, in art, architecture and literature, they made great efforts to uphold tradition and therefore created a renaissance of ancient Egyptian culture" (Karenga, 2006, p. 104).

What will it take for an African renaissance now that *Maat* has been abandoned and the artistic principles of classical Kemet have been trivialized? Since our enslavement and colonization at the hands of Europe, we have found ourselves confused, disoriented, dislocated, and unable to make the proper contribution to the society of our birth or the culture of our heritage. In the United States and Europe it is clear that Africans in the diaspora can make contributions without becoming white. One does not have to abandon his or her mother in order to assume a progressive stance against oppression or to succeed as an integrative human being. In other words, the African does not have to hate Africanity, blackness, African history, or Africa itself in order to be healthy in the diaspora.

In my view it is the acceptance of the classical African past, the rejection of self-hatred, the denial of nihilism, and the embracing of humanity that will lead to a new resurgence of African cultures. But this will take an appreciation of some commonplaces.

## Some Kemetic commonplaces

1 judgment after death symbolized by balance of scales;
2 concept of eternal life, *ankh nhh*;
3 the presence of water in primeval times as the source of all creation;
4 Ra as the master of the universe

The beauty of these Kemetic ideals is that there are correspondences in other African traditions. That is why Karenga notes that the meaning of *Maat* as natural law and order has parallels with other worldviews, notably in the traditions of the Dinka, who argue that *cieng* is a "moral-order concept and principle which means, as a verb, 'to live together, to look after, to order or put in order.' As a noun, it means morals, behavior, habit, conduct, nature of, custom, rule of law, way of life and culture" (Karenga, 2006, p. 9). What would it mean if you are not evil by nature, if there is no original sin, if there is no guilt inasmuch as guilt is a problem of individuality?

## Art

Does the reader remember how Picasso, Modigliani and other European artists were inspired to follow the themes of African art, particularly masks, in the early twentieth century as they were seeking new meanings of the human being? You remember that they created an entirely new form of European art by painting the three-dimensional abstract forms of African art onto canvases? What I am saying is that there is inspiration, based on a theme, a point of orientation, in all classical civilizations. There is no reason why Africans cannot follow the path already charted by our ancestors, but this takes the courage to be African in the world.

## Architecture

All architecture has its origins in Africa. Yet contemporary African cities, for the most part, are filled with architectural points of orientation from Europe. It is as if the European chateau or fortress or castle with moats or Tuscan highrises are the only possible example for the African architects. What would a modern city, built along the lines of classical, that is, neo-Kemetic classical, traditions look like? What if our architects simply inter-rogated the traditional designs and themes of West Africa, creating out of them new, innovative, and modern technologically efficient and convenient structures? I am convinced that if we do not locate our own revival in our antiquity others will and claim it, as they have in the past, as theirs.

We already know that the Christian churches followed the patterns of the great hypostyle-type halls of the temple Ipet Isut. Walls and columns covered with *mdw ntr* gave the early Kemetic temples a majesty that had not been seen before in the world. Greece learned from this architectural style. Nothing in Greece compared to Karnak, Ipet Isut. Consider an immense hall, 170 feet deep by 329 feet broad, with two rows of six columns each, nearly seventy feet tall, with bell-shaped capitals, flanked by seven rows of shorter columns some more than forty feet high, with lotus bud capitals. The only thing that Greco-philiacs could do was to criticize the size of the Egyptian temples, claiming that they had "no unity or structural propriety" as F. B. Tarbell wrote in *A History of Greek Art* in 1913 (Tarbell, 1913, p. 30). Versions of this type of argument occur throughout the history of Western commentary on ancient Egypt. Kemetic art and architecture were very much alive, vital, and full of unity and propriety simply because the governing principle was that of *Maat*.

## Literature

At the core of Kemetic history are the great mythological stories that embody traditions, values, and concepts that guide Kemetic society. In a renaissance of Africa it will be necessary for African people to locate their own mythologies as well as those of classical Kemet. I could see the mythologies of the Zulu, Yoruba, and Akan people as bases for re-energizing communities and societies, but inasmuch as Kemet is more ancient, complex, and diverse in its mythological character, it serves as a source for many of the later mythologies.

## Human Relationships

This is the arena of ethics, morality, and values because all human relationships deal with *Maat*. They are about holding back chaos. In a personal sense we are all on the same journey and therefore cannot disrespect the very values that constitute our own consciousness. If we trespass against another human being in our attempt to achieve some individualistic goal, are we not engaging in the death of *Maat*, the crushing of harmony, and the decline of civilization in its infinite flowering?

# 6

## The Afrocentric Idea in Education

Carter G. Woodson's *The Miseducation of the Negro* established the principles that would govern the development of the Afrocentric idea in education. First published in the 1930s, Woodson's classic book revealed the fundamental problems with the education of the African person in America. Indeed, as Woodson understood, the African American was educated away from her or his own culture and traditions and attached to the fringes of European culture. Very early in his career, Carter G. Woodson recognized that the African American's education, in order to be substantive and meaningful within the context of American society, had to deal with the African's historical experiences both in Africa and in America. This did not lead him to reject American nationality or citizenship; Woodson understood the peculiar relationship the African person had to the American nation but he also knew that for the African to assume that he or she was in the same position as the European vis-à-vis the realities of America would mean the psychological and cultural death of the African American population. That is why he placed on education, and particularly the African American colleges, the burden of teaching the Africans in America to be responsive to the long traditions and history of Africa as well as America.

In effect, the Afrocentric response to the phenomenon of dislocation was Carter Woodson's alert recognition, more than fifty years ago, that there was something severely wrong with the education of African Americans. But I also know that the problems affecting the education of Africans in the United States and Canada are nearly the same problems one sees on the African continent or in Europe and South America. Wherever Africans live in the world today, they are at the mercy of educational systems that miseducate and misorient them. Black students in Paris, London, Hamburg, Rome, and Lisbon are as dislocated by the lack of a pedagogy based on African values, interests, and concepts as children in Lagos, Nairobi, Banjul, Dakar, or Johannesburg. In African cities and villages, students often sit in classrooms where the knowledge they learn is disconnected from their own history. Afrocentricity seeks to respond to the dislocation of the African student in such an educational system by providing philosophical and theoretical guidelines and criteria which are centered in the African perception of reality.

## Focus on meaning

In education, Afrocentricity means that one provides students with the opportunity to begin study of the world, its people, concepts, and history from the point of view of the African child's heritage. Thus, the African child is not an object but a subject. No discipline of knowledge is alien to the African person from this perspective. Whether the subject is biology, medicine, literature, or social studies, the African student is centered in the reality of that discipline so that he or she is not seen as "having to get it" but rather being a part of it. What is necessary is a pedagogy that has interrogated African cultures and experiences for best practice. As far as I am concerned, "centricity" is one avenue for seeking best practice.

Centricity is the process of locating a student within the context of his or her own cultural reference in order to be able to relate to other cultural perspectives. Thus, this applies to students from any culture. The most productive method of teaching a student is to place the student within the context of knowledge. For students of European heritage in America, this goes without saying because almost all of the experiences discussed in classes are from the standpoint of European history. This is as true for a discussion of the American Independence War as it is for a discussion of Dante's *Inferno*. Even a discussion of the European slave trade concentrates on what the whites were doing instead of the resistance of the Africans. In such a world, the African student is always acted upon but seldom shown to be an actor. Centricity must be practiced in such a way that students from various cultures see themselves as participating in the flow of information and knowledge.

## Overarching propositions about education

Three propositions stand in the background of the theoretical and philosophical questions surrounding education in society. A review of all relevant literature reveals the following overarching propositions:

1  Education is fundamentally a social phenomenon; it consists in socializing children.

2  To send a child to school is to prepare the child for being part of a social group.
3  Societies develop schools suitable to the societies. A white supremacist system develops white supremacist education.

These ideas represent the core presuppositions Afrocentrists hold about education. They are not unreasonable propositions or presuppositions but they suggest the direction of my own thinking about what education is capable of doing to an already politically and economically marginalized people. The escape hatch for African Americans has to be the re-orienting of the educational enterprise by raising the same questions that Carter G. Woodson posed more than seventy years ago.

Thus, the person of African descent should naturally be centered in his or her historical experiences as an African. In education it means that we do not marginalize children by placing them in positions that cause them to question their own self-worth because their cultural narrative is seldom told. The little African American child who sits in a classroom and is made to accept as heroes and heroines individuals who defamed her people during their lifetimes is being actively decentered, marginalized, and made a non-person, one whose aim in life might be some day to attempt to "shed her blackness" as a badge of inferiority. In Africa I have seen little African children in classrooms where the teacher is telling them that some European discovered a river or a water-fall in their country. I could not contain myself on one occasion and blurted out, totally out of character for me, "The African guides led Livingstone to Musi wa Tunya." I used the African name for Victoria Falls deliberately. There is nothing problematic about centering African children in their own narra-tive as we do automatically in Western societies with white students.

One must not base any educational system on the idea of racial supremacy. However, the American system has been based on white supremacist notions which endeavor to protect white advantage in educa-tion, economics, and politics by teaching that what is white is universal, even human. On the other hand, the instruction given in such a situation is that what is black, African, is particular, specific, and cannot be human. Thus, some African writers, professors, and artists rush to deny their "blackness" because they believe that to exist as a black person is not to exist as a human being. These are the individuals Carter Woodson said preferred European art and languages to African art and languages, who believed that what was of European origin was inherently better than what their own people had pro-duced. Eurocentric curricula produce such aberrations in the African person. A truly educated person would view both African and European education as significant and useful; indeed, the white person who was educated in such a system could no longer assume any superiority based upon false education.

## The revolutionary challenge

The most revolutionary challenge to the ideology of white supremacy in education during the last half of the twentieth century in the United States was the Afrocentric idea. No other theoretical position stated by Africans has ever captured the imagination of such a wide range of scholars and students of history, sociology, communication, anthropology, education, and psychology. The challenge to white supremacist education is posed in three critical ways:

1  It questions the imposition of the white supremacist view as universal history: classical, continental, explorers, etc. (Asante, 1990).
2  It assaults ignorance by demonstrating the indefensibility of the supporting racist theories about multiculturalism.
3  It radically projects a humanistic and pluralistic viewpoint (centrism) by articulating Afrocentricity as a valid, non-hegemonic perspective in this regard.

Afrocentric education centers the child in history and culture, rather than outside it. It is therefore like any centric paradigm – one that occupies a center perspective. How alien must an African American child feel in those cases where the information being presented makes the child feel like an outsider? In most classrooms, whites are located in the center perspective position. Whatever the subject, the African person is on the outside. A truly multicultural education must initially be based on an Afrocentric initiative, otherwise the African American child will continue to be lost in the European framework.

## Afrocentricity and history

Arthur Schlesinger and others have formed what they call a "Committee for the Defense of History." But history needs no defense: only lies, untruths, inaccurate information need defending. This committee is nothing more than an attempt to buttress the crumbling pillars of a white supremacist system that has maintained its legitimacy by concealing its motives behind the cloak of American liberalism. Such a movement is in the same spirit and tradition as Allan Bloom's *Closing of the American Mind*

(1987) and E. D. Hirsch's *Cultural Literacy* (1988); both books were placed in the service of the white hegemony in education, particularly in curriculum.

Cheikh Anta Diop, the late great scholar, told me in Dakar, Senegal, in December 1980, "African history and Africa need no defense." Thus, when I heard that there were white scholars, joined by some blacks, who thought it was necessary to defend history, I knew that they must have had a lot of shoring up to perform. But perhaps, in a discussion of the curriculum that would open it up in a profound way, it was inevitable that the closets of bigotry would reveal various attempts to defend white privilege in the curriculum as it had often been defended in society. This was a predictable challenge to the thrust for pluralism. Their attempt is no more than a defense of the received interpretations of a racist history, written pre-eminently from a hegemonic, white supremacist perspective. Those who argue against the Africa-centered or Afrocentric perspective often clothe their arguments in false categories and fake terms (Keto, 1999).

Afrocentric education is not against history: it is for history – correct, accurate history. If it is against anything, it is against marginalizing African American children, Latino children, Asian American, Native American children – a true centric education is different from a racist education, that is, a white supremacist education.

What is the view that has created so much controversy in educational circles? Why has it created that discussion? What does all of this mean?

When I wrote the first book on Afrocentricity in 1980, now in its fifth printing, I did not know that in ten years the idea would help shake the country and shape discussions in education, art, fashion, and politics. Now, with the publication of *The Afrocentric Idea* (1998) and *Kemet, Afrocentricity, and Knowledge* (1990), the debate has been joined in earnest. The cultural question is the most significant piece in the curriculum discussion. The most unsettling aspect of this intellectual discussion for many white and some African Americans is that its intellectual source is the research and writings of African American scholars. Whites have always had charge of ideas in the American academy: deconstruction, gestalt psychology, Marxism, structuralism, early childhood education, and so on, have been articulated, elaborated upon, and developed by white scholars.

## Suppression and distortion

African American scholars trained in the best universities and with some of the most impressive credentials have now emerged with ideas about how to change the curriculum Afrocentrically. The forces of resistance to this transformation began to assemble around their wagons almost as quickly as the word was given that education had to treat each child equally. The attempt was to discredit the intellectual and philosophical movement because white scholars at the major universities did not start it and have not discovered how to articulate it. Yet, even without the ability to quote a single word on the theory, they write articles against Afrocentricity often criticizing it as a separatist movement, a further indication of their lack of knowledge. This is another example of the arrogant Eurocentrism that assumes that unless whites originated the idea it is unworthy of serious consideration. Have we ever called an idea that emerged out of the mind of a white thinker separatist simply because it came from a white person? The black students who study in the classrooms of some of these teachers and professors may know more about the term"Afrocentricity" than their professors because they have read the books, participated in community discussions, and viewed the Internet sites. The idea that an African American child learns from a stronger position if she is centered, that is, sees herself in the narrative rather than from the margins, is not novel (Asante, 1998) but it is revolutionary when we begin to teach teachers how to put the child in his or her history.

## The conditions of education

Institutions such as schools are conditioned by the character of the nation in which they are developed. Crime, education, politics are different in different nations because of the societies. In the United States we have practiced a whites-only orientation in education. This has had a profound impact on the quality of education for all children. The African American child has suffered out of proportion to white children, who also are victims of diseased curricula. One value of Afrocentric education is that it teaches discipline, that is, it empowers the teacher because discipline is based on the quality of ethical authority that comes from truth. Children submit to discipline to show devotion to a group.

## The transformation of perspective

Afrocentric education represents a new interpretation of productive transmission of values and attitudes. Students are made to see with new eyes and to hear with new ears. African American children learn to intepret phenomena from themselves as centered; whites learn to see that their own centers are not threatened by the space taken by African Americans or others.

It is good for all children because it is correct, respectful, and accurate. During the past five years, I have had white students and parents come up to me after presentations in tears or angry about the absence of information about African Americans. Recently at a major university in the northeast a young white man said to me, "My teacher told us that Martin Luther King was a commie and went on with the class." The fact that this student's teacher did not discuss King's ideas meant that the student was kept ignorant about Martin Luther King. The vast majority of white Americans are ignorant about African American history or culture. Very few white professors have ever taken a course in African or African American Studies and therefore are unable to provide systematic information about African Americans. Unfortunately, much the same is true of black professors who have usually been taught by white professors.

We are victims of the same system. Our children do not know the names of the African ethnic groups who comprise our population; we do not know any names of sacred sites in Africa; we can hardly tell you what the Middle Passage was and meant to Africans; and we have forgotten the brutality of slavery and celebration of freedom. Faheem Ashanti developed the Ashanti Brainwashing Test in which he took test items from questions that high school students should have been able to answer and gave them to African American and white students at various colleges. Amazingly, to me, the students' scores were almost identical on Afrocentric and Eurocentric information. For example, they all did fairly well with the year of the Declaration of American Independence but all did poorly on questions such as the year of final emancipation of Africans from enslavement in the United States, and the meaning of the word *oba*. Of course, they knew what the word *king* meant. When African American children come out of that experience you can rest assured, as Martin Luther King once said, "they have clouds of inferiority floating around in their mental skies." Again this phenomenon is found all over the African world. It is as much at work in South Africa as it is in Brazil; it is as strong in Kenya and Nigeria as it is in Jamaica and Ghana. I know that there are Afrocentric schools that have tried to intervene in the process of education but they are often fighting against Africans who are brainwashed, self-hating, and anti-African in their attitudes because they have internalized inferiority. When African-Mexican children in Mexico are prevented from learning about their own history because of the notion of *mestazaje*, mixture, in which the attempt is to wipe out Africa or the First Nations people, the result is the same as in North America.

# The tragedy of ignorance

There is a deep inadequacy in African people's knowledge about their own history. Our children have little understanding of the nature of the capture, the transport, and enslavement of Africans. How many of us were truly taught the horrors of being taken, shipped naked across twenty-five days of ocean, seeing others leap singing to their deaths, being broken by abuse, indignities of all kind, and then dehumanized to a thing without a name? If we knew, perhaps our behavior would be different. If our children had to read the slave narratives, the ship captain's words, they would be different, the white children would be different; America would be a different nation.

They should have been exposed to the historical narrative of how the barbaric treatment began, of how the African's dignity was stolen, and how culture was destroyed. They should know the story of how death swam next to the ships in the dreaded Middle Passage. A few Africans recorded their experiences: Jacob and Ruth Weldon, an African couple, give the most detailed account ever discovered (Feldstein, 1971, pp. 33–7). They wrote that the African, having been captured and brought onto the ships, was chained on the deck, made to bend over, and branded with a red-hot iron in the form of letters or signs dipped in an oily preparation and pressed against the naked flesh till it burnt a deep and ineffaceable scar, to show who was the owner.

The Weldons say that those who screamed were lashed in the face, breast, thighs, and backs with cat-o'-nine-tails wielded by white sailors. Every blow brought the returning lash pieces of grieving flesh. The Weldons continue that they saw "mothers with babies at their breasts basely branded and lashed, hewed and scarred, till it would seem as if the very heavens must smite the infernal tormentors with the doom they so richly merited."

The children of America should read the words of the Weldons who said that the male slaves were chained two by two, at the arm and leg. Women were stowed away without chains but naked, and all were packed away in the holds of ships for the five-to-eight week trip across the sea. The Africans could not even sit upright, the space between the decks being only two feet in height. On fair weather days the Africans were allowed to come on deck and dance for exercise. This they did in leg irons and chains to prevent them from escaping. Even some of the slave ship captains said the "groans and suffocating cries for air and water coming from below the deck sickened the soul of humanity." Compelled to weep and wail the long hours of night away, with no water to quench the tormenting thirst, and just enough oxygen to prolong their suffering, some of our ancestors vowed in those dark, damp, dank hellholes of horror that we would be free one day. African children are systematically denied knowledge of this story, both in the diaspora and in Africa. And white children do not know the story. If they were taught the Afrocentric perspective on the Great Enslavement, I suspect that we would have a different response to diversity. Remembrance is a necessity for humility and understanding. This is why the Jewish community has rightly campaigned to get the European Holocaust taught in schools and colleges. Such monstrous human brutality should remind the world of how humans have often violated each other. Teaching about the African Holocaust is just as important for some of the same reasons; essentially it underscores the enormity of the dislocation of Africans, physically, psychologically, and economically. Without understanding the historical experiences of Africans, one cannot truly make any headway in dealing with the problems of the present.

There are those who will say that education should begin with the arrival of Africans in the English colonies because that is where African American history begins. That would be a mistake for several reasons. In the first place, 1619 was not the first time that Africans were in the Americas. Furthermore, on the slave ships it is true that the weak perished and that the strong stayed alive, meaning essentially that America became something of a home for those who survived. Yet the experience on the ships created an entirely different history for Africans than for whites who came willingly to what they thought would be a better life. No African came to the Americas with that in mind. No, on the slave ships, the captives' sleeping and resting places were often covered with blood and mucous and the horrid stench of the dead, breeding yet others for death, and some cursed the crime that forced them away from their homes. They were not looking for a better place; they were at home and in the land of their ancestors with no reason to leave. Those who survived often looked upon the dead beside them and intoned "gone to she own country" or "gone to he own friends."

## Testimonies

The slave captains spared not even children and infants from terror. The Weldons tell of a child of nine months being flogged because it would not eat. This failing, the captain ordered the child's feet placed in boiling water which dissolved the skin and nails, then the child was whipped again. Refusing to eat, the child had a piece of mango wood tied to his neck as punishment. When nothing would make this baby eat, the captain took him and dropped him from his arms upon the deck. The child died instantly. The mother was called and asked to throw the dead body overboard. She refused and was beaten. Then she was forced to take it to the ship's side, where "with her head averted so she might not see it, she dropped the body into the sea."

When those slave ships reached land, whatever the land, whatever the condition, nothing, Africans thought, could be as bad as the Middle Passage, with its long bloody night of violence and terror. However, on land, the situation was often worse. Mothers were often forced to leave their children alone in the slave shacks while they worked in the fields. Unable to nurse these children or to care for them, they often returned from work at night to find their children dead (Feldstein, 1971, p. 49).

If they could really read history and see the relationship of Africans to cotton, women and children working till

> the blood runs from the tips of their fingers, where they have been pricked by the hard pod; or if they could see them dragging their baskets, all trembling, to the scale, for fear their weight should be short, and they should get the flogging which in such a case they know they must expect; or if they could see them bent double with constant stooping, and scourged on their bare back when they attempted to rise to straighten themselves for a moment . . .

they would treat each cotton shirt or dress as a sacred piece (Feldstein, 1971).

They should have heard the testimony of Henry Bibb who said:

> I was born May 1815, of a slave mother . . . and was claimed as the property of David White, Esq . . . I was flogged up; for where I should have received moral, mental, and religious instructions, I received stripes without number, the object of which was to degrade and keep me in subordination. I can truly say that I drank deeply of the bitter cup of suffering and woe. I have been dragged down to the lowest depths of human degradation and wretchedness, by slaveholders. (Feldstein, 1971)

Few contemporary schools teach this history the way it should be taught to transform students who enter schools or colleges. The Afrocentrist is concerned with total education of the child and we tend to have a belief in the ability of individuals to take information and use it wisely for moral and intellectual growth. There should not be a problem with students being exposed to this type of education. What is needed is a pedagogy of veracity built upon the actual facts of history as far as we know them.

*Correcting distorted information*

Hegemonic education can only exist so long as true and accurate information is kept from people. With information, people have new inputs into reasons, whether they want to follow these paths or not. You can no longer be comfortable with teaching that Greece is the origin of philosophy if you realize that the Greeks taught that Africa, specifically Kemet, was the home of the origin of philosophy. You cannot teach the European origin of art if you know about the black people of ancient Kemet. Hegemonic education can exist only so long as whites think that Africans have never contributed to civilization. It is largely upon such false ideas that invidious distinctions are made.

Not only did Africa contribute to human history; African civilizations pre-date any that we know about since humans originated on the continent of Africa. This is true whether you take archaeological evidence or biological evidence. Let us leave Greece and the Greeks and return to study the Egyptians and Egypt. Let us study the first philosophers: Kagemni, Khunanup, Ptahhotep, Kete, and Seti. But since our education about ourselves is so disjointed, we have no way of seeing an organic relationship of Africa to the rest of human history. With our enslavement came an attack on our psychical and spiritual being. The ontological onslaught caused some Africans to opt for suicide; enslavement was a living death, the brutality of the slavocracy is unequaled for its psychological destruction of African Americans. This gave us a freedom faith. However, the result was often dislocation, disorientation, and misorientation, all conditions of being decentered. The African in this situation is one who has "shed" or tried to shed race, to become raceless. One's basic identity is self-identity which is ultimately cultural identity. Without cultural identity, you are lost. You can no more divest yourself of your race or your culture than you can stop breathing oxygen and still live. We are African and human; others are European and human; there is no contradiction in either position.

*"Wade in the waters, children, don't you get weary"*

We have been mesmerized, tranquilized, and paralyzed when it comes to the education of African American children. But we must face up to and defy the predictions. That has been our history. How is it that our ancestors built colleges with pennies and dared to call them universities and some teachers and administrators want to say that African American children cannot be motivated?

*Symbols of resistance*

There is the idea that there are two discourses about multiculturalism. Different adherents to the theory have different views on what it means. There is only one discourse that is relevant to the liberation of the minds of African and white people in the United States and that one is based upon the acceptance of Africa as central to African people in terms of place, location, foundation, history, as the starting point for any discussion. Diane Ravitch argues that there is a pluralist multiculturalism and a particularist multiculturalism. This is nonsense. These ideas exist only in Ravitch's imagination. Either you are for multiculturalism or you are not. The divisions she advances are really to conceal her position. You either support the maintenance of white supremacist teachings in education or you do not; there is no other possibility. Support of these positions depends upon keeping other people ignorant. Information must be distorted, suppressed, books never written or if written, never published, and if published, banned from the school district. All of the tactics are the tactics of those who prefer Africans on the mental and psychological plantation. Diane Ravitch has been called the leader of the professors who are opposing multiculturalism. But since their positions are indefensible they argue that they are for multiculturalism which means when you read their works that they are for a white perspective on everybody else's culture. I call these professors resisters because they are attempting to resist the progressive transformation of a mono-ethnic curriculum. The resisters say that Afrocentricity is anti-white. If Afrocentricity as a theory is against anything, it is against racism, ignorance, and white hegemony in the curriculum. This is not anti-white; it is pro-human. Others have written that it brings about the tribalization of America but America already has ethnic diversity; Afrocentricity provides all Americans an opportunity to examine the perspective of the African person in this society. No one raises an eyebrow at Chinatowns in America; it is only when the African seeks to create from his or her center that reaction sets in to deny the transformation.

Pluralism is recognition of our difference. America is already divided if you speak of opportunities afforded in education to children. The white child, by virtue of the protection provided by society and enforced by the curriculum, is already ahead of the African American child in the first grade. We have got to concentrate on giving the African American child opportunity at the kindergarten level. But the kind of assistance the child needs is as much cultural as academic. Indeed, if the cultural information is provided, the academic will follow. The aim of the Afrocentric curriculum is not to divide America; it is to make America flourish as it ought to flourish.

Some resisters claim that history is being created simply because they do not know the facts. No one has ever proved that history was being created. Can you imagine how arrogant it is for someone to speak of "fantasy history" and "bizarre theories" simply because they have never read the facts or heard the arguments? What they have pointed to is the fact that they did not know something. But it is very arrogant to claim something is created just because you have never heard of it. The only reigning initiative for total change proposed and led by Africans is the movement to transform the curriculum. Instead of getting on board to fight against white hegemonic education, some whites and some blacks too have decided to plead for a return to the education plantation. However, those days are gone and can never be packaged as accurate, correct education again.

### Myths about education

The educational system does not need a tune-up; when it comes to understanding African American children, it needs an overhaul. We know that our children have been maligned. Our history has been maligned. Our continent of origin has been maligned. We also know that our teachers have often been maligned. But let me give you two truisms about education in America. First, some teachers can and do effectively teach African American children. Secondly, if they can do it, then we can learn what their attitudes are about teaching which make them successful. Among the myths that we often hear about schools and education are the following:

#### African American children have the same advantages as whites
America has become a nation of criminals, discriminators, educators who kill little children's motivation. At no point in American history has it been the case that African American children have had the same advantages as whites. You would have to close your eyes to reality in order to make a statement supporting the equality of opportunity. There is not a predominantly African American school in any community in America that is considered the equivalent of the predominantly white school in the same district. I am not talking about brightness of students; I am talking about treatment of the students and expenditures on the schools. The experiences of the Africans are not the same. No other group of people has had such a long campaign against its history and culture. The aim has been to wipe out African identity. There are several myths which add to the misinformation about education. Those who provide information are often operating on the basis of these false myths.

*Treatment of African American children is the same as for whites*
If you believe this myth, then you are ready to be sold the George Washington Bridge. Whether you speak of the historical relationship to school environment, textbook publishers, boards of education, or teacher responses to the children, our children are not treated equally. I am not saying treated the same; I am saying treated equally. Most of all, context for learning is different, names of buildings, models for learning experiences, trips to places of cultural value to the students, and invitations to writers and speakers.

*There is ample information about Africans in the curriculum*
School curricula see Africans as guests; consequently there is little modeling of events and personalities. White students may ask the teacher that teaches about Africans, "Is it going to be on the test?" If not, then they often do not consider the information as an organic part of the subject under discussion. Why should a little African child have to see herself as a guest when her ancestors are interwoven with the fabric of the nation?

Every part of the nation is attached to the African American past.

## Strategies for implementation

There are several steps necessary for implementing a curriculum for change. Indeed, the attention to language in the scope and sequence of the curriculum is one of the easiest ways to assess the situation in a school curriculum. What type of words and terms are used to refer to African peoples? Are these words pejorative? Can they be changed to reflect the realities of the situation? Among the steps to be considered are the following points for discussion:

1 Language issues: pay attention to terms such as slavery (enslavement), bushman, pygmies, minority, co-culture, sub-cultures, like a bunch of wild Indians, etc.
2 The essential involvement of parents, teachers, and community leaders in the school program.
3 The understanding of the ideas of scope, sequence, and objectives as they relate to curriculum.
4 The de-biasing of attitudes as well as facts by identifying assertions that are biased in the way they are stated.

The meaning of Afrocentric education is that African people have something to contribute to the world perspective but it must be contributed from the viewpoint of African people. Afrocentric education is therefore a fundamental necessity for anyone declaring competence in almost any subject in America; otherwise the person remains essentially ignorant of a major portion of the world. Multiculturalism, to be authentic, must consider the Afrocentric perspective which is the proper stepping-stone from the African American culture to a true multiculturalism. If this step is skipped, we are likely to see an idea of multiculturalism as defined through the eyes of whites without any substantive African American information infused in the curriculum. This can be avoided and should be avoided for the mutual benefit of all Americans.

# 7

## Sustaining a Relationship to Black Studies

## Origins

In the United States, the Black Studies revolution of the late twentieth century profoundly impacted the curricula of most institutions of higher education. Universities and high schools were changed and their curricula expanded to include African content. Taken together with the infusion of students of African origin and the presence of multinational Africans as faculty, the advancement in curriculum at American colleges and universities is a quantum leap from what it was at the end of the nineteenth century. No traditional discipline, such as anthropology, history, sociology, or literature, has been the same since the revolution that brought Black Studies into existence.

"Black Studies" was a term that grew out of the political and academic climate of the 1960s. When students at San Francisco State University campaigned in 1967 for courses that reflected the experiences of African people, they called for "Black Studies" since so much of the curriculum was "White Studies" parading as if it were universal studies. Merritt Community College students in Oakland, California, were at the same time demonstrating for more black faculty and African American history courses. The California spirit of revolution in the classrooms had taken root in the organic struggles for equality carried on by African American students who had been radicalized by Martin Luther King and Malcolm X. Motivated by the political, social, and economic ideas of self-determination and self-definition, students led by the US Movement and the Black Panther Party, whatever their own differences, were united around the establishment of Black Studies. Almost simultaneously the movement caught on nationally and chapters of Black Student Unions were created to express the pent-up intellectual energy felt by African American students.

The immediate academic aim was to create the opportunity for "a black perspective" in the American academy in social sciences, arts, and humanities. A number of names emerged to describe the course of study and group of subjects under the umbrella of "Black Studies." Among the more popular names were "Afro American Studies" as in the UCLA Center for Afro American Studies; "Africana Studies" as in the Cornell University Department of Africana Studies; "African American Studies" as in the Temple University Department of African American Studies; "Africa World Studies" as in the Miami University "Africa World Studies" program; "African Diaspora Studies" as in the PhD program at UC Berkeley; and "Africology" as in the Department of Africology at the University of Wisconsin at Milwaukee. A few departments, such as Ohio State University and California State University, Long Beach, retain the title of "Black Studies." Increasingly, and for critical reasons, the term "Africology" has gained recognition as a name and objective of our intellectual pursuit.

### A historical note

During the early days of the campaign for Black Studies the most critical need was for faculty guidance about the courses being proposed. Students often developed syllabi, courses of study, and bibliographies and presented these to the various deans of universities as indicative of what could be the core of Black Studies. But the list of faculty who could assist the students was limited. Eventually, this would lead to the issue of black faculty to teach the courses. Most major universities had a few token blacks who had been on campus for several years, but many of them did not relate to the innovations sought by the students.

At UCLA, the Harambee Club took the leadership in 1966 to compile a list of possible courses that could be taught at university level. Similarly, students across the nation met day after day, night after night, in the most intense drive for academic freedom at the curricular level in the history of American education. No movement for curricular reform had ever been so widespread and as thoroughly universal in its intellectual commitment as the Black Studies movement. Its energy came directly from its organic link with the people who were experiencing a persistent white racial domination in the classroom. These were not theorists who had studied at some elite graduate school; most were undergraduate students or graduate students who were the first-generation college students in their families. They could not afford to "mess up," that is, to fail to graduate from college, and yet they knew that they would be "messed up," that is, psychologically disturbed, if they took into their brains the white racism that was being taught to them as if it were universal knowledge. They reacted strongly as one massive national block with a political drive that was demanding and they were ultimately heard. Their pursuit, and ours even now, was for a discipline that would begin its study with African people as subjects rather than objects of the European imagination (Asante, 1998).

However, in the process many young people were lost in the tumult that accompanied the birth of the new field. When students completed their tomes of syllabi and bibliographies, they would often march to the offices of the university leaders with their work in one hand and a list of demands in the other. They wanted, among other things, additional black faculty members, black cultural centers, lecture programs of outstanding black scholars, and sensitivity classes for white faculty members. The institutional leaders were quick to call the police to the campuses. Many African American students were arrested during that period and some were given unfairly long jail sentences. They remain the heroes of the struggle for equal education and their legacies are in the thousands of students who have been taught in African American Studies, though those early pioneers often seem forgotten. The system of racial privilege favoring white students and white information in the classrooms did not end easily; it held on and may even persist in some institutions today.

## A search for faculty

Another issue that faced the incipient movement was who would teach the courses and where would the university find professors. This proved to be a critical issue, one that has continued to shape and, in some senses, to distort the field. The terminal degree for most social sciences and humanities disciplines is the doctorate and for the arts it is often the Master of Fine Arts. While there were hundreds of African Americans with the degrees in the 1960s, the overwhelming majority of them taught at predominantly black institutions in the South. The only other sources of African-descended doctorates and MFAs were continental Africans who had been educated in the United States.

African Americans entered the predominantly white institutions of higher education in large numbers in the late 1960s but it would be several years before Black Studies departments would have the benefit of their education and, even then, there would be inherent theoretical and philosophical issues. Eager to attract and hire black professors, many universities hired continental African professors. This proved to be a challenging action both for the professors and the students who had campaigned for their hiring. In the first place, as I indicated in my book *Afrocentricity*, the emphasis on the race of the professors to be hired led African American students to a dead-end when some black professors, continental and diasporan, were less knowledgeable than some white professors (Asante, 2003a). Insistence on biology always leads to a misunderstanding of the cultural, social, and psychological experiences that are necessary for empathetic relationships. One might say that biology, at some point, is important but it is not defining in terms of who should teach African American Studies. The continental Africans who had doctoral degrees were usually trained by white professors who had very little appreciation of the history of African Americans. This meant that the continental Africans had to be quick students in the African American experience in order to be successful as professors in Black Studies. They had to abandon the attitudes of some of their white professors and adopt a consciousness that was African American which usually meant a stance against racism, a belief in the ability of blacks to govern and control their own destinies, the acceptance of the African origin of civilization, and the maintenance of a sense of confidence. The scores of African professors who found their postures in this arena were exceptionally brilliant in the classroom. Some were heroic and memorable such as Boniface Obichere, a Nigerian by birth, who taught me African History at UCLA. Some made this change quite easily; Chike Onwauachi and others found it rather difficult. The problem was often that these continental professors had not taken on the issues of the African Americans and fell victims to the same racism that the students had complained about prior to their hiring. Indeed, some continental African professors found the task daunting and opted to join more traditional departments.

In some cases the universities, desperate to find faculty, opted to employ African Americans who were degree-less or who did not have the terminal degree although they had other degrees. This meant that significant community activists could teach in their own fields of expertise and achievement. Prominent individuals who came to lecture at universities under those circumstances were Sonia Sanchez, Bayard Rustin, Gwendolyn Brooks, Eldridge Cleaver, Amiri Baraka, Margaret Walker, Charles Fuller, and numerous others. Some major universities, to gain African American professors, even raided the faculties of predominantly black institutions such as Howard, Fisk, Tuskegee, and Hampton. Arna Bontemps, nearly retired, left Fisk to join the faculty at Yale University, for instance.

## The general revolutions

There have been three movements for academic enrichment within the general revolutions initiated by the Black Studies Movement. Each movement was pegged to one of the terms for the concentration: Black Studies, Africana, and Africology. Furthermore, each of these movements had as its political objective the freeing of the minds of the students so that they might reflect on the vast and diverse universe of knowledge usually kept from them.

## The Black Studies Movement

The Black Studies Movement in the United States did not arise out of a primordial Nun, but rather from an organized group of ideas that formed a core philosophy for use in confronting the status quo in education. There was a powerfully raw energy to the creation of the Black Studies Movement. It was unlike any other transformation in the American Academy. Groups of students from various colleges, acting simultaneously, almost as if they were collectively programmed, passed through the same processes in order to establish Black Studies on their campuses. First, it was necessary to define the missing links in the institutional chain of delivering information; subsequently, the students would insist that those links should be supplied with information and scholarship; and finally the students oversaw the initiation of the programs to assist the institutions. All over the United States from Boston to San Francisco, from Detroit to Miami, the African American students projected their vision. It was often resisted, students were arrested, and many attacked by police. In the end, when the dust had settled, African American students had opened most of the doors at major American universities.

It is clear to me that the time for such Afrocentric renewal will soon come in Europe with the increased numbers of Africans. No society can operate a system of education that disconnects students from their own historical experiences without creating internal dissension and factional contention over the education of children. In Rome, one sees this with the growing demand of Ethiopian Italians for a voice in the education of their children. This is repeated in France, Spain, the United Kingdom, the Netherlands, and other countries of Western Europe with the growth of immigration. One is already seeing in Paris and other cities in France the Movement Noir Fier, Black Pride.

However, one asks, what constituted the Black Studies Movement in the United States? Like the Black Power Movement and the "Black is Beautiful" Campaign, the Black Studies Movement was a move for self-definition, self-determination, and mental liberation. In this regard it was in line with the most radical elements of the contemporary objective of securing for African Americans a more positive place in the curriculum. By its projection as

"Black," the Movement suggested its ethnic and cultural energy and by its use of the word "Studies" indicated its intellectual component. This was new and different because never before had "Black" and "Studies" been used in the same term. Most white Americans could not conceive of anything "black" being connected to anything intellectual. In answering the grossest questions from the white community about the nature of the intellectual study, Black Studies "closed the mouths" of the nay-givers.

The defining moment in the Black Studies Movement was the publication of Maulana Karenga's *Introduction to Black Studies* (2002 [1979]). When this book was published, about ten years after the establishment of the field, it was the first attempt to draw the boundaries of a new area of study. What Karenga did in *Introduction* was to state precisely how the field should be conceptualized, discussed, and projected. One could no longer assume that the field of study did not have precursor ideas, a core of intellectuals, and approaches to phenomena that constituted a whole new area of inquiry. This book was first published in 1979 and immediately created a stir in the field because until its appearance no one had conceived of Black Studies in such a wholistic fashion. Karenga organized the field into seven key areas: history, mythology, motif, ethos, social organization, political organization, and economic organization. These divisions were possible within the context of the Kawaida philosophy that had been the foundation for the creation of numerous self-defining experiences in the African American community.

## Africana Studies Movement

Riding on the tide created by Black Studies, the Africana Studies Movement was carried to new shores in the Academy in the early 1980s. However, this movement was not of a different species than Black Studies; it was in fact a new name for Black Studies. The National Council for Black Studies was the first professional organization in the field and it had increasingly referred to the field by the name "Africana" so that by the mid-1980s there were a good number of departments with that name. The aim was to make the field more academic and less political by changing the name of the departments around the nation. The Africana Studies Movement was initiated by members of the Cornell University faculty who were among the first to adopt the name Africana Studies for their department. The term was quickly adopted by other departments in the northeast part of the United States and soon spread to the Midwest because of the popularity of the professors from Cornell. Seeking to offset any criticism, the faculty who subscribed to the utility of the name "Africana" presented two arguments for its acceptance. First, Africana was meant to embrace the African world. Secondly, it was intended to de-politicize the study of African phenomena. As such Africana was meant to be a step away from confrontation, that is, black versus white. To say "Africana" was more than saying "African American"; it was a statement about the nature of the African experience in the world. This meant that the scholar could embrace the Caribbean, South America, and the African continent as a part of the field of study. Indeed, Black Studies that had been limited to the African American experience was now enlarged to include African issues on the continent, political upheavals in South America, literary developments in Haiti, and numerous other issues. One could just as easily research and discuss the Esie stones of Nigeria as one could the meaning of economic liberation among African Americans in Stone Mountain, Georgia.

## The Africological Movement

The Africological Movement, emerging in the mid-1980s, was trans-generational and transcontinental in scope. In my book, *Afrocentricity*, written initially in 1980 and revised several times since, I had spoken of a discipline of "afrology." This term was refined to "africology" by the University of Wisconsin professor, Winston Van Horne. I have since employed this term, using the definition I once gave afrology, that is, "the Afrocentric study of African phenomena."

Temple University's doctoral program established in 1987 quickly adopted the new movement as a way to advance a disciplinary approach to the area of study. Africology promised to be more than an aggregation of courses about African people. One could find at a number of institutions a list of courses on African subjects, but it was only when there was a discipline, as defined by philosophy, methods, and orientation to data, that one could speak of a discipline. Africology was being used to signal that there was no longer a field, but a discipline of study. It had become fashionable to speak of Black Studies or Africana Studies as a field of study with numerous disciplines contributing to the study of African people. This was based on the old ethnic studies or area study model. For the Africologist this was a dead-end model that would not lead to the growth of the study of African phenomena, nor to the advancement of scientific methods. The reason this was so had to do with the fact that knowledge could only expand if researchers were able to think outside the traditions. This was not about to happen with Black Studies scholars who had not committed discipline suicide, that is, who had not abandoned their traditional or doctoral areas of study. Thus, to think outside the box, so to speak, one had to believe that there was enough in the study of African phenomena, meaning in the United States and everywhere else where African people exist, to warrant strong methodological and philosophical study.

Africologists repeat the dictum that a department is not a discipline and a discipline does not constitute a department. A department is an administrative, not an intellectual, project. Although it takes intelligence to organize a department so that the administrative functions of the faculty members can be carried out, the real intellectual discourse is around philosophical orientations and theoretical emphases that create a discipline. It is clearer today than ever before among scholars who articulate the Africological Movement position that there are numerous interests, such as social work, social institutions, literary studies, historical experiences, psychological questions, and linguistic issues, but only one discipline. Those who accept this view are growing in numbers as well as in influence. Fundamental to this project is the belief that Cheikh Anta Diop was correct to argue that until Africans dare to connect ancient Egypt to the rest of Africa there could be no true interpretation of African history (Diop, 1974). Diop understood the significance of examining the classical civilizations of Africa as a prelude to any discourse on anything African.

Separating the study of African culture or civilizations by the West African Ocean (Atlantic Ocean) is a peculiar saline demarcation that does not exist in any real sense. Thus, to speak of a black Atlantic makes no real intellectual sense when you assume that Brazil, Venezuela, Nicaragua, Jamaica and Panama do not have anything to do with Africans in England or the United States. Indeed, all Africans on both sides of the Atlantic are inextricably joined by a common experience and a common cultural response, however tailored the response is to specific histories. Diop was the first African to articulate so powerfully the necessity for our linkage. Such clarity, on the part of the late Senegalese scholar, made him, alongside W. E. B. Du Bois, one of the greatest intellectuals of the twentieth century. When Diop died in 1986, he had already become the single most important historian of ancient Africa and consequently the patron of a new historiography that would elevate the writing of African history to another level of Afrocentricity (Keita, 2000).

## Issues of theory and method

The challenge to scholars in the postmodern era is to devise ways to explore African phenomena that avoid the worst pitfalls of Western theories and methods. This means that the source of the theories must be in the historical and lived experiences of the African people wherever they appear in the world. Congruent theories of African phenomena have symmetry to African life. This does not mean that we cannot learn from theories developed in other places, but rather that symmetry to one's own phenomenological history is a better way to view reality. I think that the issues of method are similar. You cannot stick your head in the sand and assume that the methods often used by non-Afrocentrists in an effort to predict and control our behavior can be readily applied to African phenomena without modification.

To examine theory and method is to confront the problem of Western science's attempt to bifurcate the study of human experiences. In most departments of Africology we are faced with deciding whether we are in the social sciences or the humanities. Here we are at Eshu's crossroads, presented with a choice. If we claim to be social scientists, studying the nature of human behavior, we wonder about our interests in the creations of human beings, in art, literature, and music. If we claim to be in the humanities, then we are left asking questions about our interests in how African people survive under the pressures of racist brutality and discrimination. So we are caught between the Limpopo and the Zambezi; if we cross the first we are leaving behind the Great Zimbabwe and if we cross the second, we also leave behind the Great Zimbabwe. The resolution of this issue can only come from our own cultural center. As we stand on the pinnacle of the Great Zimbabwe, we must see our world going out to the various ends but not being defined by one or the other.

All departments of Africology should have the ability to articulate both interests as a part of the philosophical project. In the first place the study of African phenomena for us does not subscribe to a division where you separate behavioral studies from creative studies. Our concentrations in Cultural Aesthetics or in Social Behavioral Studies is intended to suggest that what passes for social sciences includes far more than psychology or sociology and what passes for arts and humanities includes far more than writing and dancing. All human behavior is a creative product and all human creations are evidence of human behavior. Therefore, we cannot and should not be boxed into choosing one side or the other; we do both and our discipline is one whether or not for administrative purposes a university wants to keep us in social sciences or humanities.

Afrocentric metatheory is the leading approach to the examination of African phenomena. This metatheory exists as a place in which Afrocentric theories can be generated to deal with practically any issue in the African world. A study by Ama Mazama of the way Africans have created language in the Americas is an example of how a scholar can creatively position the Afrocentric theory. Mazama is convinced that the language of the Africans of Guadeloupe is an African language, not some bad French (Mazama, 1997). She writes of a first measure for understanding the relationship of the Africans in Guadeloupe to Africa this way:

> La première consiste à réfuter le mythe du vacuum linguistique et culturel dans lequel nos ancêtres se seraient trouvés en arrivant dans les Caraibes afin de démontrer, au contraire, la continuité historico-culturelle qui existe entre l'Afrique et les Caraibes, ainsi que je m'y suis attachée dans ce livre. La deuxiéme mesure à prendre est l'identification de la composante africaine des langues caribéennes. (Mazama, 1997, p. 124).

An Afrocentric theory is one that is constructed to give Africans a centered role in their own phenomena. It is an attack on marginality and peripherilization of Africans. There can be as many Afrocentric theories as scholars seek to create, all operating within the same general Afrocentric framework. While the Africologists can explore the relationship of other theories to the phenomena of Africans, the sine qua non of the africological adventure is Afrocentricity.

The discipline of Africology is grounded in the principles of *Maat*. Those ancient African principles seem to hold for all African societies and most African people trans-generationally and transnationally. The principles of *Maat*, as recently clarified by Maulana Karenga, include harmony, balance, order, justice, righteousness, truth, and reciprocity. What the Africologist seeks in his or her research is the pathway to harmony and order in society. This is why the ancient people of Kemet called this concept *Maat*. This is not about observing and experimenting in order to control your behavior but rather this is about making humans whole.

When I created the first PhD program in African American Studies in 1987 at Temple University, I had to keep uppermost in my mind the fact that African intellectual traditions were not anti-people. In fact, the doctoral program in African American Studies had to be a people-affirming program. Writing and defending a program that was considered to be far from the usual university development fare had its disappointments and rewards. I understood precisely what we were up against when the proposal went to the Graduate Committee of the College of Arts and Sciences. Not only were there people with Neanderthalian ideas but some who did not want to see any challenge to the hegemony of European education even if it meant that they would be less educated if they did not know the information. They were in bliss in their ignorance. They would soon be confronted with a proposal that met the university's requirements in every way. Furthermore, I was a professor who was more published than any of my white colleagues and had created two previous graduate programs, the MA in Afro American Studies at UCLA and the MA in Communication at State University of New York at Buffalo. I soon had a parade of white professors tell me why they could not approve the MA and PhD in African American Studies at Temple. The argument, whether from History, English or Sociology, was the same argument: there was no guarantee that the program was going to be a quality program. What this meant to me was that they were concerned that the principal faculty handling the courses and the program would be African American. Of course their objections had nothing to do with quality since our faculty was more "qualified" than some of those raising the objections. Emma Lapsansky from the Dean of Arts and Sciences office went so far as to write a two-page letter decrying the establishment of an "intellectual ghetto" on campus. My response to her was pointed: the entire university was already one big intellectual ghetto and I was only trying to open it up. When the first 35 graduate students entered the university in the fall 1988, they changed for ever the nature of education at predominantly white institutions in America. But they changed something else as well: the intellectual basis for African American Studies. The only way that I could justify the creation of a doctoral program was that we were teaching something that was not being taught anywhere else. This meant that those of us who worked in the department had to commit discipline suicide from our old doctorates and work feverishly to flesh out this new discipline that was not African American history, not African American literature, not Women's Studies, not African American sociology, and not Studies in Racism.

We confronted the turf wars with other departments and won on the merits of what it was that we were doing. We found the energy and the time to write the texts and establish the sequences that would demonstrate that we were as much a discipline as any other group of scholars. The process is not over; it has really only just begun. In Africology it ought to be possible to point to texts written by scholars in our field, not in literature, English, sociology, and history, as significant for our graduate students. We are doing more in this regard with the annual Cheikh Anta Diop Conference, the student conferences, the *Nommo* symposia, and the publication of fundamental works such as The African Intellectual Heritage, and the editing of numerous journals. The pursuit of Africology is nearly completed but will not be truly accomplished until contemporary Black Studies departments begin to refurbish their faculties with PhDs who have completed the terminal degree in the field. When we have reached the level of having more than half of our faculty members with degrees in African American Studies, we can say that the discipline is secure.

# 8

## Afrocentricity and History

Afrocentricity as a theory of human liberation and intellectual critique was initially a project of practical social reform for highly industrialized, complex heterogeneous nations. As such it challenged the continuation of white racial hegemony over all symbols and social systems by opposing archaic structures of race based on the imposition of a particular cultural reality as if it were universal. Afrocentricity is presented as one way out of the impasse over social and cultural hegemony. One arrives at an understanding and rapprochement by accepting the agency of the African person as the basic unit of analysis of social situations involving African-descended people. This is a critical step in achieving community harmony. It becomes absolutely necessary to accept the subject position of Africans within the context of historical realities if progress is to be made in interpretation, analysis, synthesis, or construction. What this means, however, is that every system that has depended upon the degradation of the African worldview, the denial of African humanity, and the ignoring of African achievements in civilization in order to enhance its own rationalizations must be confronted. With the end of the Great Enslavement in 1865 there were nearly four and a half million African refugees in the United States. Within the next thirty-five years the literacy rate leaped from five percent to nearly fifty percent in one generation in one of the most remarkable expressions of educational interest in the history of the world. This was generated by a period of Reconstruction from 1865 to 1877. It would barely last twelve years but during that time it would mean that the African people could exercise freedoms that had been denied for nearly 250 years.

During Reconstruction, the African population voted and ran for political office and once in office created many innovations such as public schools and public highways. However, with the signing of the Hayes-Tilden Compromise that allowed the rebellious southern whites additional privileges, the Union Army that had protected the four million Africans of the southern states was withdrawn from the South and a reign of terror literally set back the clock of social progress for generations. Whites organized vigilante groups to pursue, hound, and harass Africans out of government offices. The Ku Klux Klan organization was born with the express purpose of terrorizing any African who had the courage to register to vote, or who voted, or ran for office. The southern landscape was littered with the corpses of Africans who simply attempted to express the right to vote. Such harsh measures meant that soon blacks had been completely eliminated from legislative and administrative posts in the southern part of the United States.

An entire league of African reformists sought remedies and relief but was met with even more lynching and brutalizing of African people. In the United States the top of the twentieth century was devoted to the campaign against mob rule and the denial of citizenship rights. By the time Martin Luther King, Jr., and his brothers and sisters, started the Montgomery Bus Boycott in 1955, many religious African Americans had come to believe that it was possible for whites to reform their actions, change their racist behaviors.

Indeed, King's strategy was to appeal to the principal documents in which white Americans believe: the Bible and the American Constitution. Some change was brought about and the results were that King was considered a hero by many Americans. Yet the final results would reveal the hollowness of the victory of that romantic age, the decade of the 1960s.

There was a growing sentiment after Malcolm X, and perhaps in response to him, that what was needed among African Americans and Africans in general was a more self-defining and self-determining attitude about all social, economic, political, and cultural issues. It was understood that reform was necessary, but the reform was to be of the African person. In fact, it was to be an intense interrogation of the African person's concept of space and time. Being was held to the light of history and it was revealed that for five hundred years African people had been moved off all terms. We were operating, so to speak, on someone else's intellectual space and within someone else's time frame. This meant that we could not actively pursue our own course of agency and direction for African people without conflicting with the received idea that whites would have to change before progress was made. The Afrocentrists redefined the meaning of progress, charged the receivers of violence and oppression with as much complicity as the ones who carried out the initial crimes, and went on the warpath. To change one's situation it would be necessary to change oneself became an innovative dictum of power during the Afrocentric movement.

I think it is crucial that we have a clear understanding of how Afrocentricity emerged as a paradigm of theory and practice in the arena of African American Studies. Afrocentricity enters the critique of European hegemony after a series of attempts by European writers to advance critical methods of the construction of reality in the context of Europe itself. But Europe has been unable to satisfactorily critique itself from outside the racist, hegemonic paradigm established as the grand narrative of the European people. It is here that Afrocentricity provides the first deep analysis of the social and political situation inherent in hegemonic societies. It is as if we cannot learn from Europe in the area of human relations because everywhere Europe has been it has been the destroyer of equality and respect for diverse humanity. In no place where Europe has appeared with non-European people has Europe sought to live in mutual peace with other people. Everywhere Europe has sought domination, defeat, ethnic cleansing, and conquest. All European ideologies from dialectical materialism to postmodernism protect the ruthless Eurocentric idea of white triumphalism and hegemony.

What remains problematic with European thought is its inability to allow space for other cultures and therefore it becomes self-absorbed in some notion of Europe as the categorical universal for the world. Such self-centeredness has left the rest of the world searching for a theoretical corrective. Among the principal ways that Europe has approached its own rendezvous with destiny has been the establishment of schools of thought that have answered some of the questions of displacement, economic inequality, fragmentation, universalism, grand narratives, and ethical issues. In order to ascertain how and where Afrocentricity enters the picture in the context of the Western world, I will discuss some of the relevant Eurocentric approaches and suggest how they differ from Afrocentricity. In fact, one of the chief ideological positions of most Western scholars is the privileging of Western science as a mode of acquiring knowledge. Rather it should become essential that a discourse on the nature of rational inquiry that produces knowledge be grounded in cultural understandings.

## The science issue

Marvin Harris, for example, writes as good an apologia as anyone for the value of Western science as a unique and precious contribution of Western civilization. His theme is that no other way of knowing is based on a set of rules explicitly designed to transcend the prior belief systems of mutually antagonistic peoples, nations, classes, and religious communities in order to arrive at knowledge that is equally probable for any rational mind.

Therefore, according to Harris, the real alternative to science is not anarchy, but ideology; not peaceful artists, philosophers, and anthropologists, but aggressive fanatics and messiahs, eager to annihilate each other and the world if need be in order to prove their point. He is willing to characterize the scientific approach as superior to others and to claim that it is uniquely rational among systems. He engages fully in the Eurocentric thesis that other societies are societies of nonscientists. He readily admits that there are domains of experience the knowledge of which cannot be achieved by adherence to the rules of scientific method. Nevertheless Harris sees this "nonscientific" knowledge, particularly the ecstatic knowledge of people he refers to as mystics and saints as well as the visions and hallucinations of drug users and of schizophrenics alongside the aesthetic and moral insights of artists, poets, and musicians, as beyond his understanding. This is almost fantastic, an admission that he cannot distinguish between the euphoria of drug users and saints or schizophrenics and the insights of artists and poets! But Harris has a deeper problem.

Harris's characterization of what he calls the Western scientific method is by no means unique. Yet his ability to denigrate other ways of knowing creates a false impression of deeper modes of inquiry. Science does not exclude moral or aesthetic insight. The special disciplines and rigors of the arts and the regularized, methical procedures of the so-called mystics cannot be easily discounted, for they have added knowledge and richness to the human experience. What Harris and other apologists of this peculiarly narrow version of the scientific adventure argue against is what they perceive as the random, mystical type of discovery. They see it as valuable only when it is transformed into precise, logical verification. Thus, discovery is separate from verification. In effect, Harris's view would dismiss the creative process, divest itself of discovery, and concentrate on the verification process. My desire is to see a paradigm of complementarity that integrates discovery with verification where necessary. In this manner, Afrocentricity expands the repertoire of human perspectives on knowledge.

Harris's judgment is cloudy on the issue of science inasmuch as science is not unique to the West. It cannot be described as solely a creation of the West and it is unlikely that it can be considered a method originating in the West. One does not have to look far for some answers to this situation. When Imhotep, the architect of the Sakkara Pyramid, built his massive monument for King Djoser in 2750 BC he did not wait for Western scientists or philosophers to work out theories, methods, and procedures for his work. He did this himself two thousand years before the mothers and fathers of Greek thought, the first in the West, appeared. In fact, rational thinking as a principal means of discovery and verification occurred in Egypt long after the Egyptians had begun to teach the Greeks philosophy.

## Afrocentricity and Africanity

Because the Afrocentric idea is unthinkable without African agency, I feel compelled to resolve the confusion surrounding the terms Afrocentricity and Africanity. How one approaches these concepts in large measure determines the efficacy of a challenge to hierarchy. The substance of one term is not that of the other, and the consequences of one can create problems for the other. In other words, one – Afrocentricity – seeks agency and action, and the other – Africanity – broadcasts identity and being. Actually, Africanity refers in its generality to all of the customs, traditions, and traits of people of Africa and the diaspora.

On the other hand, Afrocentricity is very specific in its reliance on self-conscious action. To say, for example, that Afrocentricity has no role in Africa because the people there already have an African perspective is to misunderstand the practical dimensions of Afrocentricity. To be African is not necessarily to be Afrocentric. It is possible, however, to develop a nexus between Africanity and Afrocentricity in order to generate a more productive architectonic African culture of balance and harmony. A major part of my Afrocentric quest has been to bring the consciousness of rhetorical structure to the study of African communication, particularly discourse. This is why I set a conceptual field for exploring the Afrocentric perspective on discourse in other works as well. Such a conceptual field allowed for the explanation of the rhetorical condition as a phenomenon with an implicit structure and did not negate the position of a metatheory for African communication. The oratory of African Americans could then be examined as the totalization of the Afrocentric perspective, emphasizing the presence of *nommo*, the generative and productive power of the spoken word, in African discourse and in specific instances of resistance to the dominant ideology. In the oratorical experience, much as in the jazz experience, the African person finds the ability to construct a discourse reality capable of calling forth *nommo*. One can see in this type of quest that different human objectives are derived from different historical and cultural experiences. What occurs in any science or art is a debate over mode, structure, and condition; that is, the guidelines for the valid discussion of discourse are at the center of any polemic. But hearing the voice of African American culture with all of its attendant parts is one way of creating a more sane society and one model for a more humane world.

## Dialectical materialism

It was the European concern with industrialism and capitalism that gave birth to dialectical materialism. We must never forget that these concerns were not expressed the same way universally. Other nations arrived at industrialization in different ways. In fact, Marx was very much Eurocentric in his focus. There was no global idea to his initial formulations. One might even say that there is a bias against modern notions of culture, whether as cultural relativity or cultural materialism, because there is simply a fascination and intense concern with the position of Europeans in the world. I am not criticizing this inasmuch as I believe that what the dialectical materialists sought was the revivification of Europe. This was their task because they saw it as their obligation to Europe itself. When one reads the *Communist Manifesto* one grasps the ideas of Marx and Engels clearly when they say "The history of all past society has consisted in the development of class antagonisms." In a later edition Engels corrected this idea when he wrote that the notion "all past society" should be the "history of society" since the evolution of the state. Engels wrote the book, *The Origin of the Family, Private Property and the State*, which was the centerpiece of Marxian social thought for nearly thirty years. Lewis Henry Morgan had written *Ancient Society* (Morgan, 1877) and had influenced works by Engels and Marx. They thought that they had seen in Morgan a corroboration of the materialist conception of history. Yet *Ancient Society* was interested in causality as much as germ ideas and natural selection. The idea of trying to impute causality to original germ ideas demonstrates how Eurocentric writers have periodically been fascinated with an interest in essentialist theories, yet quite ironically it is the Eurocentrists who now try to demonstrate that Afrocentrists are essentialists. As African American ancestors often said when the hounds of the slave owners would be trying to track those who ran away, "they are barking up the wrong tree." Engels never transcended the limitations of Morgan and his book, *The Origin of the Family, Private Property and the State*, is now seen as flawed in its methodology. There was no attempt to provide an infrastructural explanation for the development of the clan lying at the heart of village and chiefdom social structure (Harris, 1980, p. 161). The reason for this inability of dialectical materialism to deal with some of the issues outside of Europe is because the work falls in line with the entire narrative of European history where anything that is pre-capitalist, non-European, and external to the capitalist system is literally outside of history.

The key contribution of dialectical materialism is its understanding and appreciation of the infrastructure, the material conditions of society. To the degree that dialectical materialism establishes theoretical principles that undergird the primacy of material conditions, it is distinguished from Afrocentricity which argues that the constant interplay of infrastructure and structure, the material conditions and matter, so to speak, is the proper way to understand society. It is like nature or the relationship between lovers.

Thus, Afrocentricity is the answer to questions that are left open by dialectical materialism's fascination with the industrial realm in European development. In saying this I am not saying that Afrocentricity is the opposite of dialectical materialism, as the dialectical materialists might say, but rather stating that Afrocentricity must not be seen as counter to Eurocentricity.

The idea behind Eurocentricity in its most vile form, whatever its theoretical manifestation, is that Europe is the standard and nothing exists in the same category anywhere. It is the valorization of Europe above all other cultures and societies that makes it such a racist system. On the other hand, there should be nothing incorrect about European people wanting to have motifs, ideas, narratives, concepts that are derived from their history. That is to be expected, but what is not to be expected is the idea that Europe somehow has a right to hold a hegemonic banner over all other people. Afrocentricity does not seek African hegemony; it seeks pluralism without hierarchy. We will replay this discussion in a different light when I return to the dangers of avoiding structure or content in symbols, society, infrastructure, and text.

## Structuralism

While dialectical materialists were having a problem maintaining the character of their work on a consistent basis, the French intellectuals under the guidance of Claude Levi-Strauss were actually defining the most influential Western system of analysis, structuralism. Most of what we read in the social sciences in the West in the nineteenth and twentieth centuries is influenced by structuralism, whether it is a support of it or a rejection of it. Structuralists are fundamentally antipositivist, ahistorical and idealist. But like all theorists each structuralist would have a commentary to make on the type of structuralism practiced. For example, there are those who argue that they are not idealists because they accept the idea of infrastructure as primary in analysis. Idealism normally makes everything consist in ideas, denying the grounds for material bodies, and in the extreme having belief in nothing except percipient minds and ideas. Yet Levi-Strauss, the founder of the theory of structuralism, had said that he wanted to deal with superstructures that Marx had not dealt with, namely, the psychological structure of sociocultural systems. He saw ethnology as psychology where this type of structuralism and ethnology impact on Africans is at the level of research itself. If you assume that there are certain molds that must fit some societies, hence, people, and other molds that must fit other people, you are likely to establish a hierarchy of molds. This is what the Eurocentric writers did in following Emile Durkheim's idea that society is a conscience collective, collective consciousness or collective conscience, all meaning the same thing in French, as identified as a set of exterior ideas that have a coercive force over individual thought. Durkheim may have given the classic essentialist position when he wrote: "The collective consciousness is the highest form of the psychic life since it is the consciousness of the consciousness. Being placed outside of and above individual and local contingencies, it sees things only in their permanent and essential aspects, which it crystallizes into communicable ideas" (Durkheim, 1915).

As I have tried to indicate in previous works, structuralism in some of its guises raises questions that Afrocentrists are interested in because they question the psychological mode of thinking, the collectivity of Europe as a creator of images, and the motivations behind the actions that destroy, maim, and stifle human personality and community. But Afrocentricity is not structuralism; it is more than structuralism because, like dialectical materialism, structuralism does not answer the issues the Eurocentric ground creates itself. For example, while I share structuralism's interest in developing a system that considers "superstructures," Marx's "infrastructures," that are not evaluated in dialectical materialism, such as the psychological or even cognitive structures of society, I have a problem with the inability of structuralists to self-analyze. This lack of self-analysis leads to a paralysis of interpretation, explanation, and meaning whenever the structuralists are confronted with white racial supremacy. It is more complicated when the ideas of white racial supremacy are inherent in the discussion of social confrontations among people who are presumably defining themselves as whites. The structuralists and almost all European theorists have a loss of words when it comes to properly explaining white racial supremacy. Starting from this idea as a normative idea means that Africans are automatically thrown into the categorically other. The Afrocentrists reject this notion and therefore understand that structuralism cannot handle the contradictions of white racial supremacy any more than the dialectical materialists or their relatives, the cultural materialists. They are blinded by a white racial ideology that is only a little more sophisticated than that of the sociobiologists.

# Modernism and postmodernism

Of all the European narratives on society, postmodernism is the most difficult to define and locate because of its continuing flux in areas of art, music, film, literature, sociology, communications, and technology. Those who call themselves postmodernists know that Europe is in a deep cycle of social danger and they are thrusting around for another venue for explanation and sense having found most of their social theories abandoned after the Nazi Holocaust, the interminable hatreds of Ireland, the Balkans, and ethnic rivalries in numerous nations of Europe. This flux in social and political life appeared constant and so after the 1960s with the decade-long sorting out of values we found European writers, mainly literary scholars, attempting to create some new response to the crises of culture and identity. Even without a formal definition it is possible to view it as a set of ideas about literary, artistic, and social life that emerged during the decade of the 1980s. Was it intended as a counter to the newly found voice of African agency with the emergence of Afrocentricity in the 1980s or was it by chance that these two approaches to social phenomena arose to compete in the African arena? I take the position that Afrocentricity is an intellectual advancement on the idea of democratizing scholarship, philosophy, economics, and social discourse. In this sense, it is not a competition, but a transcendence of a thematic regime and ideology of phrases and counter-phrases because its foundation is a new cosomological space.

Postmodernism emerges out of modernism's aesthetic sensibilities and, in some ways, may be seen as a reaction to the twentieth-century Ideas of European art forms. Modernism was a movement of the visual arts, drama, literature, and music which transcended the Victorian rules of what constituted art. There was a period of "high modernism" between 1910 and 1930, taking in the disintegrating period of the First Great European War (1914–18). At this time as Europe sought to redefine its own value systems on the battlefields, the writers Rilke, Joyce, Eliot, Pound, Proust, Mallarmé, Woolf, and Kafka undertook a radical alteration in the way people viewed poetry and fiction. Europe's literary modernists must include these writers as among the founders of twentieth-century modernism. They held in their minds and put on their pages the seeds of postmodernism.

Among the leading characteristics of postmodernism are fragmentation, reflexivity, the rejection of high and low cultural forms as elitist, and hegemony, and an intense subjectivity that allows for self-consciousness in writing. In some senses these were also the elements of modernism as seen in the stream-of-consciousness and highly subjected forms of modernist writers such as e. e. cummings and Rilke. The difference between modernism and postmodernism relies on ways of viewing the decentered, destructured, and destabilized state of our existence. Actually, the modernists had dismissed the decentered, destructured and destabilized from significant consideration. It was a regime against the democratizing iconography of postmodernism or Afrocentricity. Postmodernists, however, would not rely on works of so-called classical art to produce anything of value, certainly not a more stable, or a better, society. The modernist view was that art could bring stability, unity, and a degree of coherence to human society as long as we could conceive of an elitist, superior-educated humanity. A rejection of this view has enthroned postmodernism as the principal literary mode of the European experience at the dawn of the new millennium. Thus, the attack on grand narratives remains in full force and may, if wrongly perceived, constitute a major assault on the works of African scholars, poets, and novelists seeking to bring about a revolutionary change in society that postmodernism has failed to achieve.

It is extremely important to appreciate the source of European fears of uncertainty, the lack of place, and lack of anything solid, certain, either as belief or as fact. I trace it back to the ghastly war fought in Europe in the late 1930s and 1940s, to the reconstruction of the German economy by the West, to the dispersal of European Jews to Israel, to the unsettling of the Roma, to the continuing drive of the Anglo-Germanic elements to define a separate identity from the rest of Europe, and to the inability of Europe to agree on a collective consciousness in the Durkheimean sense. What this meant was that the uncertainty of persons created alienation, unrest, insecurities, and a sense that stability was not only fleeting but useless. If people knew who you were, then they could bring danger to you, harm your family, resurrect some old crime, entangle you in a web of red tape and Kafkaesque bureaucracy, so why not be someone today and someone else tomorrow? Unfortunately, this has been the result of some postmodernist critics who, for fear of losing place, power, and even their Western-fixed identities, have embraced alienation and a nihilistic detour in order to regain Western security. The same path has been walked upon by some African scholars as well.

The African writer Manthia Diawara in his recent book, *In Search of Africa*, claims as much for himself. He is a Parisian, New Yorker, Guinean, or Malian, according to him, in a most postmodern expression. This is precisely the problem as the Afrocentrist would see it unless one means it in the sense that there is no hegemonic determinism. One can live in many places, but one's identity may be transformed by circumstances and conditions. However, basic personality structure and all the elements that go into culture are negotiable by you regardless of your venue. Nevertheless, the Jew cannot escape his Jewishness by claiming that he is an American citizen. He simply adds a layer onto his identity. He could be a citizen of France, Britain, or Germany, but he remains a Jew. In the same way, Diawara remains an African. Perhaps, as in the case of the eagle in our parable, the culture has to be learned.

The problem here is that the African has found a way to negotiate identity, based on an African cosmology and value system, that is, after five hundred years of being off-center from this source, different from the West. Afrocentricity announces that there is no longer any warrant to discuss identity as a fixed idea, but as an infinite quest to regain, reclaim, or construct identity. Afrocentricity further advances this position by claiming that one often has to learn culture or negotiate this identity. Neither modernism nor postmodernism articulates a thesis for supplanting the dominance of Europeans as Europeans; both are stuck in a Western dichotomous mode, although it is fair to say that the postmodernists have gone about as far as one can go to throw off this mantle of self- righteousness. If the English will not give up Englishness as the Tiger does not give up Tigerness, then we must create new and more radical ways to create a surge in human understanding. Suggesting the death of a constructed identity or the end of culture or the completion of history as the postmodern nihilists have done is nothing less than a betrayal of the oppressed.

Therefore, the Afrocentrist must re-examine the cosmological foundation of the current intellectual regime. Since it is difficult to find any intellectual support in the major avenues of European thought we must seek closer to home, that is, to the traditions that have helped to make African thought what it is today. Thus, I have sought to discover in the study of African civilizations and culture, and the reading of several African authors, an understanding of Africa, African culture, and linkages to Afrocentricity. Nothing in my Western education adequately prepared me for the possibilities inherent in the African world. Indeed, as I have shown elsewhere, not even Africans trained in the West have understood the power of their own cosmological systems.

## Linkages to Afrocentricity

If Afrocentricity is a response to Europe it is only so as a response to the conditions of African people at the hands of European oppression for five hundred years; it is not a response to European intellectual theory and does not find its energy in any European system of thought. Critics sometimes speak of the Afrocentrist's use of European languages and the use of logical arguments as indications that the Afrocentrist is really incapable of abandoning European influences. Even the suggestion is an attempt to place Europe at the center of all discourse. To discuss anything intellectually, they would claim, means that one has to be doing European discourse.

There are several responses that can be made to such a charge but the important one, particularly as it relates to language, is that English and French are increasingly less English and French. In fact, English has been changed permanently by the black speakers of the language and there are more people who are non-English speaking the language now than there are English speakers of it. The same holds true for French where the French speakers of French are among the minority speakers. English and French are truly contested languages. Beyond this fact, however, is the fact that the Afrocentric discipline protects the Afrocentrist in the matter of language choices. This was one of the initial developments in the Afrocentric theory development because I understood that the first liberation had to be language liberation. A considerable literature has grown up around this particular point and I do not need to repeat it here except to say that Afrocentrists are aware of this charge regarding language. You will never read an Afrocentrist writing of "Black Africa," "African tribes," "primitive huts," "Africa, South of the Sahara," and such expressions because of the discipline.

The statement about logical argument is less serious. Logic is not the exclusive purview of any people. Indeed, logical argumentation itself, as far as actual presentation of arguments is concerned, goes back to "Khunanup's Defense Before the Judges," often called by Europeans "The Eloquent Peasant" (Asante and Abarry, 1996). Khun-anup's piece appears more than a thousand years before the existence of Thales of Miletus, the first Greek philosopher. Using logic is a human activity and to set one's arguments in a certain fashion is not following Europe but Africa. Just as when Europeans use introductory greetings at the beginning of their speeches, they are following the patterns of the ancient Nile Valley Africans.

Three intellectual currents are directly linked to Afrocentricity: Negritude, Diopian historiography, and Kawaida. While each influenced the early work in Afrocentric theory, the development of Afrocentricity itself must be seen as linked to each one differently. Afrocentricity shares with Negritude its promotion of African agency, though Negritude was unable to deliver African centeredness. Afrocentricity and Diopian historiography share the same epistemology, but Afrocentricity is much broader in its reach in an effort to shape the discourse around the African world. Afrocentricity and Kawaida share the same epistemology but have emphasized different theoretical and philosophical methods. Kawaida is much more concerned with ethical aspects of actions than Afrocentricity which is more concerned with the structures that encourage moral decisions.

## Negritude

The main proponents of Negritude were Léopold Sédar Senghor, Aime Césaire, Jean Rabemananjara, and Leon Damas. It was a school of thought that emerged in Paris in the 1930s and 1940s as a reaction to the totalizing idea of culture as presented by the French scholars. To the French, in the European fashion, Africa was without culture, that is, without self-conscious art or an artistic tradition. As students in Paris, the young continental Africans and South American and Caribbean Africans came together to defend their own historical tradition as legitimate and valid within the world context. They were the first line of resistance to the virulent racism of white supremacy in the area of art, particularly in poetry, drama, and literature. On the fringes of this movement, Cheikh Anta Diop, Alioune Diop, and Pathé Diagne operated as fellow travelers, encouraging the Negritudinists, writing historical essays, and creating spaces for writers to assemble and publish.

Senghor wrote "Negritude and Humanism" (2007) as one of the central essays in the definition of the movement. It was Senghor who unfortunately characterized the African as concerned with emotion and the European with reason. Widely misunderstood and badly interpreted, Senghor could never live down the dictum: "L'émotion est nègre, la raison est hellène." Of course, Senghor knew, if any one did, that all human beings shared emotion and reason and he was simply trying to place an emphasis on the degree to which Africans and Europeans had distanced themselves from each other as one embraced and the other distanced life.

Césaire has grown over the years as the greatest poet of the African race as his work in *The Return to My Native Country* is called the best poetry of the Negritude period (Césaire, 1954). He is at once, serious, playful, surreal, symbolic, and culturally sensitive to the various moods, directions, contours, and crevices of the African condition. As a voice of Africa, Césaire remains, at least, in his poetry, clairvoyant.

From Negritude, Afrocentricity learned the constituents of resistance to oppression were action and agency, although Negritude itself did not give us the kind of agency that would be revealed in the work of the Afrocentrists. In fact, Afrocentricity was a much broader paradigm than Negritude which depended upon Africanity much more than Afrocentricity to thrust its place in the discourse of social change. Africanity is not Afrocentricity. One can have an appreciation of African cultural behavior, participate in it, and still not be Afrocentric. One is a state of being; the other is a state of consciousness. The value of one is that it is what we might be doing existentially, but the other allows us to see what is possible, even in the area of consciousness. Afrocentricity establishes a window on African culture but does not see the culture merely as a good photograph; it must be a moving picture that takes into consideration all of the ways African people express agency. It is not simply about poetry, or about blacks in poetry, or about beautiful black women in poems, but about a way of viewing the images that move in and out of our sight as we carry out our lives.

## Diopian historiography

Cheikh Anta Diop, the late Senegalese scholar who had written for the Negritudinists, went beyond their work with a new historiography of Africa. Indeed Diop may be considered the most significant African scholar of the century because of his demolition of the European construction of ancient Africa (Diop, 1974; Diop, 1981). He did it almost singlehandedly, without African or European support, when he initially started his research. In the end he established conclusively that the ancient Egyptians were black-skinned Africans and that the origin of civilization must be traced to the Nile Valley. A school of historians calling themselves Nile Valley historians arose to lend support to his thesis. Among the principals in this discussion and debate were the African Egyptologists, Theophile Obenga and Maulana Karenga. Obenga had been a protégé of Diop since the 1970s and after Diop's death Obenga continued his work in the United States, initially at Temple University, in the midst of the Afrocentrists, and then at San Francisco State University as Professor of African American Studies. At Temple University the first graduate class in the ancient Egyptian Language and Culture was organized and taught by Theophile Obenga and myself. Karenga, who has been active in every Afrocentric movement, organized the first conference around the Diopian methodology and founded the Association for the Study of Classical African Civilization. In addition, he published several key books on ancient Egyptian civilization that gave direction to a new field of research culminating in his second dissertation, a comprehensive study of *Maat*, ancient Egyptian ethical system, written for the University of Southern California.

Although it is true that Afrocentricity borrows from Diopian historiography in the arena of historical epistemology and methodology, Afrocentricity is much more far-reaching than a discussion of history. As we used to say in the late 1960s, African American Studies and history are two different disciplines. You cannot limit Afrocentricity to Diop's historiography any more than you can limit soccer to a ball and soccer shoes; these are necessary equipment but one must have all the other elements, rules of play, field, etc., to make the game. The Afrocentric idea engages all sciences, social sciences, family sciences, and arts and consequently must be viewed as an innovative paradigm in the discourse around African people. When Theophile Obenga and I taught the Ancient Egyptian Language and Culture course at Temple University, we were not simply reproducing Diop; he had already done his work. The scholarship of Miriam Maat Ka Re Monges, Troy Allen, Mohammed Garba, Cynthia Lehman, James Naazir Conyers, Katherine Bankole, and others actually followed in the line created by Diop but added Afrocentric dimensions that articulated the best methods and practices of the Afrocentrists.

## Kawaida

Maulana Karenga, while in graduate school, proposed the theory of Kawaida as a corrective for what he observed were cultural problems within the African American community (Karenga, 1997). In Karenga's view, any examples of alienation, degradation, dysfunctionality, self-hatred, and criminal activity were directly related to a misplaced consciousness. How to regain a sense of culture or to introduce a sense of national culture into a community that had abandoned its best ideals in the face of oppression and white racial supremacy was the challenge confronting Karenga. Contending that the cultural crisis was the main element in the dysfunctionality of many in the African American community, the philosophy of Kawaida expressed an orientation toward corrective action that included the reconstruction of cultural values on the basis of African traditions. It was to be a reconstruction, in the sense that what Africans had lost in the five hundred years of involvement in the West with European domination and racism had to be regained through conscious action, but it was also a rediscovery, in the sense, that what was possible existed within the epic memory of the people themselves and only had to be appealed to in ways that the masses would respond to with action.

Kawaida was dependent upon collective action. Karenga perceived the truth of the organic relationship of leadership to community and articulated a belief in the possibility of mass education resulting in mass revolution in the sense that people would do better if they knew to do better. The real revolution, he was fond of saying, had to be in the mind of the people or else no other revolution was possible. His appreciation of the role of the masses in all modifications of society was a major contribution to the radical movement of humans from a condition of dependence to one of liberation.

The tenets of Kawaida were prescriptive; the concepts of Afrocentricity proved normative in terms of what was happening in the African American community. Afrocentricity sought to use the Kawaidan critique of culture as a starting place for suggesting African agency in two radically different kinds of phenomena. In the first place, agency must be sought in all human behaviors influenced by the environment, large or small, in any given situation. This meant that the superstructure or infrastructure along with the structure or content had to be seen as loci for agency. What is the role of the African in such-and-such a story? How are we to examine the position of the African person during the Constitutional Debate in Philadelphia? Did the enslaved African have a choice in his or her enslavement? What role did Africans play in resistance against oppression? These are questions that get at the phenomena of the infrastructure and structure, but what of phenomena that is more mental? What about the thoughts and emotions we experience within our heads? I mean, what is to be done with the researcher's silent questions regarding phenomena that seem racist, white supremacist? To explain the mental processes of the African people in Brazil, Jamaica, Ghana, the United States, Britain, or any other nation means to have some idea of the symbols, myths, motifs, concepts that exist within those cultural realms. Even so, the explanation can only be partial since it is not possible to reproduce the behavioral processes or mental processes of any people with one hundred percent certainty. We can only speak of plausible approximations. Yet I know enough as an Afrocentrist to know that an African in Britain, say, would have different things going on in his or her head than an ordinary white English person during a discussion of racism in the workplace.

## We are free at last!

The escape from the Western hegemony is not easy and, just as we have announced our escape, we recognize that the Fortress West is not going to let us leave the mental plantation without a struggle. Afrocentricity seeks to obliterate the mental, physical, cultural, and economic dislocation of African people by thrusting Africans as centered, healthy human beings in the context of African thought. Every conceivable concept, movement, institution, and office will be placed at the disposal of those who would argue against the self-determination of African people. To be for oneself is not to be against others; this is the most authoritative lesson that can be learned from the Afrocentric school of thought. Only when there is an effective mass movement of Africans from the margins of Europe to the center of their own reality, in a self-conscious way, can there be a true revolution. This would, of course, mean the end of white world hegemony.

# 9

# The Black Nationalist Question

One of the genuinely brilliant minds of the last half of the twentieth century was Harold Cruse whose enigmatic and sometimes provocative critiques of culture caused consternation among many socialists. It was Cruse's belief that there was no consistently revolutionary sentiment evident in the white proletariat (Asante, 1998). What was necessary in his mind was a new ethic that would cause the black leadership in the academic world and culture to become the vanguard in an authentic black movement. Research into the African American community shows that Black Nationalism is an abiding ideology in the United States, generated by the continuing privileging of whiteness within society.

Michael C. Dawson, the William R. Kenan Jr. Professor of Political Science and the College, and director of the Center for the Study of Race, Politics, and Culture at the University of Chicago, has written an outstanding study of black political ideologies in which that sentiment is clearly revealed (Dawson, 2002). Over the past decade Dawson has established a reputation as one of the best survey researchers in the United States and the leading authority on political opinion in the African American community. *Black Visions* is Dawson's most ambitious work to date. Nevertheless, as in some cases of survey research, the lapse in the time of data gathering and the time of data reporting plays havoc with conceptual synchrony. Dawson has dealt with this issue by presenting a strong narrative analysis of the data and a warning that we must guard against assuming that ideologies are "themselves fixed throughout time and place" (2002, p. 7). Of course there is some truth to this statement but it must be seen as a nod to the postmodernist corner. Inevitably the votarists of Marxism, liberal capitalism, and postmodernism see themselves as constituting a cadre of individuals who are committed to certain intellectual practices that are consistent with a form of solidarity of opinion, if not fact. They are fixed ideas, at least, fixed long enough to allow use of the central tendencies in discourse and critique.

If Dawson is correct, and I suspect he is, then the ideology of Black Nationalism remains an essential current within the thinking of African Americans. There is no reason to challenge his data on this issue since it has been a permanent factor in the African American community since the first data were collected. Not surprisingly, Dawson records that the idea of self-determination, self-definition, and self-actualization in which the people articulate a vision of their own agency is central to the ideological discourse in the African American community.

*Black Visions* is lucid, stunning in its detail, with a transparent narrative style that allows the reader to participate in the author's method of analysis. So Dawson receives high marks for presentation and style. More troubling, however, is the fact that Dawson seems ambivalent about his own data, particularly regarding what to make of this heavy emphasis on Black Nationalism within the African American community. It is as if Black Nationalism, one of several ideologies analyzed, should not have such importance in the African American community but since it does, according to the data, it must be explained in terms that negate the data. Of all the political ideologies in his framework, Black Nationalism is the only one that he scrutinizes for redefinition and re-organization. It is almost as if he is afraid to follow the data. Nearly thirty years ago, John Gwaltney's work *Drylongso* established in an anecdotal way the truism discovered in Dawson's interviews. The majority of African Americans see themselves as a nation within a nation, a people distinct and different from an ethnic group.

Dawson identifies "six historically important black political ideologies" (Dawson, 2002, p. 14) as Radical Egalitarianism, Disillusioned Liberalism, Black Marxism, Black Conservatism, Black Feminism, and Black Nationalism. As with all classificatory schemes, one could reasonably argue that Dawson's fixation on these six ideologies is based on a misreading of the data, but that is not the point I want to make here.

It is my intention to discuss the problems with this type of research. Unfortunately there are two problems with this classificatory scheme. In the first place Dawson misreads the notion of "black political ideologies" and analyzes instead ideologies that are accepted by some segments of the black community. Indeed it is questionable whether one could reasonably call Marxism, liberalism, feminism, or conservatism, however swarthy the adjectives, black ideologies. They are Eurocentric and European ideologies that have been bought into by many black adherents. To call them "black political ideologies" is a stretch of the imagination.

Those ideologics are based essentially on the writings and philosophies of European theorists and philosophers about white people. Conceivably,

Black Nationalism is the only true black ideology since it finds its source in the early writings and discourses of Africans who resisted enslavement and racism. One can argue that this ideology, admittedly with many variants and interests, reflects the authentic sentiment of the overwhelming majority of black people in the United States. It is a healthy and meaningful assertion of black humanity. The second problem is that, even if one accepts Dawson's ideological classifications, his discussion of the nature of the relationships between the classifications and their roles in the political lives of African Americans appears incomplete. For example, to say that Black Nationalism is "the second oldest" (Dawson, 2002, p. 21) ideology in the black community is to mis-state the nature of the early affirmation of culture and resistance to racism articulated by the first Africans to land in the English colonies. All indications from history are that the earliest enslaved Africans felt a burning need to return to Africa and to escape the horrible condition of servitude to which they had been brutally subjected. They were not interested in some "radical egalitarianism" with whites. This radical egalitarian type of thinking would come only after many years when some Africans had moved away from the daily routine of surviving whippings, abuse, rape, violence, and degradation during the enslavement and when they had been introduced to European concepts of equality. On the other hand, they were always nationalistic, believing as David Walker believed that the "white Christian Americans" were the cruelest and most barbarous people on the earth (Walker, in Asante and Abarry, 1996, p. 627).

I believe that Dawson's work is driven by his political conceptualization and social philosophy rather than the data. What I mean is that it appears that the data are forced to fit the conceptualization rather than the other way around. He has a clear idea of what it is he wants to establish and discovers in his data answers to his questions. His version of the record situates Black Nationalism in the nebulous world of chaos and nihilism. Whatever the social repertoires or political agendas his analysis seeks to serve, it has missed the authentic response of Africans to their reality.

The works of Robert C. Smith, FeFe Dunham, and Ronald Walters have frequently used other ideological themes that could have been important in Dawson's analysis. As we often say, it is the orientation to data, not the data, which reveals more about a study than anything else. In this case, the terminology long established in the African American intellectual tradition for political ideologies such as Integrationism, Accommodationism, Separatism, and Nationalism are abandoned by Dawson but may have been useful in providing a clearer understanding of how African Americans perceive themselves. Integration, Accommodation, Separatism, and Nationalism are terms that have grown out of the African American tradition; in fact, they are clearly conceptualizations from an internal agency. What is clear in Dawson's work is the absence of a conceptual framework based on Afrocentric agency. Without an appreciation of the agency of African Americans, that is, the role African people have played in defining political ideologies, it is easy for Dawson to misunderstand history and to impose an external framework on the data.

Thus, it is easy for Dawson to claim a "vulgar and brutal misogyny" (Dawson, 2002, p. 41) for Eldridge Cleaver and Kwame Toure (Stokely Carmichael). This terminology clearly does not apply to Carmichael and in the case of Eldridge Cleaver only applied to him *prior* to his "Black Nationalist" days. To argue that their misogyny, hatred of women, fueled the black feminist camp organizations and literatures is overreaching. The evidence does not show this conclusion. Few men loved women as human beings more than Kwame Toure and this love was reciprocated by the many women who found inspiration from his Black Nationalist stand during his life. Near the end of his life his friends, mostly women, mounted a celebration of his life in struggle that brought about 2,000 people together. Dawson's comment on Black Nationalism, like so many misrepresentations of the dominant African American political ideology, is an aggrandizing bow to feminism which has many legitimate strengths of its own without this exaggeration of Black Nationalism's position on women. I am not familiar with any theoretical or philosophical discourse in the Black Nationalist ideology that is anti-woman. On the other hand, Black Nationalists, as opposed to the radical egalitarians who tend to be mostly Christians, have advanced an African idea of gender complementarity. This is a more progressive position it seems to me than either that taken by Christian Socialist egalitarians (Michael Dyson, Cornel West) or the Social Democrat Marxists (Abdul Alkalimat, Manning Marable). I think the reason for this distinction is that patriarchy is at the root of most class and race issues in the West; it is after all at the base of both Christianity and Marxism. Patriarchy is responsible for all forms of hierarchy and consequently the Marxists have it wrong to say that racism is a product of capitalism; it would have existed and did exist under socialism and communism and was expressly not dealt with in Marx and Engels because they came out of patriarchal societies. Of course, one may make the argument that under capitalism the idea of racism reached its highest form as in the case of African enslavement and the Jewish Holocaust. In the same vein, one can say that female oppression was most evident under the patriarchal domain of European culture.

Nevertheless, Dawson's 1993–4 National Black Politics Study (NBPS), developed prior to the Million Man March or the Million Woman March, is a remarkable survey. The data were obtained from telephone interviews of 1,206 people over the age of eighteen. Each interview lasted about forty-five minutes. The study was conducted between November 20, 1993 and February 20, 1994. The principal aims, according to Dawson, were to provide instrumentation for the analysis of the relationships between black ideologies and their determinants and consequences, and the relationship of black worship to black public opinion.

The overwhelming conclusion in this study supports the view that the black population remains committed to the ideology of Black Nationalism. In this sense, it would have been possible, had Dawson's study been reported earlier, to predict the success of the marches on Washington and Philadelphia. Given the fact that the data show a powerful ideological commitment in the African American community to Black Nationalism, Dawson seeks to create an elaborate classification of the ideological tendencies and to redefine the nature of the dominant Black Nationalism by introducing the term "community nationalism" (Dawson, 2002, p. 120). He accepts the idea that community nationalism is "black empowerment politics" (Dawson, 2002, p. 120) but seeks to advance Louis Farrakhan as the model Black Nationalist.

This is problematic in and of itself inasmuch as many nationalists see Farrakhan as a fringe part of the movement. More importantly, I am at a loss to see how community nationalism differs from other forms of Black Nationalism that seek to present the calling cards of self-definition, self-control, and self-determination as the principal icons of the ideology. Trying to isolate Louis Farrakhan from the equation is unnecessary to the main argument of the data in this survey. When Dawson claims "the community nationalist variant of black 'nationalism' enjoys strong mass support," he follows his data (Dawson, 2002, p. 101). Delimiting separatism and withdrawal from the state from community nationalism increases the numbers of adherents. But to include separatism and withdrawal from the state in any current definition of Black Nationalism is to assume that there is no shift in the ideology. What is called community nationalism is perhaps the only salient nationalism of the 1990s. Dawson's redefinition of Black Nationalism generally and the shift to community nationalism may be more decoration than anything else in his construction of the black community's interest. Separation and withdrawal from the American state became a part of the rhetorical discourse during the intense period of KKK racial activities in the early turn of the twentieth century and remained a part of the discourse until the 1960s. After the deaths of Malcolm X in 1965 and of Martin Luther King, Jr. in 1968, Black Nationalist ideology banked away from the theme of separation and withdrawal of the state due to increased participation in electoral politics. Yet the essential core concerns of the Black Nationalist ideology remained constant as Dawson's data show.

Dawson's aim is to supply answers to questions such as: what political ideologies are supported by blacks? Who is most likely to support what ideologies? How does residential location shape ideological orientations? How do black ideologies shape black public opinion? What is clear after one reads the analytical narrative is that one cannot measure what one did not conceptualize. In the dissertation "More'n a Notion: The Determinants of the Appeal of Black Nationalism in the Post Black Power Era," and a conference paper, "Countenances of 'Collective Grace and Communal Availability': The Appeal of Black Nationalism in the Post Black Power Era," National Council for Black Studies, San Diego, March, 2002, FeFe Dunham demonstrates that "the appeal of Black Nationalism is a result of that part of the culture that nourishes and affirms collective grace and communal availability," terms first used by Lerone Bennett.

Just as the African American community has undergone an evolution in self-identification from African, Negro, Colored, Afro American, Black, African American and back to African again, we have also experienced a similar movement in ideological commitments, nomenclature, and purposes. Take the term "radical egalitarianism," for example, it is referred to, with the same coordinates, as "capitulation" by some Black Nationalists. What is called Black Nationalism, on the other hand, is called "black separatism" by some Radical Egalitarians. This has not been adequately sorted out in Dawson's work. This is not a criticism that needs to stand in the way of appreciating the monumental manner in which he has grappled with the issues of African American ideologies. He admits in the preface to his book that he is a political scientist and not a historian (Dawson, 2002, p. xiii) and while this is a reasonably good admission it nevertheless handicaps how one can use what he has discovered in this study.

There are many useful attributes of *Black Visions*. Clearly, Dawson's discussion of identity and black feminist ideology challenges the reader to rethink much of what we see as group identity politics. One would have wished, however, that Clenora Hudson-Weems's notion of Africana Womanism might have been examined more closely since Hudson-Weems argues for a pro-female stance that is not anti-male. This is certainly a growing movement among African American women who are not feminist, but who are pro-woman. Other women writing in this vein are Patricia Dixon and Yaa Asantewa Reed. Dixon's book *We Want for Our Sisters What We Want for*

*Ourselves* (2002) and Reed's dissertation are two works that suggest the mass of African American women are supportive of women's rights but are also not anti-male. Concentrating on feminism as an ideological theme without attention to Africana Womanism is a major problem for many readers.

Dawson's work is a triumph in many ways but it is clouded by provocative dislocations about Black Nationalism based primarily on the same old traditional canard about Black Nationalism being a response to disillusionment with being outside white America. This is a total misunderstanding of the legitimate affirmation of culture and respect for identity and heritage that has little or nothing to do with white people. Dawson is worried that the liberals have nothing to offer because "there is little sign of a vibrant mass movement, and clearly there are high levels of disillusionment in the black community about race relations in America. As always, particularly with the collapse of the left and the isolation of the feminists, the nationalists are waiting in the wings" (Dawson, 2002, p. 280).

*Black Visions* will remain an important document despite its many flaws because it is a reasonable attempt to make sense out of very complex data. However, Dawson's work might be seen as an effort to explain away the dominant ideological current in the black community as only a reaction to not being "accepted" by whites. If this is the case, it is an unfortunate rendering since it means that the readers will never understand the internal agency of those who just plain like being who they are without reacting to anybody else!

If a work could take Dawson's data, add a mixed Marxist idea, and a reaction formation to Black Nationalism, and produce confusion better than Algernon Austin's *Achieving Blackness*, I have yet to read it. One comes away from reading Algernon Austin's *Achieving Blackness: Race, Black Nationalism, and Afrocentrism in the Twentieth Century* (2006) with the belief that the palimpsest in Austin's thinking is anti-Africanism. It is possible to see this in his assault, almost at the outset, on the most powerful theoretical and practical tools Africans have produced to deal with discrimination, hegemonic white cultural practices, racism, lack of agency, fluidity of identity, vulgar hegemony, and marginality.

One does not "achieve" blackness as one does not "achieve" whiteness or brownness. The cleverness in the title traps the author from the outset in a netherworld from whence his discourse never recovers. In the twenty-first century world, one is born into a culture with no effort on the part of the subject, all expenditure of energy having already occurred by the parents prior to the subject's birth. However, a location of Austin's idea of achieving blackness suggests the false idea that the only possible explanation for blackness existing as a category of human thought and culture is that it has been "achieved" by those who express blackness in their ordinary lives. But we must be careful here to reject the notion that blackness is something that is arrived at when one completes a certain goal. Actually, we could be born into a black community and not be fully aware of the extent of our blackness, but we cannot be wholly without knowledge of it. When I say "not be fully aware," I am thinking of the people who must always discover anew in each generation that Africa had civilizations before Europe, that African people were not uncivilized, and that Africans in America were robbed of their labor and so forth.

There are some interesting aspects to Austin's thinking, but there are also some awful misunderstandings about Afrocentricity. If he were conscious of his mistakes one could claim malice, but since I sincerely believe that he missed the point of the Afrocentric idea I simply believe that he got it wrong legitimately. I will try to right the ship in my critique.

It occurred to me while examining Austin's reasoning that he knew very little about some of the topics he chose to write about in *Achieving Blackness*, although I noticed that he had read some important works. He still was not sufficiently well-read or interested in the literature to dump some of the simple-minded stuff left over from the 1990s when Mary Lefkowitz's *Not Out of Africa* and Arthur Schlesinger Jr.'s *The Disuniting of America* created a fire storm that kept serious scholars from examining Afrocentricity. It was all hype, but it did a propaganda job on the public in the United States and Austin's discourse shows him to be a child of the "black scare" of that period. He is not aware, for instance, that I debated Lefkowitz three times and Schlesinger once on the question of Afrocentricity, or that my book, *The Painful Demise of Eurocentrism* (1999), obliterated the false arguments in Lefkowitz's book.

Yet I think Austin has a fairly good idea about Black Nationalism, but knows little of the original research writings on Afrocentricity and insists on speaking of *Afrocentrism* when he means something totally different. Afrocentrism gives the idea of a religion in the sense that misled Patricia Hill Collins to write badly about the intellectual idea as a civil religion. Austin falls into a similar trap. He further confuses his readers because he misunderstands the difference between Afrocentricity and Africanity. What he is usually describing is *Africanity*, not *Afrocentricity*, and when he thinks he is writing about Afrocentricity he calls it Afrocentrism which is a false construction for debating tactics.

Austin's inveterate attack on Afrocentricity strikes me as staged and managed by an incessant need to interrogate concepts, ideas, and images that have nothing to do with Afrocentricity and yet to cast them in the light of Afrocentricity. This is not only bad scholarship, it smacks of the acceptance of the popularized notions of Afrocentricity that have been generated by various anti-African schools of thought. Afrocentrists are serious scholars who have questioned the fundamental ideas projected by Western social scientists and humanists about African people. This, alone, is enough to have black and white Eurocentrists up in arms in defense of a failed racist ideology.

Algernon Austin, founder and director of the Thora Institute, seeks to argue in a postmodern way that "races are social creations." The problem with this type of thinking is that the postmodernists rarely go far enough to tell the readers who established the creations. The fact that race and races may be social creations does not lessen the impact of racism, based on the social creations, in the lives of millions of people. I think the most serious fault of Austin's argument is that he allows the racists, those who practice racism, to slip the hook by arguing that "Oh, there is no such thing as races." Regardless of the idea of "social creations," races exist in the way humans respond to these creations, which is mostly at the biological level, and they persecute, discriminate against, and brutalize people because of these "social creations." I am not certain it helps us to explain racism to say "races are social creations."

While it is popular to argue that "somebody" who is never mentioned "created" the idea of race and got people to believe in the idea, it is rarely demonstrated how those same people used racism to oppress. Austin uses the euphemism that race became "a tool that can be used in new or redefined situations of conflict." Whatever the truth in this statement, the overwhelming consequence of Austin's work is to take a position against an African theoretical idea in a great flourish of anti-African theorizing about agency.

Turning now to the question of Afrocentricity, let me underscore that Austin has missed the point completely. Let me try in fairness to reconstruct as best I can his argument. He believes that one way to examine the racial dynamics in the United States is to look at how blackness has moved from one level of meaning to another. There may be potential in this line of reasoning but Austin does not find it because he has become trapped in the Aryanist notion of attacking any African drive for self-definition, self-expression, self-determination, or self-actualization. He explores the way the Nation of Islam developed in the early days of the movement with the idea of the "Asiatic" black man. There is certainly a problem with the construction of identity in the early days of the Nation of Islam. I am not certain what point is being made here since Islam is clearly a religion and neither Black Nationalism nor Afrocentricity claim to be religions. If anything, they are mostly anti-religious. However, Austin moves from this position to claim that the Black Power era was the time when Negroes became black and forced "white" black people into acting more like blacks. Well, there are several problems with this thinking. In the first place, there have always been African people who proudly saw themselves as black. Indeed, the word *Negro* itself carried with it the meaning of black in both Spanish and Portuguese. It was not the African people who changed the meaning of this word but whites who infused it with meanness and villainy. The rejection of Negro by Africans in the United States was not a rejection of blackness but the rejection of something that had become soiled, stained. As to Afrocentricity, Austin argues that it was based on defining the condition of Africans as a culture of poverty. This is highly suspect as an argument. As the author of many articles and books on Afrocentricity, I am unaware of any theorist who has made such an argument. The Afrocentrist would argue that there is a misappropriation of culture that leads to poor cultural esteem but has nothing to do with the arguments for or against self-esteem issues. Indeed, black people do not have major self-esteem issues; our problem, if we have one, tends to be a group or cultural esteem problem.

Thus, Austin writes of Afrocentricity from a Marxist class position and sees a middle-class phenomenon. He announces that the votarists of Black Nationalism, which is a political philosophy, and Afrocentricity, which is an intellectual perspective on data, have succeeded in demonstrating that the ideas are not just limited to the poor and underclass but are middle-class ideas. The truth of the matter is that Afrocentricity is classless because it assaults the psychological and intellectual terror on black people from all angles and all classes. There is no specific class appeal or class doctrine in the responses of Africans to the idea of African agency. In addition, it should be noted that the Afrocentrists claim no easy wins over the forces of the right, but one thing is for certain, that the Afrocentrists cannot be both right and non-right or left and non-left. The truth lies in this fact: Afrocentricity does not claim a political or economic policy; it only claims the minds of the oppressed who will then determine the best political and economic strategy for African redemption.

# 10

## Race, Brutality, and Hegemony

The instruments of African dislocation are truly awesome. I shall seek to show the extremes on a continuum of psychological violence. Nothing is so violative as the physical brutalization of the African because of race. It is impossible to create the illusion that humanity was crushed, smashed against the wall of ignorance, and eliminated, and nothing happened. Then there is the postmodern attempt to eliminate the African by suppressing discourse on ethnic and cultural identities. One often hears in the United States politicians and some English professors railing against "identity politics" by which they mean the political use of group identities, such as gay/lesbians, women, blacks, Latinos. But as an African American, I am a child of groupness not simply by my own estimation but by that of the dominant society.

I was born in south Georgia in the same year that a black man was lynched after having been dragged through the dusty streets of Kill-Me-Quick, a rundown section of Valdosta. Lynching has never been out of my mind and I have always been keenly aware of what racial hatred and animus can create in a society. I also know that the silence of the white citizens in southern Georgia was the same silence felt throughout the South by blacks. We heard no voices brave enough to condemn or confront the lynch mobs.

Anne P. Rice tells us in the book, *Witnessing Lynching* (2003), that we were not all alone and that there were others who spoke on behalf of the brutalized. There were those brave men and women, black and white, who responded to these raw and vile attacks on African Americans. Rice has chosen to highlight works by authors who lived and wrote during the most intense periods of the lynching madness. Among the more well-known authors who spoke out against lynching were Frederick Douglass, Ida B. Wells-Barnett, Frances Ellen Watkins Harper, Paul Laurence Dunbar, Mary Church Terrell, W. E. B. Du Bois, James Weldon Johnson, Theodore Dreiser, Carl Sandburg, Claude McKay, Countee Cullen, Langston Hughes, Sterling Brown, Erskine Caldwell, Richard Wright, and Jean Toomer.

The lynching of Africans in the South is one of the most brutal chapters in America's history. In 1872, twelve Africans were lynched but by 1892 the number had reached 255. It would continue to increase until Benjamin Brawley, the historian, could write that in a period of thirty-five years more than 3,200 Africans had been murdered by crowds of white people. Georgia, Mississippi, Texas, Louisiana, and Alabama constituted the heart of the lynching South. Indeed, between 1889 and 1919, these five states had 1,683 lynching deaths; nearly six black people were killed each month during this period in just these five states. When you add the numbers of murders in states like Tennessee, South Carolina, Arkansas, and Florida, the horrendous nature of the lynching disease becomes ever more heinous.

*Witnessing Lynching* is a remarkable book because it allows us to re-inter-rogate the nature of our societal relationships. In fact, those who wrote against the institution of lynching were courageous in their attacks on the system of injustice because they were also in danger of the lynchman's noose for their outspokenness. The novelist Theodore Dreiser's description of a black man in the vise of the killers is chilling: "The sickening sight was that of the Negro, foaming at the mouth, bloodshot as to his eyes, his hands working convulsively, being dragged up the cellar steps feet foremost. They had tied a rope about his waist and feet, and so had hauled him out, leaving his head to hang and drag. The black face was distorted beyond all human semblance" (Dreiser, quoted in Rice, 2003, p. 165). In this essay called "Nigger Jeff," Dreiser is dealing with his own complicity as a white man who witnesses a lynching but does not do anything to stop it. How many whites shared this dilemma? A lynching could attract thousands of whites, men, women, and children, as if to a picnic and the voice that would raise a caution or call the mob to rationality would be gone in a moment of madness turned on the prophet. So most whites who witnessed lynching did nothing about it. Blacks, too, saw themselves as helpless in the face of the overwhelming insanity of mob violence against one of their own. To raise one's voice in protest would have meant sure death. There would have been another murder instead of just the one caught in the grasp of the mob. Thus, the black compatriots felt sorrow at both their weakness and their fellow African's misfortune.

One could argue that most of these writers lived in the North, a long way from the "heart of Dixie" where the most violent crimes took place. But this is not a just criticism given the fact that these writers had the courage to speak out against mob rule in America where the possibility of denial of opportunity to make a living, censorship, or discrimination, even threats of death, could keep the writer from working. America itself was guilty of this crime and the incidence of lynching may have occurred most in the South but the provenance was national.

What the witnesses saw in the lynching phenomenon was a nation in moral chaos. How do you report on moral decay? When you see thousands of men, women, and children in a festive mood at the lynching of a human being, what do you say? *Witnessing Lynching* is a moving book because it provides the reader with a clear understanding of the agony experienced by those who were often falsely accused because of this outbreak of savage brutality. I came away from *Witnessing Lynching* with a remarkable appreciation of the impact that the lynching phenomenon had on contemporary witnesses.

## Against racism

Periodically there appears an argument about race that runs counter to the wisdom of experience in the African American community. *Against Race* by the sociologist Paul Gilroy is just such a book. Gilroy, a British scholar, made a reputation in the United States with the postmodern work, *The Black Atlantic*. I see this book as a continuation of that work's attempt to deconstruct the notion of African identity in the United States and elsewhere. Of course, it runs squarely against the lived experiences of African Americans. The history of discrimination against us in the West – whether the United States or the United Kingdom or other parts of the Western world – is a history of an assault on our dignity because we are Africans or the descendants of Africans. This has little to do with whether or not we are on one side of the ocean or the other. Such false separation, particularly in the context of white racial hierarchy and domination, is nothing more than an acceptance of a white definition of blackness. I reject such a notion as an attempt to isolate Africans in the Americas from their brothers and sisters on the continent. It is as serious an assault and as misguided as the 1817 Philadelphia conference that argued that the blacks in the United States were not Africans but "colored Americans" and therefore should not be returned to Africa. To argue as Gilroy does that Africans in Britain and the United States are part of a "Black Atlantic" is to argue the "colored American" thesis all over again. It took us one hundred and fifty years to defeat the notion of the "colored American" in the United States and I will not stand idly by and see such a misguided notion accepted as fact at this late date in our struggle to liberate our minds. We are victimized in the West by systems of thinking, structures of knowledge, ways of being, that take our Africanity as an indication of inferiority. I see this position as questioning the humanity and the dignity of African people.

It should be clear that Gilroy's book, *Against Race*, is not a book against

racism, as perhaps it ought to be, but a book against the idea of race as an orga-
nizing theme in human relations. It is somewhat like the idea offered a decade
or more ago by the conservative critic, Anne Wortham, in her reactionary
work, *The Other Side of Racism* (1981). Like Wortham, Gilroy argues that the
African American spends too much time on collective events that constitute
"race" consciousness and therefore participates in "militaristic" marches typ-
ified by the Million Man March and the Million Woman March, both of which
were useless. The only person who could make such a statement had to be
one who did not attend. Unable to see the awesome power of the collective
construction of *umoja* within the context of a degenerate racist society, Gilroy
prefers to stand on the sidelines and cast stones at the authentic players in the
arena. This is a reactionary posture. So *Against Race* cannot be called an anti-
racism book although it is anti-race, especially against the idea of black cultural identity, whether constructed as race or as a collective national identity.

Let us be clear here: *Against Race* is not a book against all collective identities. There is no assault on Jewish identity, as a religious or cultural identity, nor is there an attack on French identity or Chinese identity as
collective historical realities. There is no assault on the historically constructed identity of the Hindu Indian, nor on the white British. Nor should
there be any such assault. But Gilroy, like others of this school, see the principal culprits as African Americans who retain a complex love of African
culture. In Gilroy's construction or lack of construction, there must be
something wrong with African Americans because Africa remains in their
minds as a place, a continent, a symbol, a reality of origin, and source of
the first step across the ocean when they are really not African. But Gilroy
does not know what he is talking about here. This leads him to the wrong
conclusions about the African American community. The relationship
Africans in the Americas have with Africa is not of some mythical or a mystical place. We do not worship unabashedly at the doorsteps of the continent although we have an active engagement with all that it means. Are we
always conscious of it? Of course not! You will not find all African
Americans walking around the streets of Philadelphia or Chicago or Los
Angeles thinking about engaging Africa, yet we know almost instantly that
when we are assaulted by police, denied venture capital, or criticized for
insisting on keeping Europe out of our consciousness without permission
that Africa is at the center of our existential reality. We are most definitely
African, though modern, contemporary of Africans domiciled in the West.

Actually Gilroy spends a considerable amount of time in this book
explaining how race, a false concept, "is understood." He writes: "Awareness
of the indissoluble unity of all life at the level of genetic materials leads to a

stronger sense of the particularity of our species as a whole, as well as to new anxieties that the character is being fundamentally and irrevocably altered" (2000, p. 20). I do not know how Gilroy can move from this position to indict the African people as the carriers of this anxiety about "race," clearly a concept that was never promoted by African people in this country or on the continent. It is essentially an Anglo-Germanic notion, manufactured and disseminated to promote the distinctions between peoples and to establish a European hierarchy, as well as a hierarchy among Europeans themselves. In fact, it is more likely the result of a drive for patriarchy in which there is a declaration of leadership, mastery, and control. No wonder it was patriarchy and not capitalism that gave rise to the idea of racism in the first place.

I am of the opinion that Gilroy has no understanding of what Randall Robinson means in *The Debt: What America Owes to Blacks* (2001). In fact, Gilroy would proclaim Robinson's work of the genre that does not extend "beyond the color line." But it is not color that creates problems in the Western world between African-descended people and whites. It is rather a strange belief on the parts of whites that they are superior to Africans, that they have a right to establish and maintain a hierarchy over blacks by force of arms or customs or laws or habits.

Gilroy's notion that "anti-racism" has lost credibility and authority and therefore there has to be a new language "beyond the color line" seeks to get us to renounce race-thinking as a dramatic strategic gesture. The problem with this line of thinking, however, is that those who practice racism, those who support it in their workplaces, and in their daily lives, and in the institutions that discriminate against people on the basis of their "race," understand what they are doing. What is absurd is our belief that they are ignorant of the false divisions that are maintained by the ideology of white racial domination.

It may be true that fascism is a major political orientation of national wills in the last century, as Gilroy contends, but fascism's most daring and dangerous manifestation has always been in white racial domination and white supremacist notions. This is true whether they have been expressed in Germany, Britain, Australia, or the United States. To deplore or criticize African fraternal gatherings without an appreciation of the successful historical reactions to racism and white supremacy in the American public by Black Nationalism is to miss the point of this century. In no society in the contemporary world has the struggle against racism been any more successful than in the United States and that is by virtue of the aggressive action against it by black people. The most exacting antidote to white racism has been African American nationalism where African agency, self-determination, and self-actualization allow Africans to live their lives regardless of white racial insanity. Otherwise, in violent reactions or in acquiescence, the African person becomes lost in the same madness of race as the white racist.

One of the advantages of having an organic relationship with the ordinary people of the African American community is that one does not forget what the issues are in the struggle against racial domination. Ordinary Africans in the United States are not wrestling with the identity issues of the elite classes who are seeking ways to express an abstract cosmopolitanism devoid of actual contact with African people. I believe that Gilroy's issues are those of Africans who are trying to de-Africanize Africans in order to make us more acceptable to whites. This was the old canard when the issue was our hair, our skin color, or our speech. But we knew even then that these were false issues and that nothing could please the racist but the annihilation of the African. Unfortunately, instead of the racist having to perform the task of making Africans invisible, now scholars like Gilroy rush to demonstrate that there is something wrong with being an African.

The reality is that any new language about race or identity ought to be straightforward, blunt, and uncompromising. It should say that one does not have to give up his or her heritage, ancestry, or color in order to exist in the world. Why should African-descended scholars be promoted for advancing ethnic abstractness? I prefer the language of my late father who said, "If you cannot accept me as I am and for who I am, then that is your problem, not mine." I do not believe that this is arrogant or militant; I believe it is the only authentic voice that is necessary to bring about a new language of race in this century.

There is much to applaud in Gilroy's visionary statement about an intercultural society but it is not the "raceless future" aspect of his argument. First, I do not look forward to such a colorless, heritage-less, abstract future, and do not see why anyone should look for it. Only those who have a need to escape from their own histories have a need for such a raceless future. On the contrary, it is much more hopeful that we defeat the notion of racial superiority and establish a broad new moral vision based on mutual respect for all human beings. I cannot believe that racelessness, whether that means racial amalgamation or the obliteration of the African phenotype, would amount to anything except the diminishing of the world. Where Gilroy has a point is in his intense desire to counter the rise of European fascism, but I think that he has the wrong idea about how to counter that resurgence. To me, it is not in the elimination of race or races, but in the elimination of racism, the defeat of the ideology of white racial domination, that we will discover the way to a new humanism.

I think it is important that we have some clarity about how this ideology has affected the intellectual environment in which we work. Without a clear appreciation of the depth of racist ideology in the textual and symbolic fabric of Western society, we will miss the real threat to human relations between people from different gene pools. I am convinced that hegemony, based on patriarchy, must be confronted. Inasmuch as different nationalities of Europeans become "white" in the American society, it is not so much an ethnic issue, as it might be in Africa, but a search for privilege over black people in the great leap to whiteness by joining the Eurocentric hegemony. Nowhere is this accession to whiteness more demonstrative than in the Eurocentric hegemony in the Academy.

## Hegemony in the Academy

I think that the intellectual project of Eurocentric hegemonists continues the objective of domination established in the earliest days of Western social theory as a corollary to political and economic imperialism, although it was inherent in the drive to enthrone patriarchy over the natural form of matriarchy at the very dawn of human history. Thus, it is through a rhetoric of triumphalism that the principal concepts of Western thought as a universal mount a globalizing tendency. It will always fail to produce positive human relationships because at its base it advances one racial/cultural idea as best for all. It undermines the art, science, and culture of other cultures except the globalizing one. I will suggest the need for a transforming ethic.

It is not my intention to answer all of the attacks on Afrocentric intellectuals but rather to establish the framework for future examination and discourse by critiquing the perverse ideas that mask the mystique of power parading as science. Since Afrocentricity remains a profound challenge to the theory and behavior of racial domination, those who support hegemony will always criticize it.

## The rhetoric of triumphalism

It is easy to believe that the Western Academy of the twenty-first century is literally comprised of a cadre of individuals whose purpose is nothing more than the creation and maintenance of a collective literature of European triumphalism based upon the idea that all theories and philosophies not rooted in European historical consciousness are unreal. Such an attitude is not only articulated by white Americans; it is also taken up by some compradors like Peter Gran, the Palestinian historian, who claimed that "he starts with the premise that Afrocentricity is false" (email memorandum to Susan Herbst, Molefi Asante, and others from Peter Gran, November 2005). This idea is expressed in numerous ways in the colleges and universities of the West. In case after case, African American, Native American, Asian American, and Latino scholars who present their cases for tenure or promotion at higher education institutions discover that the reviewers have established artificial and arbitrary barriers grounded in white triumphalist rhetoric of maintaining standards, which is another way of declaring that they are maintaining dominance. In one situation, a professor was denied tenure and promotion although she had published eight books (Asante, 2003b). Another professor at a major university in the eastern part of the United States was denied promotion to full professor with four books and 37 articles. The extent of the anecdotal information betrays any claim of innocence on the part of these institutions and they do not seek innocence; they seek control and power over the voices of those who are defined as outside.

I recall that the standards have been flipped time and time again as more Africans, Latinos and Asians have entered the competitive academic arena. Since people other than whites publish, it is no longer good enough to publish in peer-reviewed journals and be considered an intellectual who has reflected on one's subject; you must now publish in the "right" meaning literally "right white" journals. Beyond that, if you publish a book, some universities do not count that publication as valid unless it is published by one of the few unencumbered university presses. They insure that you do not publish with an African American or African press because, with one exception, there are no African American university presses.

A nearly-forty year battle for African American history to be taught in the Philadelphia School District ended in 2003 when the School Reform Commission asked me to write courses on African American History, African History, and the African diaspora. Why did whites so vehemently resist the educational initiative for forty years? What would be the danger in teaching all children the history of Africans in the United States? What could have agitated the school district's administrators and boards of education prior to 2003 in such a vigorous reaction to this modest proposal?

There remains in the psyche of many people of European descent the idea that the world was created for their use alone (Memmi, 1991, pp. 8–9). Furthermore, there are those who seem to insist that the only legitimate history is European history and that nothing written by Africans, Asians, Latinos, or First Nations people really matters. This represents an arrogant villainy in intellectual discourse.

Now more than ever the untenable position of many Eurocentric intellectuals has created an erosion of credibility in the social and human sciences. It is no longer enough to argue for Universal Man or Classical Standards and mean by the arguments something unique about Europeans. Of course, there are enough anti-racists and radical sociologists to point the way to new forms of human understanding; that is why I am not indicting the entire sociological, behavioral, or critical enterprise. I also know that the reconstruction in the arts and sciences has been going on for at least three decades. But we have not yet achieved the ultimate turn away from racism, classicism, and sexism that is necessary for a more productive and civilized remaking of reality.

## An overview of the intellectual situation

A general survey of Western history and philosophy reveals several themes that serve to disrupt the stability of human society. These themes or strands in Western thinking have often become part of the imperial ambitions of the West in regard to scholarship. What concerns me is that this triumphalist notion of scholarship is attached to some of the main components of Eurocentrism, including aggressive individualism, chauvinistic rationalism, and ruthless culturalism. Armed with these swords of domination, the cultural hegemonist seeks to decimate any cultural or social center that is not fully within, that is, under the control of, the European way of thinking.

I will show that these concepts of a new theology of victory over all others are nothing more than calling cards used to give the impression of European dominance. Like skin-color racism, they are built upon a fake idea of superiority of the European culture and seek to establish "whiteness" as the standard for that superiority. Ultimately, in the context of globalization, the subversion of concepts, theories, and ideas from Africa, Asia, and South America is the principal agent undermining the radical transformation of the world economy. It is not merely the control of concepts that accompany Europe's thrust (by Europe here I am referring mainly to the Anglo-Germanic tyranny of discourse) into the world but the power to assert the productive means of shaping and disseminating those concepts to humanity that stabs social science and truth in the back and makes vulgar cultural caricatures of Africans, Asians, and Eastern Europeans.

# Aggressive individualism

The concept of aggressive individualism is derived from the notion that the standard of value can be reduced to an individual. Although humans exist in society and communities, the individual is the primary unit of reality in all social systems and must be preserved and supported beyond the community, which is nothing more than a collection of individuals. Nothing is above the individual.

This means, of course, that every person is an end in himself and should not be required to give up anything for the sake of another individual. Set off on his own mission to conquer the world, the aggressive individualist carries aspects of the classical individualist in political terms with the more self-interested and ego-centered aspects of a gross individualism. According to this ideology, each individual stands on his own ground and achieves on his own against the world. While aggressive individualism is not isolationism, it does have some of the aspects of the lone hero. The philosophical concept of individualism relies on the belief that the individual is the primary unit of society. In sum, the political and social ideology of aggressive individualism celebrates self-reliance, autonomy, personal independence, individual liberty, and triumphalism over others.

Among the more prominent features of individualism as a political ideology are the promotion of individualistic materialism and the promotion of the rights of the individual at the expense of responsibility toward others and the society at large. This leads to the advancement of a culture of contract over a culture of trust and promotes individualized medicine over the needs of public health (Cummings, 2005, p. 33).

The Afrocentrist's concern is not so much with individualism per se but with a form of autonomic aggressive narcissistic individualism that opposes humanistic collectivism and hence, destroys any possibility for seeking group interests and the collective well-being of society. It is this gross form of aggressive individualism that threatens the idea of human community. One must make these distinctions because there are many examples of individualism that are current in sociological discourse. When Max Weber claimed in *Economy and Society* (1968, first published 1922) that methodological individualism was a way of showing that social phenomena resulted from individual actions that had to reflect back to motivations, he was attempting to establish the outline of Talcott Parsons's "action frame of reference" (Parsons, 1937, pp. 43–51). This set the tone for aggressive individualism as a doctrine although it could not itself be considered as favoring such a position. But neither Weber nor Parsons knew anything much about black people or African cultures and they certainly did not write about Africans on the continent. They were essentially involved in a European discussion about method, but Weber was at least clear in asserting that methodological individualism was not in any conceivable sense an aggressive individualistic system of values (Weber, 1968, p.18). This position was to be advanced by other European writers feeding off of what they considered to be the Weberian view, however distorted.

The extraordinary destructiveness of aggressive individualism is evident. It aligns itself against community and the goodwill of society in order to elevate the individual. Nothing escapes the self-interested party, not even the will of the group to survive, in its attempt to assert its own interest. Clearly, the African culture is in conflict with this attitude about reality. It is not me against the world that is the unit of importance in the universe of humanity, but me as a part of the greater good in the world. I am not against my brother or sister, but for the advancement of the human personality in all of its dimensions. This does not mean that I am not a person; I am profoundly a person with deep personal commitments. But I am not an aggressive individualist with no regard for community or group interest. I survive because we survive and my survival as an individual is meaningless if there are no other people. I am defined by my relationships and there are no great values in some narcissistic monastic isolation (Opoku, 1978).

## Chauvinistic rationalism

The idea that European thinkers are more rational than other writers and thinkers is a part of chauvinistic rationalism. This is not to be confused with the continental rationalism expounded by René Descartes or certain forms of modern rationalism based on the three theses: (1) the Intuition/Deduction Thesis; (2) the Innate Knowledge Thesis; and (3) the Innate Concept Thesis. The Intuition/Deduction Thesis usually holds that intuition is a type of rational insight that allows us to "see" something to be true. The Innate Knowledge Thesis is that we know certain things a priori as just part of our nature. This is neither intuition nor experience, but knowledge based upon our humanity. The Innate Concept Thesis holds that certain concepts are a part of our rational nature and may be brought to consciousness by some experience.

Theophile Obenga has explained that the Greco-Germanic tyranny regarding ancient Egypt had a lot to do with the idea that philosophy, as a part of the Western concept of the rational, played a role in dismissing African knowledge and ideas (Obenga, 1989, pp. 277–85). What the

Eurocentric hegemonists did was to claim philosophy for Europe. I have called this a form of chauvinistic rationalism which I define in an exact sense to mean a political and social concept designating a claim on discursive reasoning by a particular culture.

Thus, a dogma is produced which claims that philosophy is European or rather that it is Greek. It captures the term and the idea for Europe, thereby leaving out any other regions of the world as producers of philosophy. And since philosophy has been seen as the greatest or highest of Western sciences, giving birth to other fields such as history, physics, and music, it demonstrates the power of the Western ideal. In fact, there is no other region of the world where philosophy, in the sense of the rational discourse, exists. The First Nations create myths but not philosophy. The Hindus may have produced religious texts but not philosophy. The Chinese may have given the world wise sayings but not philosophy. The Egyptians may have produced metaphors and figures of extraordinary gods but not philosophy. Yoruba may have legends and stories but not philosophy. Indeed, in the thinking of the hegemonists, Greece is the sole possessor of philosophy. Such unitary claim sets up the foundation for claiming Western superiority in the area of logical thinking. If philosophy is Greek and can be found nowhere else, then it is European and white and no other people have the same ability to make rational arguments or to come to rational conclusions. Europe is singular in this regard, according to this ideology of triumphalism.

The word philosophy comes into the English language from the Greek but it is not of Greek origin. We have come to understand its meaning to be "lover of wisdom" by breaking down the Greek word thusly: *philo* means "lover" or "brother" and *sophia* means "wisdom" or the "wise." Therefore, philosophia means "lover of wisdom." The Greek etymological dictionaries say that the origin of the word "sophia" is unknown. When a European says it is unknown, nine times out of ten the person has not bothered to look at African languages. When one examines the African record it is clear that the word *seba* corresponds to *sophia* in Greek. The first mention of the word *seba* is on the tomb of Antef I around 2052 BC. The word is taken to mean "the wise" or "wisdom." It does not appear in Greece until nearly a thousand years later. So the word "philosophy" is not of Greek origin and, hence, philosophy itself could not have developed in Greece where they did not have a word until it came to them from Egypt.

The first philosophers considered Greek philosophers were Thales and Pythagoras, both of whom studied in Africa. Before the seventh century BC, there was no tradition of philosophy among Greek writers. However, in Kemet, called Egypt by the Greeks, the tradition of philosophy was ancient by the time the first Greeks began to write intelligent sentences in their language. The fact that this is not widely known nor widely taught has a lot to do with the chauvinistic rationalism of modern Eurocentric thinking. A discourse on the origin of philosophy cannot be conducted without a fundamental recourse to the works of Ptahhotep, Amenemhat, Merikare, and Duauf, among other Kemetic authors. Yet the attempt to define rational thinking as the property of Europe or white people, as has been done by numerous writers, makes a mockery out of historical fact. Nevertheless, the continuing surge of intellectual work being done by young Afrocentric scholars in Africa and its diaspora will completely revise the imperialistic text of Africa's history written by the proponents of what Martin Bernal calls the Aryan thesis of civilization (Bernal, 1987).

Perhaps one of the most troubling moments in modern Western intellectual history occurred when Mary Lefkowitz, an erstwhile important classicist, wrote the book *Not Out of Africa*, seeking to counter what she considered to be the advance made by Afrocentrists in toppling the Greek–Roman hierarchy in ancient classical studies. It was no secret that the Afrocentrists had argued that there was a significant African influence on ancient Greece, showing in numerous writings that the impact on art, architecture, geometry, mathematics, law, politics, medicine, astronomy, and religion was astounding and overwhelming. What is more is that the Afrocentrists had argued that the Africans who made this impact on Greece were black Egyptians (Asante and Mazama, 2002, pp. 18–19)!

Rushing to attack the Afrocentrists without a careful consideration of the evidence, Lefkowitz produced, with the support of several conservative foundations, a political tract that sought to reassert the Aryanist tradition of scholarship by raising straw arguments to be knocked over by her superior scholarship. In doing these gymnastics, she failed to deal with any of the real arguments advanced by the Afrocentrists. Nevertheless, her book was widely hailed by conservative scholars and columnists. George Will of *Newsweek*, and Roger Kimball of the *Wall Street Journal*, saw fit to bless Lefkowitz's book. Will saw the book as a sort of "white hope" or as a "definitive moment in intellectual history" (Will, 1996). It was no such moment. Kimball gloated that readers should savor the "definitive dissection of Afrocentrism" (Kimball, 1996). No such definitive dissection took place; rather there was a definitive exposure of the principal assumptions of a racial structure of classical knowledge. Yet one could expect writers in a tradition that praised the dominant mythologies of race in the history of the West by diverting attention to marginal issues in the public domain to write such commentary.

Lefkowitz sought to demonstrate that Greece did not receive substantially from Kemet. In order to do this, she ignores the African influence on Greece in the ancient works of Aetius, Strabo, Plato, Homer, Herodotus, Diogenes, Plutarch, and Diodorus Siculus. A reader of Lefkowitz's book is placed in a peculiar position of deciding whether to believe the ancient writers or a twentieth-century author with a bone to pick. This was a racial argument that was clearly fast back-stepping.

Chauvinistic rationalism should not be imposed and Greece cannot impose itself as some universal culture that developed full-blown out of nothing without the foundations it received from Africa. Actually it is neither Greece nor the Greeks that have sought to make this imposition, but many racist writers out of the Aryanist school of thought who have limited knowledge of ancient African history, philosophy, and culture.

Unfortunately, chauvinistic rationalism is accepted doctrine in some circles and some people will go to great lengths to uphold it. They usually commit four fundamental flaws: (1) they attack insignificant or trivial issues to obscure more important issues; (2) they will make assertions and then offer their own interpretations as evidence; (3) they will undermine writers they previously praised in order to maintain the fiction of a Greek miracle; and (4) they will announce that both sides of an issue are correct, and then seek to discredit African agency. Let us see how these flaws are revealed in reality.

## Attacking insignificant or trivial issues

Lefkowitz has three main axes to grind in her book. The first is that a student told her that she, the student, believed that Socrates was black because of some references made to him in the ancient texts. The second point that Lefkowitz takes issue with is the idea that the Greek gods came from Africa. The third point she wants to make is that George James's famous book, *Stolen Legacy* (1954), is based on freemasonry. The main point asserted and defended by Afrocentrists is that Greece owes a substantial debt to Egypt and that Egypt was anterior to Greece in human knowledge. Lefkowitz attempts to avoid this issue. I do not know any African scholar of note who argues that Socrates was black, although it is possible for one to make such an argument given the record. But it is a trivial point, as is the question of whether or nor Cleopatra, descendant of Ptolemy, had any African ancestors. On the question of the Greek gods coming from Africa, Herodotus writes in the History that "nearly all of the names of the gods came to Greece from Egypt." George James's work has stood the test of many attacks for more than fifty years. His arguments cannot be obfuscated by appealing to freemasonry; as a scholar of Greek and Latin he makes important intellectual arguments on what the Greeks received from the Africans.

## Making assertions and offering interpretations

Lefkowitz says: "In American universities today not everyone knows what extreme Afrocentrists are doing in their classrooms. Or even if they do know, they choose not to ask questions" (Lefkowitz, 1996, p. 1). She never gives one example of an extreme Afrocentrist in any city at any university. Nor does she tell us what these "extreme Afrocentrists" are teaching that is so wrong. The reader is made to believe that something exists where nothing exists. No matter how passionate the statement, assertion alone is not evidence.

What Afrocentrists do teach is that to begin a discussion of world history with Greece or with the Greeks as the mothers and fathers of civilization is to ignore thousands of years of human history in Africa and Asia (see Hilliard, 2002, p. 51). Thus, it is clear that creating clouds of suspicion about academic colleagues in order to support a racial mythology developed over the past centuries to accompany European enslavement of Africans, imperialism, colonialism, and exploitation will not dissipate the fact that Greece owes a cultural debt to Africa.

## Undermining ancients to maintain a fiction

Herodotus was once considered to be the father of history until he was adopted by African scholars as a key player in the ancient world for his description of African culture and African people. It was Herodotus who declared in Book Two of *History* that the ancient Egyptians had "black skin and wooly hair." This statement alone has upset many white and Eurocentric historians who are now ready to say that the venerable Herodotus did not know what he was seeing. Furthermore, Herodotus claims that the Greeks could never think that their gods originated in Greece and he glorifies Egypt in relationship to Greece. But he is not the only ancient to be dismissed by the Aryanists. Aristotle reported that the Egyptians gave the world mathematics and geometry. Lefkowitz claims that Herodotus did not know what he was talking about when he wrote on ancient Egyptian contributions to Greece. She says that you cannot trust Homer, Iamblicus, Diogenes Laertius, Plutarch, or Strabo. Her position is that Strabo, like Herodotus, depended too much on what the Egyptian priests told him. Every Greek who wrote on the overwhelming impact of Egypt (Africa) on Greece (Europe) is discredited or set up to be discredited by the Aryanists. The idea to abandon the Greek authors rests on the belief that these ancient Greek writers cannot be counted upon to support the theories of white supremacy.

*Both sides are correct – so choose the European side*

Lefkowitz could have admitted that Egypt during the times of the Pharaohs, whatever interpretation you have of that ancient society, for example, as ornamented with Mystery Schools or simply filled with keepers of mysteries at the temples of Ipet Isut, Edfu, Kom Ombo, Esna, Philae, Dendara, Abydos, or other cities, was the source of much of Greek knowledge. Rather she claims that the only impact of Egypt on Greece was in art and architecture. This is to state an obvious fact in order to obscure the deeper influences in science, astronomy, geometry, literature, medicine, mathematics, religion, politics, law, music, and philosophy. To maintain a position of chauvinistic rationalism, it is impossible for her to admit that Africans had reason before Greece. In fact, she would rather believe that the ancient Egyptians who completed most of the large pyramids by 2500 BC did so without rational knowledge because the Greeks would not come until 1,500 years later!

This is what we know from science and history:

- Ancient Egyptians (Kemetians) during the Pharaonic Period, according to ancient sources, were black-skinned Africans (Herodotus, *Histories, Book Two*; Aristotle, *Physiognomonica*).
- Egyptian civilization preceded that of Greece by several thousand years.
- Philosophy originated in the continent of Africa in the Nile Valley and the first Greek philosophers (Thales, Isocrates, Pythagoras) studied in Egypt.
- Greek students of Africans included Plato, Eudoxus, Isocrates, Pythagoras, Thales, Homer, Herodotus, Lycurgus, Solon, Anaxamander, Anaxagoras, and Democritus.

What is the project that Mary Lefkowitz and other Aryanists seek to uphold? She states it quite simply in her own words: "Any attempt to question the authenticity of ancient Greek civilization is of direct concern even to people who ordinarily have little interest in the remote past. Since the founding of this country, ancient Greece has been intimately connected with the ideals of American democracy" (Lefkowitz, 1996). For Lefkowitz, to question the false position established by early classicists with an imperial bent is to cause trouble with the American ideal. If truth about the ancient world will create problems for the American ideal, then that ideal sits upon a weaker foundation than I ever imagined.

*Ruthless culturalism*

Ruthless culturalism is the promotion of the American ideal as the most valuable and valid form of human customs and traditions. Any assault on this ideal is considered emotional, irrational, and immoral. Thus, the practitioners of ruthless culturalism believe in their framework as uniquely legitimate and superior to any other form of human organization. They defend this construct with numerous machinations of science, politics, statistics, and literature.

Obviously this means that there is a bankruptcy of culture in the West because the ruthless culturalists think that by asserting it against all other forms of culture they can save it. I like C. L. R. James's statement about the intellectuals of "bourgeois civilization" as an apt description of the ruthless culturalists. James said of the bourgeois intellectuals that they "run to and fro squealing like hens in a barnyard when a plane passes overhead. Not a single philosopher or publicist has any light to throw on a crisis in which the fate not of a civilisation but of civilisation itself is involved" (James, 1992, p. 153). We find nothing but chattering by neoconservative hacks whose only prescription for the human crisis caused by their arrogance is more empty political prescription. Logic has disappeared. Generosity is nonexistent. And we are confronted with brute force and blunt talk but not discourse.

Marimba Ani has written in *Yurugu*, "the cultural other is a creation of the European culture, constructed, in part, to answer the needs of the European *utamaroho*. The *utamaroho* is expansionistic. This, as a cultural characteristic, is itself very important to understand. The ego seeks to infinitely expand itself. This kind of self-expansion should not be confused with the desire to 'give of oneself,' to 'merge self with other' or to 'become one with the world'" (Ani, 1994, p. 403). In fact, Ani claims that expansionism is the projection of the cultural ego onto the world (p. 403).

In the past twenty years, the level of intellectual debate in the United States, one of the neoconservative leaders in the West, has plummeted. Of course, there are those who would attribute a great deal of the pessimism to the September 11, 2001 attacks, but much of the rhetoric of ruthless culturalism coming from neoconservatives in the United States existed long before planes flew into buildings. Take the theme-announcing tract, *The Disuniting of America* (1992) by Arthur Schlesinger, Jr. As a designated great American historian, he was supposed to know something about America and about African American scholarship, his ultimate target. However, pontification remains one of the most obvious attitudes of hegemonic thinking in cultural matters. You have to come away from this document with a certain distrust of Schlesinger as well as call into question his perspective on American society. This is doubly so if one is an African American accustomed to thinking that the author of *The Age of Jackson* (1945) and *A Thousand Days* (1965) had shown a real metamorphosis in the twenty years between those two books. However, twenty-seven years, nearly a generation, after he wrote the book about the Kennedy presidency, he produced a piece of intellectual trash that initially came with all of the bells and whistles of the American public advertising campaign that Whittle Communication could muster.

*The Disuniting of America* was widely attacked as it should have been by Afrocentric scholars as inaccurate, bullish, and insulting. It represented a classic example of ruthless culturalism by a writer who had rarely been considered in the conservative column, although this book demonstrated how far right the American intellectuals had moved since the 1960s.

The problem with this kind of ruthless culturalism is that the vision of America set forth by Schlesinger was one found in an outdated vision of America as a white country. After all, the American state was founded upon the First Nations' land, a fact that is largely forgotten in the writing of the most liberal white American. Schlesinger argues for an America where Anglo-Saxons define the protocols of the American society and white culture as the ideals to which all others were expected to aspire. In this vision, this history of America, there is no genocide of the native people, no enslavement of the African people, and no dispossession of the Mexican people. In effect, this ruthless culturalist perspective argues that disunion is caused by Africans, Mexicans, and others who questioned the values of American society. The proponents of ruthless culturalism claim that adjustments might need to be made to smooth out the ripples in an otherwise perfect society, but that the issues raised by those exploited and discriminated against are minor. This vision is corrupted by the arrogance of political, academic, and cultural dominance.

Schlesinger is unable to see the contemporary American reality and I believe he has missed the point of the past as well. The evidence suggests that he holds a nearly static view of American society. And perhaps the whiteness of his youth, his academic life, social relations, and business acquaintances, kept him away from a more authentic version of the American reality. There is, of course, a nightmarish side to Schlesinger's fantasy. He has peopled his vision with negations, colored by axioms that support no social or economic truth but which are ultimately structured to uphold the status quo of white male privilege and domination. This mixture of fact and fiction presents itself for analytical de-invention, not national disunity.

Of all the issues that might have attracted Schlesinger's attention for disuniting America – unequal protection under the law, gender inequity, taxation without representation in Washington, DC, economic class antagonisms, corrupt politicians, rampant anti-Africanism, growing anti-Semitism, pollution of the environment, robbing of the First Nations – he finds the African American challenge to the ruthless culturalist educational system in America to be the premier disuniting element. Indeed, he sees it as a frightening development. Why should African Americans fighting for the infusion of the African American content in the curricula of the American nation's schools create such an uproar if not because the ruthless culturalists prefer to maintain curricula of exclusion of information about Africans?

There is no doubt in my mind that many of the ruthless culturalists seek to maintain their hegemonic imposition by creating symbolic, economic, and cultural domination. Yet I know that hegemonic thinking is like a person standing on the lid of a manhole. The fact that someone will rise out of that manhole means that the person standing on the lid will have to change positions or be toppled off. A lifetime of delusion that denies Africans and Africa a place in human history creates a basic disbelief in facts that are presented in an Afrocentric framework. Scores of African scholars have abandoned Eurocentric ways of looking at the world and have begun to view reality from the standpoint of Africans as agents and subjects within their own stories. Doing this pushes Europe from the center of studies about Africa. Schlesinger's fear is that Europe will no longer dominate the imagination and consciousness of African people.

One must learn to be factual and in trying to be factual I have learned that primary description is better than secondary interpretation. Thus, when Afrocentrists claim that George Washington and Thomas Jefferson were slave owners, inter alia, who did not believe in equality for Africans, that is a descriptive statement about the facts. Washington held more than 300 Africans in bondage and brought seven with him to Philadelphia when he accepted the presidency under the Constitution. When Ona Judge, one of the enslaved women, ran away, Washington wrote furiously to people he knew trying to bring her back to bondage. Jefferson, it is known, had a child by a fourteen-year-old African girl, Sally Hemings. One can excuse the facts on the grounds of interpretation, one can claim ignorance, one can argue that the presidents' good points outweighed their bad points, and so on; but the fact is that they believed in the inferiority of Africans. Arthur Schlesinger would insist that we not mention the racist heritage and character of the "founding fathers" because that would create disunity. If that be creating disunity, not only am I guilty as he claims in his book, but I will create more disunity because nothing is more valuable than the truth in bringing about national integration. Schlesinger seems to operate in a closed system of thought and such systems inevitably produce closed minds. Education in such a system is found to produce those who speak a certain restrictive language, use a handed-down arcane political vocabulary, and believe in elves.

The danger, quite frankly, is that Schlesinger's attitude toward difference creates insiders and outsiders, the definers and the defined. I can paraphrase Memmi here when he writes of the colonialist that "his racism is as usual to his daily survival as is any other prerequisite for existence" (Memmi, 1991, p. 70).

Ruthless culturalism is based upon three major ideological constituents: (1) the belief that white culture is superior to all other cultures; (2) the aggressive assault on African or other culture in order to deny them any standing; and (3) the use of persistent and constant propaganda to discredit all African intellectuals who articulate a view of the world based on their own agency.

The first constituent is found in nearly all places where Europeans exist with other people. It is derived from the last five hundred years of imperial domination and, although it is coming to a close, the impulse to fight for this antiquated idea of racial superiority is a hard nut to crack. The assault on African culture is almost like a "strike first" action, a sort of George W. Bush attitude about "pre-emptive strikes" against those you think might do something bad. This is nonsense but it is the kind of fuel that racism runs on and it is difficult to rein in the horses once they have been let out. Propaganda attacks on African intellectuals often become ludicrous. Schlesinger and others would like to claim that African American scholars are badly educated because they insist in demonstrating that the educational systems of the country poorly educate black children. These are the arguments you make when you have run out of things to say. The conviction that we will defend the rights of all cultural expressions, not just the

Greco-Roman-Hebraic-Germanic-Viking cultures, remains at the core of the Afrocentric idea.

Neither the aggressive individualist, chauvinistic rationalist, nor the ruthless culturalist can offer us a future world based upon respect for the diversity and heterogeneity of humanity. They are bankrupt ideas tied unfortunately to a worldview rooted in an imperialistic past and connected to the most oppressive forms of political and economic expressions. These are the terms that have often disempowered, decentered, de-culturalized, dehumanized, and de-politicized ordinary human society. Such ideas can be accused of taking our art and politics out of ethical circulation, thereby rendering humanity powerless, without any efficacy to transform our situation. It will be for those intellectuals still seeking to make the world a good home for humanity to rise up in constant intellectual struggle to see that truth outdoes falsehood and culturally-based morality, which overcomes the perpetual childhood of legal morality, conquers all forms of individualistic terror. We can do this by working vigorously to reconnect academia to host societies which are increasingly reflective of multiethnic and multicultural realities.

# 11

## Blackness as an Ethical Trope: Toward a Post-Western Manifesto

### The parameters

In the latter half of the twentieth century, Africans in the United States and Brazil and throughout the black world went through a profound change in cultural nomenclature. Africans were no longer Negro. The term "Negro" had been loaded with too much baggage from enslavement and colonialism to make it to the twenty-first century without a dramatic transformation. A Spanish word for "black," the term "Negro" assumed connotations that ran from the bizarre, like "the Negro type" which had no validity in an African continental sense, to "the Negro problem" in the heterogeneous and multicultural United States. So now "Negro" is a museum relic. However, as we passed from Negro to an accepted blackness, there was the possibility that an essentializing ethic might appear in the discourse. This is why it has become necessary, in an Afrocentric sense, to launch a new approach to the question of identity in the African world.

The philosopher Ama Mazama (2003a) raises a profound question about Frantz Fanon's understanding of the idea of blackness. What Mazama seeks to demonstrate is the fact that the brilliant Fanon, like so many black thinkers, had not thought through his own dislocation although he had made a strong analysis of the effects of colonization on African people. Indeed, Fanon had been born in Martinique in 1923 and lived most of his life under the colonization of the French in the Caribbean and in Africa. Colonization was a preoccupation of his writing and he understood, as presented in his book, *Black Skin, White Masks* (1967), that it was possible for Africans to be deeply alienated from culture because of the violence of the colonization process. However much Fanon might have wanted to do so, he could not distance himself from the continuing predicament of Africans who had experienced self-hatred, self-rejection, and the pathological doctrine of white supremacy. Blackness emerged as an obstacle to unfettered injustice and became, in the moment of psychological terrorizing, the ethic of resistance.

Therefore, it is clear that to be black is not merely a color nor simply to use the language of black people, but to use it to express the most progressive political, cultural and ethical interests that, in a racist society, must always be for human liberation and, thus, against all forms of oppression. Thus, it has become over the decades a trope of strong ethical dimensions with implications for a post-Western construction of reality.

A preacher from Jackson, Mississippi, went to Chicago to preach. He complained that the people did not respond to him the way that they responded to him in Jackson. He said, "I spoke in the people's language, used the proper idioms, and they sat there like I was not talking to them." The preacher assumed that the mark of blackness was language alone or, at least, the ability to speak the idioms of the people. However, idioms represent only one aspect of the meaning of blackness.

What the preacher missed is the fact that to be black is to share the evolving political and social interests of oppressive people. The language is essential, but it must be devoted to the liberation struggle of oppressed people. Language is more than a personal skill: it is a commitment, a belief, an emotion. Thus, some people may have mastered all the technical elements of Ebonics and still not be considered "black" by those with sentiments born of political and social situations. There are therefore degrees of blackness as there are degrees of Ebonics. No one has ever come full grown into blackness; no one ever will. However, there are individuals that we say possess "charisma" but what does this mean in the sense of blackness? It means that the person has found a commitment to the emotional, political, and social interests of the black community and knows how to master the language of community ambitions.

There is a reason that African Americans felt that Malcolm X brought the persona of morality when he entered a room. The meaning of this is that he brought with him the full complements of blackness, the expected rhetoric against oppression, the optimism of victory over evil, courage to speak his mind, and the validity of struggle for a good cause. It was often said that Malcolm X was the fulfillment of the culture of the African American because he was immersed in an environment of consciousness of all forms of humanity. Every thought, action, and motivation appeared to be connected to the totality of the people's will and desire. This was his meaning; indeed, it was the meaning of black culture or rather he was the meaning of the culture, a cultured person. Malcolm understood the nature of blackness as a trope in the American consciousness and his persona was an explicit presence of its power.

Lewis Gordon (2000, p. 12), writing in *Existentia Africana*, claims "race has emerged throughout its history, as the question fundamentally of 'the blacks' as it has for no other group." While Gordon is not here concerned with blackness as a trope, he is definitely interested in seeing how blackness operated within the context of a racist society. He knows that the question of Africana philosophy has been "the only situated reality that has been conditioned by blackness" (2000, p. 12). The fact of the matter is that race matters are not simply matters of "chromosomal makeup or morphological appearance" in Gordon's terms, but rather they are matters of "the values placed on what has been interpreted as given" (Gordon, 2000, p. 12).

## Isolating a perspective

Blackness is certainly not seen as a form of confraternity among all people who are black in complexion. If it were the basis of confraternity, we could well argue that it had taken an essentialist turn. However, when I am in Paris and I speak to an obvious African by phenotype – indeed, a very black French-speaking African who is with a French woman – he is likely to ignore me with the implication, "We have nothing in common." Thus, blackness is not merely a phenotype phenomenon. It is more concretely a phenomenon of time and place. Mark Christian noted in *Multiracial Identity* that some black British spoke of blackness as a "belonging" (Christian, 2000, p. 35).

I am dealing here with situation and history.

Frank Thorpe, my twelfth-grade history teacher, had a profound impact on my conceptualization of the world. He was, however, most distinguished by his pedagogical method that might be described as a provocative inquisition of young minds.

"Why were some people made black and some made white?"

"Who is responsible for racism anyway?"

"Why are white people white?"

He would pound his fist on the desk and then say, "If you can't answer the questions leave the room and return with the answers." Sometimes he would leap out of his chair and shout, "What is blackness if it is not the color of the universe? If you cannot answer the question, you all know what to do." No one ever left the classroom and he did not intend that we should leave even if we could not answer his questions. The joy, in Thorpe's classes, was to be in pursuit of answers; it was the one activity from which no one escaped. Blackness itself is a pursuit.

I am in pursuit of the full complements of blackness in the context of twentieth-century foundations and twenty-first century possibilities. Of course, I know better the foundations than I do the possibilities since I do not frame my inquiry as either a prophetic fragment or prophecy. I am much more realistic and ordinary in my objective. Yet I do not find this pursuit unfamiliar turf since as an Afrocentrist I have been convinced always by the arguments of history that African people have moved off of or been moved off of their own philosophical, cultural, economic, and political terms for a long time. Thus, the discussion of blackness itself as an attribute of a people is an unnecessary marginalization of what is a central philosophical and pragmatic action of our times. This should become clearer in the tension between blackness as taxon and as practice.

## Taxon and practice

The notion of blackness as taxon yields different results than blackness as practice. The first is based on an Aristotelian essentialism. It is therefore founded upon what we have come to call a Greek tradition. The second derives from an assertion of humanity that struggles against the chaos of domination. It is from the Kemetic tradition of the ancient Nile Valley, the classical home of African cultures. Both traditions have helped to advance science. Nevertheless, these two notions of blackness have often been confused in the literature and orature of proponents and detractors of blackness. Resolving this issue so that all the pieces are in place will require a step-by-step analysis.

One of my intentions, therefore, is to establish the fact that the Aristotelian patriarchy of taxonomic essentialism is responsible for much of the confusion surrounding the concept of blackness. In this way I hope, in my discussion, to free the discourse from unnecessary attributions. This allows me to distance my discussion of blackness from Du Bois' entrapping attribution of "double consciousness" (Du Bois, 1982 [1903]). I will then demonstrate how blackness is itself a revolutionary praxis free of any essentialist taxons. The essay will conclude with a personal statement attesting to the legitimacy of a revolutionary blackness.

## The Aristotelian patriarch

Aristotelian essentialism has been correctly termed property essentialism (Jones, 2005) because it seeks to define a thing by listing its qualities. Thus, one has various kinds of things in the world. There are many natural things, but we can know differences through attributes and characteristics of a thing. A dog is not a cat but neither is a man a dog. However, the taxons of the cat and dog are closer to each other than either one is to a man. This is the basic idea of property essentialism. If you wanted to define something, you readily sought to discover its attributes and therein was the critical difference between that thing and something else.

One sees these Aristotelian taxons in a discussion of race where Western writers subsequent to Aristotle used various taxons to create the notion of race. One was said to be of a different race if one's hair was textured differently or one's complexion possessed more or less melanin than another. Thus, property essentialism was basic to establishing the unscientific idea of biological races. A lot of emphasis is placed on the German school of the von Humboldts as promoters of the taxons of race but there are many Europeans engaged in the pedantry of race. Their legacy was to be found in the works of the greatest European minds. Furthermore, the influences of these European thinkers have penetrated the thinking of many African writers as well. The question of race is not an African question; it is pre-eminently an issue of European thinkers. No African writer espoused a doctrine of racial superiority. Indeed, it was neither in the literature nor the more generally available orature of African cultures.

## The illusion of double consciousness

The literary people among us have been trumpeting Du Bois' statement about double consciousness for the past twenty or so years to explain identity chaos or a sort of identity complication due to a racist society that privileges whiteness (Du Bois, 1982 [1903]).

However, there is no double consciousness. I announce an end to Du Bois' errant conclusion and I question the strength by which it is promoted by academic literary scholars who are often not in contact with the ordinary African person in America. The idea of "double consciousness" has fueled too many leaps into the abyss of meaninglessness and caused too many misconceptions about identity. Even if there had been a war of ideas, there is no longer any struggle between ontology and citizenship. American is not a race; it is a shared idea of society. It is not a static idea; it is nothing more than a citizenship. It is neither an ethnic group, nor a clan, nor a nation. To say "the American nation" is to talk nonsense; there is only the potential for an American nationality. It is socially constructed. There is no biologically structured American race. Furthermore, what Du Bois meant by "double consciousness" at the turn of the twentieth century has remained debatable for many decades.

Now Du Bois may have meant what he said, growing out of his own personal situation, and I am not suggesting that some Africans in America do not think they have the same personal issues, "two warring souls in one dark body," but as for me and my family, we have only one consciousness; we are black. This is not a biological statement; it is an affirmation of consciousness. As we might see later, the biological question is another matter, one that has little bearing on the question of blackness in its full complement as an assertion.

## The nature of consciousness and identity

Consciousness can only be unitary anyway. It cannot be otherwise. One can be conscious of being conscious of conflict; one could have a tortured consciousness because one wanted to be something that one was not and the something that one wanted was perceived to be better than what one was. In such a case this is not double consciousness, but madness. It is stuck in the interstices of our existence because we have permitted a dysfunction between who we are and who we are told we ought to be. Clearly all of this comes from one's society, family, and peers. We know who we are and to whom we are connected by knowing our ancestors, physical or spiritual. The more fully we know our ancestors, the rounder, the more powerful our sense of identity. This is why it is acknowledged that the fundamental requirement for slavery was the theft of history and identity, simultaneously. One way to regain what was lost is to seek a reconnection to a sense of identity and historical consciousness.

One may have a tortured consciousness but one cannot have a double consciousness. Ordinarily nothing in the African's life in America creates a clashing of consciousness. Put another way, the black man or woman living in the Deep South of Georgia at the beginning of the twentieth century did not have the "double-ness" madness. In fact, most blacks do not have it now. The tortured consciousness, mistakenly called "double consciousness," is probably the result of blacks being magnetized by white privilege and thus experiencing pangs of self-hatred. Thus, the root of the madness is not in the African but in the society. Whatever Du Bois meant was meant personally. There is no doubt in my mind that Du Bois was on a quest, like many African American intellectuals, for personal space. Lucius Outlaw points out in *On Race and Philosophy* that Du Bois' notion of "race" is best read as a cluster idea in which "elements are connected in an infinitely disjunctive definition" (Outlaw, 1996: pp. 154–5).

If you read Du Bois this way, then it becomes clear that the postmodern turn on the question of race – that is, its fluidity, mobility, and fleeting characteristics – is much more an issue of what stasis occurs at a given time along a certain continuum of human reality. Race, of course, is one thing. Blackness is another thing altogether. Where one might say emphatically that race is constructed and means one thing, to say blackness is constructed at this moment in history is to mean something entirely different. That is why the notion of a cluster idea for race might have some legitimacy if applied to blackness. To say, for example, that blackness might consist of elements that are connected in an infinitely disjunctive manner may make some sense to a lot of people. It is not to say that blackness is the same thing as race in construction, but rather to say that the cluster idea might give one a reason to look at different definitions of blackness. I am eager to see a revolutionary turn to this idea so as to annihilate the racist ideas that accompany even the cluster into the present era.

## Blackness as a trope

This brings me back to blackness. What is the meaning of blackness? Is it a color, biology, politics, race, or convenience? In one sense this is a perspectivist inquiry because the answer might depend upon where you stand. On the other hand, it is a rational examination of the evolutionary development of an American trope that represents in some primary manner and in some authentic way the maturity of the national idea. At a great party thrown by one of my friends and attended by a multicultural group of individuals, but mostly people of African descent, the conversation took an unsuspecting turn toward identity. I knew immediately that we were in for an endless evening of raucous good humor in seriousness. One of the guests, a white woman born in England, indicated that she was now an American citizen and that her husband "who is Hispanic" was a protestant preacher, at which point one of the guests asked her, "Where is your husband?" The woman looked toward the dining room and yelled, "Oh, Richard, come in here and introduce yourself." The large, round man appeared in the doorway and almost in unison, but led by the guest who had asked where her husband was, the fifteen or so other guests said, "He is a black man." The fact that the woman had referred to him as a Hispanic was a test for the trope of blackness in a truly American drama.

"No, I am not," protested Richard. "My real name is Ricardo and I am Hispanic."

"What makes you Hispanic?" a guest asked.

"I speak Spanish," said Ricardo-Richard, hoping to put an end to the queries.

"I speak English but I am not English," said the inquiring guest. "Furthermore," he continued, "just because you speak Japanese does not mean that you have become Japanese."

Another guest, a university professor, said, "My wife is Nicaraguan. She speaks Spanish but since she has not spoken tonight everyone assumed that she was black, just like they assumed you were black, by phenotype, that is, by physical traits."

Ricardo protested, "But you can see that I am not black; I have wavy hair."

So does my mother and she is black," shouted an African American woman in a long colorful African dress.

"How did you so-called Hispanics get that wavy hair?" inquired a South African accountant.

"But I am Puerto Rican and everyone knows that we are Hispanics," Ricardo insisted.

"Where did your food, music, and Santeria come from?" asked a Nigerian psychiatrist.

Ricardo was in a quandary. He could not answer the questions to the satisfaction of the audience. His wife was embarrassed.

The guests did not allow Ricardo to leave until they had pummeled him with other questions about identity. The host intervened and said that Ricardo had been a good sport but obviously he did not recognize his African heritage.

As the battered and good-natured Ricardo and his wife were leaving the party, his wife thought that she had better put everything in perspective and said, "You must understand that when Ricardo was a little boy, he was the darkest one in his family and his father used to call him the 'little Negro' and this was considered by him to be an insult. It caused him lots of pain and so now he wants to avoid any reference to being of African descent."

Regardless of Ricardo's phenotype, the Afrocentrist would say that Ricardo was not black, perhaps un-black. Blackness is not simply genetics, appearances, or color; it is fundamentally a type of consciousness, a specific consciousness that Ricardo apparently did not have nor care to have. He had been influenced by the negative connotations of blackness within the society. Had blackness been accepted by him as a positive he would not have objected; indeed, he might have embraced the idea. More importantly, had Ricardo interrogated the history of Africans in America and followed the journey of liberation and the quest for a more humane society, he might have arrived at a more ethical idea of blackness, one which he could have accepted. Unfortunately for Ricardo, he was stuck with the dominant and hegemonically-tarred and feathered image of blackness he had received from his education and the media. There is no doubt in my mind that the media, education, politics, and religion have conspired to demonize blackness as a color based on the negative images of Africa, the enslavement, and the ideas of subordination.

## "Chosenness"

Implied in any discussion of consciousness is choice, one must choose to participate. There are situations where choosing not to participate could produce historical and psychological discontinuities. Say you know someone who is phenotypically black and whose grandparents were active in the Civil Rights Movement or the Black Power Movement but who now chooses not to identify as black, that person has chosen to change identities. It is highly unlikely in a white racial hierarchical society such as the United States that a white person phenotypically would choose to be black. On the other hand, a black person phenotypically could choose to be white, that is, to claim to be white. One could see the decision as possible because of the identification of whiteness with privilege. This is one more indication that decisions are often dependent upon context. The case of Homer Plessy in the late 1890s is instructive. Plessy pleaded his case before the Supreme Court, arguing that when the conductor forced him to sit in the "Colored Only" section of the railcar he was denied "the reputation" that should have been his because he was only one-eighth black. Being seven-eighths white, by blood, should have given him the right to exercise the power of whiteness and sit in the "White Only" section of the railcar. Of course, the decision of 1896 in Plessy v. Ferguson underscored the American idea that "one drop of African blood made a person an African."

During the twentieth century in the United Kingdom, the term "black" was used to refer to either people of African or Asian, particularly Indian or Pakistani, backgrounds. Thus, it was not confined as it is in America to the idea of Africans who have been enslaved. The notion of blackness in the United States is wrapped up with the previous condition of servitude. In Britain people are identified by their color. Thus, an Indian or Pakistani is black in Great Britain. In the United States the same people are called Asians. The nature of blackness is such that it becomes an un-whiteness in England.

## Moral identity

The African American through a long struggle against domination has established a moral identity that is indestructible in the context of historical injustice and national duplicity. The concrete factors in the formulation of a moral identity of the African American are the ethical themes, not biological tenets, of the American sojourn. There are profound implications for human relationships if the lessons of our fight for freedom are appreciated as international symbols for social justice. Thus, the Dalits in India, the First Nations of Australia, and the Maoris of New Zealand, among others, have found strength in the African American's insistent and persistent struggle to bring about a moral ideal.

Our history in America remains authentic, shaped by the exigencies, conditions, pretexts, subtexts, and dramas of resistance to enslavement, segregation, and discrimination. We are not an amorphous historical body waiting for a claimant; ours is a history told in the lives of Malcolm X, Du Bois, Garvey, King, Harriet Tubman, and Zora Neale Hurston.

## What is blackness?

It is necessary to outline the argument that will follow. In the first place, blackness is not merely a color in the Aristotelian essentialist sense. Yet it is engaged in America and, in a wider context in Europe, as a taxon of race. But race itself is problematic in ways that blackness is not, as we shall see in this discussion. Furthermore, blackness is not discovered simply in the styles of dress, modes of language, or habits of a people. While one could make a case, not my intention now, for the position that certain markers do indicate an awareness of blackness through language, it will suffice to say that one cannot effect Ebonics to claim blackness. While the proper linguistic markers of black people may help to identify blackness, it is not sufficient. When the novelist Toni Morrison declared that President Bill Clinton was the first black president, she did not intend to convey anything about his biology or his speech, but about his sense of fair play in the racial arena. One could be soundly rejected as not "black enough," even if one spoke Ebonics.

The use of what one might refer to as a black idiom is not enough to count as blackness. One must also share thematic content, mainly substantive commitments to the political and social objectives of a defeat of the doctrine of white supremacy, in order to claim blackness. Thus it is a commitment more than a skill and it allows someone to say that Ward

Connerly or Clarence Thomas is not black and mean that their commitment to overturning white supremacy is absent. Strangely, it opens the door for certain people defined essentially as "white" to be seen as participating in blackness. As we shall see, the emergence of the African American movement as opposed to the Civil Rights Movement initiated the evolution of blackness. I have argued that a black perspective was necessary for the college curriculum but such an argument was never couched in terms that meant a black person needed to be in the classroom (Asante, 2003a) although a person with experiences in the black gene pool of America would most likely bring a black perspective. While I was sure that one could better the odds of having a black perspective by having a black person in the classroom, I was also aware that some phenotypical blacks were agents of white supremacy and, therefore, anti-black, meaning anti-fair play and anti-justice. Self-hatred as an abnormality of consciousness has the capacity to render people black in complexion racist against themselves.

## Separation

What separates blackness from non-blackness is the fact that blackness does not have crimes against white people in the cupboards. To say we are black is to argue that we are not keepers of secrets of conquest over others. Blackness infers no hatred of other people and black people have no arguments against the freedom of Palestinians, Kurds, Irish, or other people fighting to be left alone to determine their destinies.

Blackness is thematically against all terror perpetrated on any people. To possess blackness is to have hands free from the exploitation of the First Nations of America, Europe, Australia, Asia, or Africa. While many people, groups, nations, may have been born of strife, conquest, and domination, blackness is born of a desire for liberation and the resistance to conquest. One finds blackness disproportionately among people who are phenotypically black because we have been at the most violent edges of white supremacy. Jack Forbes has written brilliantly about white adventurers referring to Native Americans during the sixteenth and seventeenth centuries as "blacks," indicating their status as people to be conquered. As in a Marxist sense the workers' consciousness is unlike that of the capitalist, so the oppressed is different from the oppressor. Albert Memmi has pointed to this distinction in the colonized and the colonizer (Memmi, 1991). Thus, blackness becomes the antithesis to colonization, slavery, discrimination, and exploitation.

## Blackness becoming: *Khepera* syndrome

There are no Jacobins to enforce blackness, despite the fact that there are people who believe that is the case. It is neither acceptable morally nor is it necessary politically. Like the ancient Kemetic scarab, *khepera*, the glyph for "becoming" in *mdw ntr*, the idea of blackness is persistent wherever you find negativity, chaos, and ill-intent. Blackness becoming is the most authentic myth in the history of the United States, and possibly in the West during the past five hundred years.

In a penetrating article, "Race and Revisability" (2005), Richard A. Jones opined that if a person understood what the markers of blackness were then one would not have to feel "a sense of failure in not being black enough" simply because whites could not perceive one's blackness. Some people, defined by society as black, are disappointed when whites say, "I do not think of you as black." This causes some black people to question their behavior, language, actions, attitudes, and choices because they realize that if you are truly black, there should not be any mistake in your identity.

Contrary to the statements of non-Afrocentrists, there are no blackness police because no centralizing or policing force is necessary to bring it into existence. Occasionally a pundit will say, "the brothers and sisters want me to follow their blacker-than-thou philosophy." This is nonsense. One is either black or not black. There is no enforcer. One either supports the struggle against racist domination or not. There are no postmodern gray lines here; you either stand with the oppressed and against oppression or you stand with the oppressor against liberation. The shading and fading into degrees of blackness is inapplicable, as I see it, to this problem. One chooses, decides, in a transformative state, to become, thus perfecting *khepera*, the becoming.

There have been writers who expressed a desire to see an end to blackness, but this is a hopeless wish. The myth of the end of blackness is like the wish for the rainbow to cease to exist. Whenever you have histories, oral and written, of resistance to enslavement, segregation, discrimination, national expression, and white supremacy, you will discover blackness. It is the one abiding American value against the murder of hope and optimism. Thus, blackness becomes the reality of our historical activities against domination.

Of course, blackness can be altered thematically by conditions, contexts, and customs but nothing replaces blackness as the core conductor of the war against racist white supremacy. If the resistance has been intricately connected to African Americans, it is only that we have suffered the most from the promulgation of the doctrines of white supremacy. It is reasonable to assume that a major part for human liberation would be waged on the lines of black people. However, the mistake frequently made by those who have assaulted blackness is to assume that there is some genetic relationship between the thematic of blackness and race. Such a thought may have originated in the dark recesses of the minds of the Europeans who first encountered Africans, as much of the literature suggests, but the maintenance and usefulness of this connection has long since run its course.

In every sense blackness is a new type of value for the masses of the people. It possesses a political and social sensitivity and sensibility directed against all forms of human oppression. Therefore, a new people is created and by maintaining the critical themes of blackness they become the new blacks, new Africans, marked or typed by an identity rooted in their fierce opposition to all forms of domination: racism, sexism, classism, pedophilia, national terror, and white racial supremacy. These new blacks are discovered in every nation and among all ethnic groups. Indeed I have numerous friends, not phenotypically black, who are black, indeed, blacker than some individuals who proclaim that they are genetically black. Conversely, there are increasing numbers of individuals who are of African descent genetically but who are morally white, that is, they have assumed the burden of whiteness in a world in a post-Western era.

One of my graduate students, not genotypically nor phenotypically black, ran into a famous Harvard professor at an annual conference and happily announced that she was studying "Afrocentricity with Molefi Asante at Temple University," whereupon the famous professor looked her up and down and exclaimed, "Now, I have seen everything – a white student of Afrocentricity." Of course, this student never claimed to be black, appreciated the fact that being black was not mere biology, and understood, what he did not, that Afrocentricity was an intellectual enterprise. If being black in color or by some genetic formula meant blackness, then Clarence Thomas would be blacker than most people in this country. But to call Clarence Thomas "black," in terms of the struggle for justice against racism and sexism, is to stretch the trope.

By now it should be easy to see that blackness cannot be mere biology because in that case almost no people defined as black in the United States would be black. The DNA of African Americans tends to be representative of ancestors from several continents, although the core is African. Blackness is fundamentally extra-biological.

To say that someone is not black is not to pass a judgment on ethnicity. When I say that Clarence Thomas is not black, I am not saying anything about his complexion or his ancestry; I am rather speaking about virtue born out of a struggle for equality, fairness, and justice. By the same token to say that Julian Bond, Adam Clayton Powell, or Walter White, regardless of their "white" looks, are some of the blackest men in our history is to express not an ethnic or complexion statement, but a moral judgment. Some individuals may even have "black consciousness" as in skin recognition and yet not be anti-white supremacy; this is one of the peculiarities of just announcing that someone is black without knowing the meaning of the term.

Blackness is a virtue, not unlike justice, differing only in the object of application. To do justice is to participate in correcting actions deemed to have transgressed civil, criminal, or commercial codes. To do blackness is to participate in an assertive program of human equality, indeed, affirmative behavior to eradicate doctrines of white supremacy. Thus, "not by color but by their words and deeds you shall know them" might be a new axiom.

Is it possible that Picasso, in choosing the Grebo mask in 1912 as a key to his cubism, or Modigliani, in using stylized Senufo standing figures and Dan masks to develop a portrait style, might have been the first to leap at blackness as virtue? The aesthetic value of the art forms of Africa translated into ethical icons in a world stunned by the world wars that began in Europe.

What is the rhetoric of anti-blackness if it is not anti-Africanism? What is the meaning of Austin's or Gilroy's arguments against blackness? Who wishes the African to acquiesce in a pathetic arena of marginality within his own history? And why?

Ultimately anti-blackness represents the highest form of pessimism toward humanity since blackness has been posited as the post-Western trope best qualified to serve as an ethical measure of our social universe. George Sefa Dei has explored this in depth in his works on anti-racist education (Dei, 1997). In fact, African Americans who participate only in Eurocentric views can easily become anti-black simply because this is the logical extension of a virulent Eurocentric imperialism (Asante, 1998).

One only has to remember the age-old plot strategy where an author has a falsely accused person charged with a crime before the court and a chorus of others, not so accused, shouts in unison "I am guilty." In the same vein, we have achieved the purpose of the virtue of blackness as a response to white racial domination in Western society when the entire body politic, building upon an ethical plinth, adopts the strategy and says definitively, "I, too, am black."

# References

Agyeman, Opoku (1997) *Pan-Africanism and its Detractors: A Response to Harvard's Race-effacing Universalists*. Lewiston: E. Mellen Press.

Akinyela, Makungu Mshairi (1996) "Black Families: Cultural Democracy and Self-Determination: An African-centered Pedagogy." PhD Thesis, Pacific Oaks College.

Aldred, Cyril (1988) *Egypt to the End of the Old Kingdom*. London: Thames and Hudson.

Alvares, Claude (1979) *Decolonizing History: Technology and Culture in India, China and the West: 1492 to the Present Day*. New York: Apex.

Ani, Marimba (1994) *Yurugu*. Lawrenceville, NJ: Africa World Press.

Asante, Molefi Kete (1983) "The Ideological Significance of Afrocentricity in Intercultural Communication." *Journal of Black Studies* 14(1): 3–19.

Asante, Molefi Kete (1990) *Kemet, Afrocentricity, and Knowledge*. Trenton, NJ: Africa World Press.

Asante, Molefi Kete (1991a) "The Afrocentric Idea in Education." *Journal of Negro Education* 60(2): 170–80.

Asante, Molefi Kete (1991b) "Afrocentricity and the Human Future." *Black Books Bulletin* 1(8): 137–40.

Asante, Molefi Kete (1992a) "African-American Studies: The Future of the Discipline" *The Black Scholar* 22(3): 20–9.

Asante, Molefi Kete (1992b) "A Reply to the Review of My Book, *Kemet, Afrocentricity and Knowledge*." *Research in African Literatures* 23(3): 152–5.

Asante, Molefi Kete (1993) "The Movement Toward Centered Education." *The Crisis Magazine* (April/May).

Asante, Molefi Kete (1995) *Malcolm X as Cultural Hero and Other Afrocentric Essays*. Trenton: Africa World Press.

Asante, Molefi Kete (1996) "Are You Scared of Your Shadow? A Critique of Sidney Lemelle's 'The Politics of Cultural Existence.'" *Journal of Black Studies* 26(4): 524–33.

Asante, Molefi Kete (ed.) (1998) *The Afrocentric Idea*. Rev. and expanded edn. Philadelphia: Temple University Press.

Asante, Molefi Kete (1999) *The Painful Demise of Eurocentrism: An Afrocentric Response to Critics*. Trenton, NJ: Africa World.

Asante, Molefi Kete (2003a) *Afrocentricity: The Theory of Social Change*. Chicago: African American Images.

Asante, Molefi Kete (2003b) *Erasing Racism: The Survival of the American Nation*. Amherst, NY: Prometheus Books.

Asante, Molefi Kete (2006) *Cheikh Anta Diop: An Intellectual Portrait*. Los Angeles: University of Sankore Press.

Asante, Molefi and Abu Abarry, eds. (1996) *African Intellectual Heritage*. Philadelphia: Temple University Press.

Asante, Molefi and Ama Mazama, eds. (2002) *Egypt vs. Greece and the American Academy: The Debate over the Birth of Civilization*. Chicago: African American Images.

Austin, Algernon (2006) *Achieving Blackness: Race, Black Nationalism, and Afrocentrism in the Twentieth Century*. New York: New York University Press.

Banks, Reginald, Aaron Hogue, and Terri Timberlake (1996) "An Afrocentric Approach to Group Social Skills Training with Inner-City African American Adolescents." *Journal of Negro Education* 65(4): 414–23.

Bekerie, A. (1994) "The 4 Corners of a Circle: Afrocentricity as a Model of Synthesis." *Journal of Black Studies* 25(2): 131–49.

Bernal, Martin (1987) *Black Athena: The Afro-Asiatic Roots of Classical Culture*. New Brunswick: Rutgers University Press.

Bernal, Martin (1996) "The Afrocentric Interpretation of History: Martin Bernal Replies to Mary Lefkowitz." *Journal of Blacks in Higher Education* (Spring): 86–94.

Blake, Cecil (1997) "Afrocentric Tokens: Afrocentric Methodology in Rhetorical Analysis." *Howard Journal of Communications* 8(1): 1–14.

Blaut, J. M. (2000) *Eight Eurocentric Historians*. London: Guilford Press.

Bloom, Allan (1987) *The Closing of the American Mind*. New York: Simon and Schuster.

Carruthers, Jacob H. (1999) *Intellectual Warfare*. Chicago: Third World Press.

Césaire, Aime (1954) *The Return to My Native Country*. Paris: Presence Africaine.

Chambers, John W., Kobi Kambon, Jr., and Bobbi Davis Birdsong (1998) "Africentric Cultural Identity and the Stress Experience of African American College Students." *Journal of Black Psychology* 24(3): 368–96.

Christian, Mark (2000) *Multiracial Identity: An International Perspective*. London: Macmillan.

Collins, Donald and Marc Hopkins (1993) "Afrocentricity: The Fight for Control of African American Thought." *Black Issues in Higher Education* 10(12): 24–5.

Conyers, James L., ed. (2003) *Afrocentricity and the Academy: Essays on Theory and Practice*. Jefferson, NC: McFarland.

Cooksey, B. (1993) "Afrocentricity: Will This New Approach to Education Provide the Answers to a System Plagued with Inequalities?" *Journal of Law and Education* 22(1): 127–33.

Cruse, Harold (1969) *Rebellion or Revolution: Plural but Equal.* New York: Morton.

Cruse, Harold (2005 [1967]) *The Crisis of the Negro Intellectual.* New York: Monthly Review Press.

Cua, A. S. (1978) *Dimension of Moral Creativity: Paradigms, Principles and Ideals.* University Park, PA: The Pennsylvania State University.

Cummings, J. F. (2005) *How to Rule The World.* Tokyo: Blue Ocean.

Dawson, Michael C. (2002) *Black Visions: The Roots of Contemporary African-American Political Ideologies.* New York: Oxford University Press.

Dei, George Sefa (1994) "Afrocentricity: A Cornerstone of Pedagogy." *Anthropology and Education Quarterly* 25(1): 3–28.

Dei, George Sefa (1997) *Anti-Racism Education: Theory and Practice.* Toronto: Fernwood Publishing.

Diawara, Manthia (1999) *In Search of Africa.* New York: Oxford University Press.

Diop, Cheikh Anta (1974) *The African Origin of Civilization.* New York: Lawrence Hill.

Diop, Cheikh Anta (1981) *Civilization or Barbarism.* New York: Lawrence Hill.

Dixon, Patricia (2002) *We Want for Our Sisters What We Want for Ourselves.* Atlanta: OJI Publications.

Dove, Nah (1998) "African Womanism: An Afrocentric Theory." *Journal of Black Studies* 28(5): 515–39.

Du Bois, W. E. B. (1982 [1903]) *The Souls of Black Folk.* New York: New American Library.

Dunham, FeFe (2002) "Countenances of 'Collective Grace and Communal Availability': The Appeal of Black Nationalism in the Post Black Power Era." National Council for Black Studies Annual Conference, San Diego, March.

Durkheim, Emile (1915) *The Elementary Forms of Religious Life.* Trans. J. W. Swain, London: Allen and Unwin.

Early, Gerald (1994) "Afrocentrism: From Sensationalism to Measured Deliberation." *Journal of Blacks in Higher Education* (July/August): 31–9.

Ekwe-Ekwe, Herbert and Femi Nzegwu (1994) *Operationalising Afrocentrism.* Reading, England: International Institute for Black Research.

*Encarta World English Dictionary* (1999), Soukhanov, A., ed., New York: St. Martin's Press.

Engels, Friedrich (1972) *The Origin of the Family, Private Property and the State.* New York: International Publishers.

Fanon, Frantz (1961) *The Wretched of the Earth.* New York: Grove Press.

Fanon, Frantz (1967) *Black Skin, White Masks.* New York: Grove Press.

Feldstein, Stanley (1971) *Once a Slave: The Slaves' View of Slavery.* New York: William Morrow Company.

Fitchue, M. Anthony (1993) "Afrocentricity Reconstructing Cultural Values." *Black Issues in Higher Education* 10(15): 38–9.

Forbes, Jack (1993) *Africans and Native Americans: The Language of Race and the Evolution of Red Blood.* Champaign-Urbana, Ill.: University of Illinois Press.

Gilroy, Paul (2000) *Against Race*. Cambridge: Harvard University Press.

Gordon, Lewis (2000) *Existentia Africana: Understanding Africana Existential Thought*. New York: Routledge.

Gordon, Lewis (2006) *Disciplinary Decadence: Living Thought in Trying Times*. New York: Routledge,

Harris, Marvin (1980) *Cultural Materialism*. New York: Random House.

Harris, Norman (1992) "A Philosophical Basis for an Afrocentric Orientation." *Western Journal of Black Studies* 16(3): 154–9.

Henderson, Errol Anthony (1995) *Afrocentrism and World Politics: Towards a New Paradigm*. Westport, CT: Praeger.

Hilliard, Asa (2002) "Lefkowitz and the Myth of the Immaculate Conception of Western Civilization," in Molefi Asante and Ama Mazama, eds., *Egypt vs. Greece in the American Academy*. Chicago: AA Images.

Hill Collins, Patricia (2006) *Black Power to Hip Hop: Racism, Nationalism, and Feminism*. Philadelphia: Temple University Press.

Hirsch, E. D. (1988) *Cultural Literacy*. New York: Vintage.

Hoskins, Linus A. (1992) "Eurocentrism vs. Afrocentrism: A Geopolitical Linkage Analysis." *Journal of Black Studies* 23(2): 247–57.

Howe, Stephen (1998) *Afrocentrism*. Oxford: Verso.

Hudson-Weems, Clenora (1997) "Africana Womanism and the Critical Need for Africana Theory and Thought." *Western Journal of Black Studies* 21(2): 79–84.

Huntington, Samuel (1996) *The Clash of Civilizations and the Remaking of World Order*. New York: Simon and Schuster.

Jaeger, W. (1986) *Paideia: The Ideals of Greek Culture*, Vol. 1, 2nd edn., trans. Gilbert Highet. New York: Oxford University Press.

James, C. L. R. (1992) Anna Grimshaw, ed., *The C. L. R. James Reader*. Oxford: Blackwell.

James, George M. (1954) *Stolen Legacy*. New York: Philosophical Library.

Jones, Richard (2005) "Race and Revisability," *Journal of Black Studies* (August).

Joyce, Joyce Ann (1994) *Warriors, Conjurers and Priests: Defining African-Centered Literary Criticism*. Chicago: Third World Press.

Karenga, Maulana (1997) *Kawaida*. Los Angeles: University of Sankore Press.

Karenga, Maulana (2002 [1979]) *Introduction to Black Studies*. Los Angeles: University of Sankore Press.

Karenga, Maulana (2006) *Maat: the Moral Ideal in Ancient Egypt*. Los Angeles: University of Sankore Press.

Keita, Maghan (2000) *Race and the Writing of History: Riddling the Sphinx*. New York: Oxford University Press.

Kershaw, Terry (1992) "Afrocentrism and the Afrocentric Method." *Western Journal of Black Studies* 16(3): 160–8.

Keto, C. Tsehloane (1995) *Vision, Identity, and Time: The Afrocentric Paradigm and the Study of the Past*. Dubuque, Iowa: Kendall/Hunt.

Keto, C. Tsehloane (1999) *An Introduction to Africa-Centered Perspective of History.* Philadelphia: Research Associates School Times.

Kifano, Subira (1996) "Afrocentric Education in Supplementary Schools: Paradigm and Practice at The Mary Mcleod Bethune Institute." *Journal of Negro Education* 65(2): 209–18.

Kimball, Roger (1996) *Wall Street Journal*, February 14.

Lefkowitz, Mary (1996) *Not Out of Africa.* New York: Oxford University Press.

Levi-Strauss, Claude (1966) *The Savage Mind.* Chicago: University of Chicago Press.

Littenberg, Jeffrey (2003) "Patricia Hill Collins: Black Sexual Politics." September 26, http://www.bc.edu/schools/cas/sociology/vss/collins/

Longshore, Douglas, Cheryl Grills, and Kiku Annon (1998) "Promoting Recovery from Drug Abuse: An Africentric Intervention." *Journal of Black Studies* 28(3): 319–33.

Marx, Karl and Friedrich Engels (1959) "The Communist Manifesto," in L. Feurer, ed., *Marx and Engels: Basic Writings on Politics and Philosophy.* New York: Doubleday.

Mazama, Ama (1995) "The Relevance of Ngugi Wa Thiong'o for the Afrocentric Quest." *Western Journal of Black Studies* 18(4): 211–18.

Mazama, Ama (1997) *Langue et Identité.* Pointe-a-Pitre: Jasor.

Mazama, Ama, ed. (2003a) *The Afrocentric Paradigm.* Trenton: Africa World Press.

Mazama, Ama (2003b) *L'imperatif Afrocentrique.* Paris: Menaibuc.

McLaren, Joseph (1988) "Ngugi Wa Thiong'o's Moving the Centre and its Relevance to Afrocentricity." *Journal of Black Studies* 28(3): 386–97.

Memmi, Albert (1991) *The Colonizer and the Colonized.* Boston: Beacon Press.

Miike, Yoshitaka (2004) "Rethinking Humanity, Culture, and Communication: Asiacentric Critiques and Contributions," *Human Communication* 7(1) (Winter).

Modupe, Danjuma S. (2003) "The Afrocentric Philosophical Perspective: A Narrative Outline," in A. Mazama, ed., *The Afrocentric Paradigm.* Trenton: Africa World Press.

Monges, Miriam Ma'at-Ka-Re (1997) *Kush, The Jewel of Nubia: Reconnecting the Root System of African Civilization.* Trenton, NJ: Africa World Press.

Morgan, Gordon D. (1991) "Africentricity in Social Science." *Western Journal of Black Studies* 15(4): 197–206.

Morgan, Lewis Henry (1877) *Ancient Society.* New York: Holt, Rinehart.

Myers, Linda James (1988) *Understanding an Afrocentric World View: Introduction to an Optimal Psychology.* Dubuque, Iowa: Kendall/Hunt.

*New American Oxford Dictionary* (2005) Oxford: Oxford University Press.

Nkrumah, Kwame (1964) *Consciencism: Philosophy and Ideology for Decolonization with Particular Reference to the African Revolution.* London: Heinemann.

Obenga, Theophile (1989) "African Philosophy of the Pharaonic Period," in Ivan van Sertima, ed., *Egypt Revisited.* New Brunswick: Transaction.

Okafor, Victor Oguejiofor (1994) "The Functional Implications of Afrocentrism," *Western Journal of Black Studies* 18(4): 185–94.

Okafor, Victor Oguejiofor (2002) *Toward an Understanding of Africology.* Dubuque: Kendall/Hunt.

Opuku, Kofi Asare (1978) *West African Traditional Religion.* Accra: FEP International.

Outlaw, Lucius (1996) *On Race and Philosophy.* New York: Routledge.

Parsons, Talcott (1937) *The Structure of Social Action,* 2 vols. New York: Free Press.

Perry, Robert L. and Alice A. Tait (1994) "African Americans in Television: An Afrocentric Analysis," *Western Journal of Black Studies* 18(4): 195–200.

Poe, Richard (1998) *Black Spark, White Fire: Did African Explorers Civilize Ancient Europe?* Rocklin, California: Prima Publishing.

Rice, Anne P., ed. (2003) *Witnessing Lynching: American∏ Writers Respond.* New Brunswick, NJ: Rutgers University Press.

Richards, Harriet (1997) "The Teaching of Afrocentric Values by African American Parents." *Western Journal of Black Studies* 21(1): 42–50.

Robinson, Randall (2001) *The Debt: What America Owes to Blacks.* New York: Plume.

Sanders, Cheryl J. (1993–4) "Afrocentricity and Theological Education." *Journal of Religious Thought* Fall–Spring 50(1): 11–26.

Schiele, Jerome H. (1994) "Afrocentricity: Implications for Higher Education." *Journal of Black Studies* 25(2): 150–69.

Schiele, Jerome H. (1996) "Afrocentricity: An Emerging Paradigm in Social Work Practice." *Social Work* 41(3): 284–94.

Schiele, Jerome H. (1997) "The Contour and Meaning of Afrocentric Social Work." *Journal of Black Studies* 27(6): 800–19.

Schlesinger, Arthur Jr. (1992) *The Disuniting of America.* Nashville: Whittle Communications.

Semmes, Clovis E. (1992) *Cultural Hegemony and African American Development.* Westport, CT: Praeger.

Senghor, Léopold (2007) "Negritude and Humanism," in Christa Knellwolf and Christopher Norris, eds., *The Cambridge History of Literary Criticism.* Cambridge: Cambridge University Press.

Sertima, Ivan van (1976) *They Came Before Columbus.* New York: Random House.

Tarbell, F. B. (1913) *A History of Greek Art.* New York: Macmillan.

Thompson, Vetta L. Sanders and Michell A. Myers (1994) "Africentricity: An Analysis of Two Culture Specific Instruments." *Western Journal of Black Studies* 18(4): 179–84.

Van Dyk, Sandra (1998) "Molefi Kete Asante's Theory of Afrocentricity: The Development of a Theory of Cultural Location." PhD Thesis, Temple University.

Walker, Clarence (2001) *Why We Can't Go Home Again: An Argument about Afrocentrism*. New York: Oxford University Press.

Walker, David (1996) "Appeal to the Colored Citizens of the World: Our Wretchedness as a Consequence of Slavery," in Molefi Asante and Abu Abarry, *African Intellectual Heritage*. Philadelphia: Temple University Press.

Warfield-Coppock, Nsenga (1995) "Toward a Theory of Afrocentric Organizations." *Journal of Black Psychology* 21(1): 30–48.

Weber, Max (1968 [1922]) *Economy and Society*, eds. Guenther Roth and Claus Wittich. Berkeley: University of California Press.

Will, George (1996) *Newsweek*, February 12. Winters, Clyde Ahmad (1994) "Afrocentrism: A Valid Frame of Reference." *Journal of Black Studies* 25(2): 170–90.

Winters, Clyde Ahmad (1998) "The Afrocentric Historical and Linguistic Methods." *Western Journal of Black Studies* 22(2): 73–83.

Wonkeryor, Edward Lama (1998) *On Afrocentricity, Intercultural Communication, and Racism*. Lewiston, NY: Edwin Mellen Press.

Woodson, Carter G. (1933) *The Miseducation of the Negro*. Washington: Associated Press.

Wortham, Anne (1981) *The Other Side of Racism*. Columbus, OH: Ohio State University Press.

Ziegler, Dhyana (1995) *Molefi Kete Asante and Afrocentricity: In Praise and Criticism*. Nashville, TN: James C. Winston.

Zulu, Itibari M. (1999) *Exploring the African Centered Paradigm: Discourse and Innovation in African World Community Studies*. Los Angeles, CA: Amen-Ra Theological Seminary Press.

# Index

Africa: African Americans and 35–6, 135; colonial rule in 57; and diaspora 66, 75; dismemberment of 56–7; economic underdevelopment of 29, 30; ethnographical research in 46; Eurocentric education system in 27, 57, 84; European intellectual hegemony over 56, 57, 58; European names in 28–9; Europeans in 64–5; evolution of human species in 45–6; gender relations in 66; imperialism in *see* imperialism; as resource for renaissance 69, 74, 75; study of 55; tribes in 36; women rulers in 48, 66
"African": as term 47
African American Studies 102–4; and Afrocentricity 107; and history 119
African Americans: and Afrocentricity 106; as American product 36; author's family as 2; and Black Nationalism 19–20, 21, 122–3, 126; and Black Studies Movement *see* Black Studies; cultural crisis of 34–5; education of 78, 80, 88, 89–91, 151; history of, taught 139; literacy rate amongst 105; marginalization of 37; moral identity of 162; persecution of 106; and race 20
African Communities League 20
African Union: 2004 Dakar conference of 51, 55
Africana Studies Movement 98–9
Africanity: versus Afrocentricity 17, 60–1, 109
Africans: agency of 6, 16, 25, 40–1, 47, 56, 65, 120; cultural heritage of, stolen 68–9; defined 47; enslavement of 36, 37–8, 56, 85–6, 88; images of, whitened 68–9; and off-centeredness of 31–2, 57;

postmodernism 29; and self-hatred 5
Africological Movement 99–100
Africology: and Afrocentricity 101–2; goals of 53–4; subject fields of 50–1, 51–2, 53, 101; theory of 100–2
Afrocentricity: and African agency 4, 7, 11, 15, 16, 17, 40–1, 42–3, 47, 49, 56, 65, 109, 120–1; and Africology 101–2; versus Afrocentrism 17, 18, 22–3; and Black Nationalism 21–2, 24; characteristics of 41; and chronology 27–8; and cultural crisis 34–5; and culture 13, 36–7, 39–40, 43, 53; defined 2–3, 5, 7, 9, 16, 17, 49, 59, 64; and education 78–9, 81, 82–3, 87, 89, 91–2; and ethics 48; versus Eurocentrism 3, 6, 17, 26–7, 58–9; and history *see* history, and Afrocentricity; and identity 114–15; and language 43–4, 116; and location 15, 25, 27, 28, 31. 42; versus Negritude 24; perspectives of 60–1, 64; seen as (civil) religion 23–4; as weapon against oppression 31; and women 48–9
Aldred, Cyril: *Egypt to the End of the Old Kingdom* 72–3
Allen, Troy 119
ancestors: African concept of 26
Ani, Marimba 148
Ansah, King Kwame 56
anti-blackness 166
anti-racism 136
Arabs: in Egypt 69
architecture: African origins of 76; and civilization 15–16
art, African: and European artists 75–6, 166
Asante, Molefi Kete: as African American 2, 132; and African American Studies

program 102–3; *The Afrocentric Idea* 7, 18, 82; *Afrocentricity* 17–18, 99; *Kemet, Afrocentricity, and Knowledge* 18, 50, 82; *Malcolm X as Cultural Hero* 18; *The Painful Demise of Eurocentrism* 4, 129
Ashanti, Faheem: Ashanti Brainwashing Test 84
Association for the Study of Classical African Civilization 118
Austin, Algernon: *Achieving Blackness* 128–9; and Afrocentricity 129–31

Bankole, Katherine 119
Baraka, Amiri 96
Berlin Conference 57, 59
Bernal, Martin 58, 144; *Black Athena* 45
Bibb, Henry: testimony of 87
Black Nationalism 19–20, 21, 122–31; defined 21; and gender issues 125
Black Power 6. 131
Black Studies 23, 50–1, 93–8; and Africology 94, *see also* Africology; emergence of 93–5, 97; in Europe 97; faculty for 95; impact of 93
Black Studies Movement 97–8
blackness 128–9, 153–64; and Afrocentricity 24; characteristics of 162–6; denial of 80; and essentialism 156–7; and identity 153, 159–61; UK concept of 161
Blaut, J. M.: *Eight Eurocentric Historians* 58
Bloom, Allan: *Closing of the American Mind* 81–2
Bond, Julian 166
Bontemps, Arna 96
Brawley, Benjamin 133
Brooks, Gwendolyn 96
Brown, Sterling 132

Cabral, Amilcar 10
Caldwell, Erskine 132
Caribbean: African Americans and 35
Carmichael, Stokely *see* Toure, Kwame
centricity: and education 79, 83
Césaire, Aime 11, 13, 39; and Negritude 117; *The Return to My Native Country* 117
Champollion, Jean-François 44
Charles Martel 59
chicken/eagle fable 1–2

Christian, Mark: *Multiracial Identity* 155
Christianity: and individuality 71
Clarke, John Hendrik 36, 61
Cleaver, Eldridge 96, 125
Clinton, President Bill: "first black president" 162
collectivity: as African concept 73
Collins, Patricia Hill 11, 19–24, 129; *Black Power to Hip Hop* 18, 19, 19–20; on feminist thought 18–19
Colon, Cristobal 58, 59
colonization 10–11; in Fanon's work 153; and violence 12
"colored American", concept of 134
community nationalism 126
Conde, Maryse 9
Congreso Internacionale d'Estudis Africans 67
Connerly, Ward: "not black" 162
consciencism 34, *see also under* Nkrumah, Kwame
conscientization 32
consciousness: and choice 161; nature of 158
Conyers, James Naazir 119; *Afrocentricity and Its Critics* 50
Cooper, Anna Julia 10
creolization 9–10
Cruse, Harold 32, 34, 35–40, 122; on African American community 6, 34–7, on art and culture 36, 37–40; *The Crisis of the Negro Intellectual* 34; Marxism of 34, 38; *Rebellion or Revolution* 34
Cua, A. S. 74
Cullen, Countee 132

Damas, Leon 13, 39; and Negritude 117
Davidson, Basil 64, 69
Dawson, Michael C. 19, 122–8: *Black Visions* 122, 123, 127, 128; National Black Politics Study 125–7
Dei, George Sefa 166
Denon, Dominique Vivant 44: *The Description of Egypt* 62
development: problematic of 11
Diagne, Pathe: and Negritude 117
dialectical materialism 110–11; Afrocentricity and 111

Diawara, Manthia: *In Search of Africa* 114
Dinka: *cieng* concept of 75
Diop, Alioune 39; and Negritude 117
Diop, Cheikh Anta 10, 13, 51, 58, 61–2, 62–3, 82, 100; *The African Origins of Civilization* 61; on African renaissance 51; on civilization 45, 46; *Civilization or Barbarism* 61, 70; historiography of 116, 118–19; *Nations nègres et culture* 51; and Negritude 117
Dixon, Patricia 127; *We Want for Our Sisters...*127–8
*djed*: concept of 15, 16, 24, 31
Douglass, Frederick 132
Dove, Nah 14, 23; on gender relations 14
Dreiser, Theodore 132, 133
Du Bois, W. E. B. 36, 61, 100, 132, 162; and "double consciousness" 157–8
Dunbar, Paul Laurence 132
Dunham, FeFe 124, 127
Durkheim, Emile 112

education: of African Americans *see* African Americans, education of; Africans and 78; and centricity 79, 82, 83; and colonial students 33; and curriculum change 91; influence of 15; and multiculturalism 89, 91–2; pluralism in 89; and society 79–80
Egypt, ancient *see* Kemet
Egypt, modern: African connections ignored in 68–9; Arabs in 69–70
Egyptology 44–5
Engels, Friedrich: *Communist Manifesto* 110; *The Origin of the Family...*110
English 116
etymology: and Afrocentricity 28
Eurocentrism/ Eurocentricity: defined 7; and history 58; and imperialism 26–7, 58–9; and intellectual hegemony 138–9, 140, 142–3; as norm 11, 52, 111; and political ideologies 123; and science 107–8; worldview of 8; *see also* Afrocentricity, versus Eurocentrism
Europe: and Afrocentricity 115–16; as Christendom 59; and the collective consciousness 112, 114

Fanon, Frantz 11, 12, 39, 153; *Black Skin,* *White Masks* 153; *The Wretched of the Earth* 13
Farrakhan, Louis 126
fascism 136, 137
Forbes, Jack 163
French 9, 116
Fuller, Charles 96

Ga (tribe): libation practices of 63
Garba, Mohammed 119
Garvey, Marcus 10, 12, 162
gender relations 66, 125
Ghana 56
Gilroy, Paul: *Against Race* 134–6, 137
Gordon, Lewis 12; on race and blackness 154–5; *Disciplinary Decadence* 31
Gran, Peter: on falseness of Afrocentricity 139
Great Zimbabwe 101
Greece: as cradle of civilization 45, 71, 72, 73, 145, 147, 148; and origins of philosophy 143–4
Guadeloupe 9, 10; language of 9, 102
Gwaltney, John 123

Harper, Frances Ellen Watkins 132
Harris, Marvin: on science 107–8
Hayes-Tilden Compromise 105
Herodotus: on ancient Egyptians 146; on Greek gods' names 145
Hilliard, Asa 14, 23
Hirsch, E. D.: *Cultural Literacy* 82
historiography: Afrocentric 64–5; imperialist 57–8
history: and African American Studies 119; Africa's contributions to 88; Africans' ignorance of 85; and Afrocentricity 49–50, 64, 82; teaching of 78, 84, 87, 139–40; and society 140
Holocaust 86
Howe, Stephen: *Afrocentrism* 18
Hudson-Weems, Clenora 14, 23; on gender relations 14, 127
Hughes, Langston 132
human relationships 77, *see also Maat*
Huntington, Samuel: *The Clash of Civilizations* 8
Hurston, Zora Neale 162

ideologies, political 123, 124–5; black 125–6, 127

Imhotep 108

imperialism 57; and Eurocentrism 26–7, 58–9; and historiography 57–8

individualism, aggressive 141–2; Afrocentricity and 141

individuality: as Western concept 71, 73

Jaeger, Werner 71, 72

James, C. L. R.: 148

James, George: *Stolen Legacy* 145–6

Jefferson, Thomas: as slave owner 150, 151

Johnson, James Weldon 132

Jones, Richard A. 164

Karenga, Maulana 6–7, 13, 17, 23, 50–1, 118; on Africana studies 53; *Introduction to Black Studies* 98; and Kawaida 119; on *Maat* 66, 67, 73–4, 102, 118; on Nubian kings of Egypt 74

Karnak, temple of 76

Kawaida Movement 6, 13, 98, 116–17, 119–20

Keita, Sundiata 56

Kemet: African terms in 28; antecedents of 63; architecture of 76; as black African 13, 62–3, 68, 69; concepts in 75, *see also Maat*; as cradle of civilization 45, 65, 72, 73, 88, 145, 147; literature of 76–7; and neighboring lands 72–3; Nubian rulers in 74–5; and origins of philosophy 143–4; philosophers of 66, 88, 144; as resource for renaissance 72, 77

Kershaw, Terry 23

Keto, C. Tsehloane 23

*khepera* 164

Khun-anup 116

Kimball, Roger: review of Lefkowitz 144

King, Martin Luther 84, 93, 106, 162

Ku Klux Klan 106

language 43–4, 154, *see also* English; French

Lapansky, Emma 103

Lefkowitz, Mary 18, 144–5; *Not Out of Africa* 4, 129, 145–8; reviews of 144

Lehman, Cynthia 119

Levi-Strauss, Claude 111–12

Lincoln, C. Eric 21

Littenberg, Jeffrey 18–19

Livingstone, David 41, 65

logic 116

lynching 132–3

*Maat*: and Africology 102; concept of 63, 70, 73–4, 75, 77

Marx, Karl: Eurocentrism of 110; *Communist Manifesto* 110

Marxism: in African context 34; in Cruse's work 38; and racism 125; in United States 38–9

Mazama, Ama 23, 50; *The Afrocentric Paradigm* 4, 9, 18, 50; on Afrocentricity 10, 11, 13, 14, 53–4; career of 9–10; on colonization 10–11; and creolization 9–10; on Fanon 153; on gender relations 14; on language 102; *Langue et Identité* 9; *L'imperatif Afrocentrique* 18

McKay, Claude 132

Memmi, Albert 11, 42, 151, 163

*mestazje* 84

Middle Passage 84, 85–7

Miike, Yoshitaka: Asiacentrism of 4, 8

modernism 113, 114; and literature 113

Modupe, Danjuma Sinue: on Afrocentricity 41

Monges, Miriam Maat Ka Re 119

Morgan, Lewis Henry: *Ancient Society* 110

Morrison, Toni 162

Movement Noir Fier 97

multiculturalism 53, 89, 91–2

Myers, Linda James 23

Napoleon Bonaparte: in Egypt 44

Nation of Islam 21, 22, 130

National Black Politics Study 125–6

Negritude 13, 39, 117; and Afrocentricity 24, 116–17

Negro: as term 131, 153; as 'transitory person' 36

Nkrumah, Kwame 10, 32; *Consciencism* 6, 32–3

Nobles, Wade 23

Nubia 63, 65; women rulers in 48, 66

Obenga, Theophile 61, 63, 118, 119, 142

Obichere, Boniface 96

Onwauachi, Chike 96
Outlaw, Lucius 158

Park, Mungo 58
Parsons, Talcott 141
patriarchy 125, 136
philosophy: etymology of term 143; as
    European concept 142–3
Piankhy (Nubian king) 74
Plessy, Homer: case of (1896) 161
Portuguese: in Africa 56
postmodernism: and Africa 29;
    characteristics of 113–14; and white
    supremacy 72
Powell, Adam Clayton 166

Rabemananjara, Jean: and Negritude 117
racism 20, 130, 137–8; and patriarchy 125,
    136; struggle against 136; *see also* lynching
rationalism: chauvinistic 142, 145; types of
    142
Ravitch, Diane 89
Reconstruction (post-Civil War) 105
Reed, Yaa Asantewa 127, 128
reincarnation: Western concept of 26
religion: civil 23–4
Rice, Anne P.: *Witnessing Lynching* 132, 133,
    134
Robinson, Randall: *The Debt* 136
Rustin, Bayard 96

Sanchez, Sonia 96
Sandburg, Carl 132
Schlesinger, Arthur 149–50, 151
    "Committee for the Defense of History"
    81; *The Disuniting of America* 129, 149
science 107–8
Senghor, Leopold 13; on culture 39; and
    Negritude 117
Shabaka (pharaoh) 74
slavery 56, 87, 158, *see also* Middle Passage
Smith, Robert C. 124
structuralism 111–12; Afrocentricity and 112

Taharka (Nubian king) 74
Tarbell, F. B.: *A History of Greek Art* 76
Tefnakht (prince of Sais) 74
Terrell, Mary Chruch 132

Thomas, Clarence: "not black" 162, 165
Thorpe, Frank: pedagogical method of 155
Toomer, Jean 132
Toure, Kwame (Stokely Carmichael) 124
Tubman, Harriet 162

United States: and cultural multiplicity 37;
    culturalism of 148–8, 149, 151–2;
    education in 78, 80, 81, 83–4, 89–90;
    lynchings in 132–4; Marxism in 38–9;
    struggle against racism in 136; *see also*
    African Americans
Universal Negro Improvement Association
    20

Van Horne, Winston 99

Walker, Clarence: on Afrocentricity 3–6; *We
    Can't Go Home Again* 3
Walker, David 124
Walker, Margaret 96
Walters, Ronald 124
Washington, George: as slave owner 150–1
Weber, Max 141, 142; *Economy and Society*
    141
Weldon, Jacob and Ruth: testimony of 85,
    86
Wells-Barnett, Ida B. 132
Welsh, Kariamu 23
West: culturalism of 148; and individuality
    71–2; intellectual triumphalism of 138,
    140; materialist values of 48; science
    privileged in 107–8
White, Walter 166
whiteness: as ideal 57; privileging of 20, 35,
    122, 138
Wilkinson, Toby: Eastern Desert Survey
    63
Will, George: review of Lefkowitz 144
women: African, and men 14; and Black
    Nationalism 125; status of 48–9
Woodson, Carter G. 33; *The Miseducation of
    the Negro* 78
Wortham, Anne: *The Other Side of Racism*
    135
Wright, Richard 132

X, Malcolm 93, 106, 154, 162